T0365642

Knowing God Personally

God the Savior

Daouth Elias

AuthorHouse™ LLC
1663 Liberty Drive
Bloomington, IN 47403
www.authorhouse.com
Phone: 1-800-839-8640

Published by AuthorHouse 09/26/2014

ISBN: 978-1-4969-4269-2 (sc)
ISBN: 978-1-4969-4268-5 (e)

This book is printed on acid-free paper.

Dedication

This book is, dedicated to my wife Denise, and my son Anthony my parents, and my entire family all my friends. To the, fallen Heroes, for the faith, and belief. The fallen heroes, to gain our freedom, and peace for our country, and around the world.

Especially dedicated

To

My Father	My Father In Law
David E, (Daoud)Dabish	Raymond E, Causley

In The Memory

Janie D, Trenasty And Richard F, Nahabedian

Contents

Introduction

For many years been trying to write about God. My father David, and my uncle, his brother Shamaya they never gossip about anyone. Instead always talked wisdom, and taught it to everyone They were, in touch with. They often talked about good things. Comes from, the bible holy scripture.

Throughout the bible, God begging us, to choose the right path. Leading us to him. From the holy scripture Old, and new testament. We learn how to be moral, we also receive the holy spirit of God.

I made it my goal, to preach wisdom. I learned from the bible. Most of my writings, came from teaching of our Lord and Savor Jesus. I also have scientific facts from online the computer about God, and human development.

I have in this book, some stories, my father told me It made sense to me. I have no prove how true it is, but it about our life, and it meant something to me I learned big lesson from it At first I hand written all my research, and notes by hand on the regular note books Once almost complete I wanted to begin typing it. I could type but very slow. Therefore, I used a speech recognition. I was able speak to the computer in process. The computer types. It was not very easy, because of my accent. I had to train over, and over again. To have the computer to understand my dialog, I am very thankful. I managed to do it.

I am thankful, for all my friends who help me make this happen.

I basically, read the bible, and explain the way I see it and understand it. I don' t even high school diploma. I teach from my experience in life. May be someone benefit and learn something.

I speak very simple English. I used DICTIONARY/ THESAURUS to get my spellings and meaning of the words out of it.

Anyone who read the bible, will see everyone's life in it. If anyone read it, could discover answer for all the questions they may have. The answer guarantee. From A. to Z

First. few years writing this book. I was only writing notes and filled many. All the knowledge I learned from the holy scripture. I wrote down whatever came across my mine about God. Still was not the right way, writing this book.

Until one night. I had a dream. In my dream I saw a figure having white, kind of long hair Wearying ancient looking clothes. In my dream. He took me, on tour throughout old testament times, and events. At the end of my dream. I witnessed, the birth of Jesus Christ. Actually I did saw baby Jesus Christ, with his mother Mary.

When I woke up the next day, during that day my wife gave, me some books. They used to be, her father (Raymond) It is all preaching from the bible.

Until then I learned what, I was supposed to do. From that day and on. I began to go through the bible. I found what. I was looking for. From the Bible, we learn how to live our life. You'll see it

First the 10 commandments. How to, practice our faith About love. From the bible we learn

What to do, every single day we live

Parables, verses, chapters, miracles, dreams They are, all about our life, and life of others Through, old testament. God preparing, his coming.

In the new testament. The four gospels. We have book, of acts. Jesus Christ, revealing heart of God to us and personality of God. I also know that Jesus Christ did everything for us, with power holy spirit. Of one God.

Whatever question we have ? The answer, can be found in Scripture. Whatever we're feeling is there. Bible is the guidance, for entire humanity. Throughout, the holy bible God main concern for less fortunate, and the poor. Especially the hungry.

Whenever we are critical, or suffering. We should call spirit of God without any doubts or fear The needy, will never be forgotten, and there will never be dismissed by God. Psalms 9:18

God makes, the earth fertile, by the rain, and snow on it, cause the grain to grow, producing seeds, for the farmers to feed, the hungry Isaiah 55:10

Jesus Christ commandment, is to love each other, as he loved us. John 15:12-13

It is true that, the notion of loving others as our selves is. Throughout old, and new - testament. Is being mentioned constantly.

It is not only, the word love. But goes way deeper than that. Which is unconditionally doing good, toward one and another for each other. For giving each other. Feeding others. Helping others. To make sure, everyone around us. Have good, and prospective life, and to have everything they need.

Jesus Christ, died for all humanity. So they can be saved. He expects us to follow, in his footsteps. Because, he figured. If we do that, where the evil fit.

If everyone, in every corner, of the earth, know Jesus. Will not help them any. What would really will help us, and lead us to the right path, and truth. If we become, like Jesus With all our heart, with all our soul. No way no other way. If we can all, love each other un-conditionally There's no way anyone, in the world, will have, any problem.

Decent person would feel compassionate, helpful, merciful toward anyone.

About, handicapped, disable. Some handicaps, could be minor, or severe. It is great so many. Who really, and truly care. My point is, everyone in the world. Every single person, have some kind of handicap. I mean some, who are able, or capable, of doing certain things. Some aren't, Some are not mentally capable, or physically. Everyone, is different than others

Everyone is, missing something, no one is perfect. There are, a lot more reasons For entire human being. Why they, are here.

Instead of, judging each other. Is to feel compassioned, toward each other. Because everyone need help. Not, everyone is capable of becoming teacher, lawyer, philosopher, judge, politician police, fire men and all millions, of things people do. God created, everyone with certain gift Some get more, some less.

Everyone is able to get rich. But with, help of others. It is possible. Because I am not too sure, how long ago God create it, our planet earth. Thank goodness. God made it To contain, enough resources energy, and treasure to support every single person living on face of the earth.

It is crying shame. There are, people around the world whom are very poor. they can't even find a job. Some who are starving. When at the meantime. There's people, who have billions. They choose not, to at least create jobs. For people, who really need it. So they can make a decent living. In return the rich will get richer.

The fact is, the rich ones. Who help the poor. Also counting the less fortunate are very fortunate, and lucky. Because If there wasn't the poor people. The rich, they would not Have a chance. To do good deeds toward God.

Our God, and savior. Created our world this way. I mean so many. Who suffer, most of the time. It is giving the chance. For the ones. Who always, want to do good, and run to the sufferer. For rescue.

If there, isn't any good. Evil takes, over Unfortunately evil, and all the evil spirits. Live on earth. Their job, and goals are to tempt, every human being.

Lucifer, was angel in heaven, he went against God and third of angels. Therefore God cast Lucifer, and his angels followers, down to earth Ezekiel 28:17.

They become known, as Satan, or evil, and his rebellious angel followers demons. They hate, God they all are enemy of God.

All holy books, we were given instructions. How to win over evil, We need, to go by it, and follow. The commandment

A lot of us, wake up every morning. We want, to have great day. That day should be, our first choice, and goal. Is it good, to wake up every day. Hearing the news. I mean mostly horrible stories, and to become part of our lives. Or is it better, hearing peaceful, happier, a rewarding stories

So many writers wrote books, about Family values great guidance. When we feel obligated toward everyone around us. Always good things happen.

All around the world, people believe in one God. the creator. He decided, after thousands of years Predicting his coming, here on earth, to reveal to us, his personality. That was over 2000 years ago.

God has, unlimited patient he takes his time with everything he do. With him everything is possible. He is, a spirit he is able to be everywhere. At the same time. Because of the love, he has for humanity. He decided, to become the son flesh, and blood. To become a man, and divine He is the word that was with God.

He is, son of man. As well scripture is not contradiction If we examine the holy scripture It reveals to us. What means son of man. It is mentioned, throughout the old testament. God predictions of his coming.

Calling himself son of man. Because, he is awesome God. His love for humanity. He chose to become the son man.

That is, Jesus Christ our lord, and savior. He took flesh and blood of virgin Mary. He picked Joseph, to be his guardian. Jesus Christ, called himself son of man reference to his humanity Jesus Christ, became. Man by blood. Therefore, he is related to all humanity. So he can, be our redeemer. To rescue us from Sin Leviticus 25:25-26,48 In old testament. Isaiah. God referred, to himself as son of man, he also forgive sins.

Jesus Christ, have two natures divine, and human. As a person Jesus Christ claiming. He is God, in many occasions. Matthew 16;16,17. John 8;58 It said, he was also human. Philippines 2:6 Jesus said, son of man. Have the power, to forgive sins Mark 43:25. Jesus Christ, again calling himself, son of man. He said son of man, will return to earth, with his Glory to region on earth. Mark 2:10

When Jesus Christ, was asked, by high priest, if he was son of God Affirmatively, Jesus Christ, responded declaring he the son of man, who he will return, and come in power and Glory Matthew 26:63.

This is God, our God forever, and ever. He will be our guide for ever. Psalms 48:14.

If God was able, to create entire world. Don't, any of us think God. He is not, able to make himself a son ?

Jesus revealed to us personality of God. He is the solution for entire humanity. He is our savior, as well.

God himself is, the son died and raise for entire humanity. So we could be saved from evil sin. Heart of God revealed to us through Jesus Christ. Jesus revealed to us the merciful, and invisible heart of God.

In the beginning was the word, and the word was with God. He was in the beginning with God. John 1:1-2. Jesus is word of God. Because of Jesus we know God.

Author

I am a Christian. I apologize, If I may hurt anyone's beliefs, or feelings. My goal is to preach from the Bible, and not to convert anyone to any faith, or religion.

It is the knowledge, and wisdom I learned, and received from the bible. Old and New- Testament The way, I understand it.

All quotations, are taken from the bible. Verses are meant to be reference, and guidance for any or particular problem in our life.

I study the bible many times, for many years. I've discovered, spiritually therefore. I am inspired by teaching, the word, of God. That is in the bible.

I studied theology, through high school, and attended seminary. Year 1971-1973.

I believe, in one God, he is our creator. I also, learned He is God of mercy, love, peace, and grace. If anyone does anything in the name of our God. Should be only, acts of mercy, love, peace and charity. Any acts of hate, it is from evil.

God has glorification, he needed forever. If we all glorify God 24/7 ? Will not please, as much. What will really please God is If we love each other. Love is not only by word. But it goes deeper.

God want us to team together, to hold each other's hand and to see. What we needed to be done for each other. He wants to make sure, no one go without.

Mainly God concern is for the poor, less fortunate, and ones who are all alone. They don't have any one, the Orphans. Especially, God needs the goodness. Which goes on earth? From entire earth to himself.

People, for longtime being, fighting for democracy that is freedom, and for people to choose their destiny.

Democracy

We elect people, to rule over us, to take care of our daily needs. To be safe free to live in peace, and harmony. How could anyone feel free, and have any peace of mind? If they don't have any job. Always hungry, confused, and they don't know what to do.

People get tired, of not having a job, and not making enough to make a living, People get too much stressed. Real democracy, should be, making sure everyone have a job That's not government job only. Should be, our responsibilities toward each other.

Neighbor helping, neighbor. Families, friends, and relatives should be on guard for each other, to make sure everyone, have what they need. That what, will bring happiness. Freedom, and peace of mind. Knowing that everyone has what they need.

Democracy should be, backing up our government, in every way, in every field. To make sure, they remain the most, and the strongest. Democratic government, in the world. Just the way, we can never succeed without our government. The same our government cannot succeed without us

Throughout, history. Only one person, understood what democracy meant what democracies are about. That is, Jesus Christ. He knew, it was all about people.

He made sure everyone got to eat. Everyone who, needed to be healed. He healed. He made sure, everyone is safe he treat it everyone equally. He brought peace into everyone's heart. He gave mercy, beyond our imagination. He taught us how to love respect obeys. Also taught us how to love, our enemies. He taught us, how to lay ourselves for a friend. Even if we have to die, for a friend.

The only way. We fully, pleases God. If we become, like vine yard owner. In the New- Testament. Matthew 20:1-16.

Two meaning, for the parable. First, it is heavenly. Second preparation, for the kingdom of heaven.

That man, he was generous, kind, merciful and thoughtful. He made sure, everyone have a job Because, he knew, they needed to make a living. Maybe they have children, need to feed or payments they have to pay. He wanted, to take the pressure off them. His generosity, went far and beyond, the morning, midday, evening workers. They all got same amount of pay. It was not

because, he was a mean person, or unfair. He knew, those workers dependent on that one day of pay He also knew they did not have a steady work. Where they knew. They were going to work the following day.

It is wonderful, rewarding to take pride, into our faith, and beliefs. However as long, as we believe in one God, the creator.

We are, debating, which religion, is right, or which one is wrong, or who is closer to God.

How many people did you help a day?

How many people did you feed a day?

How many people did you clothes a day?

How many people without jobs found them a job a day?

How many sick people you gave comfort to a day?

How many people did you forgave a day?

How many homeless people you took in a day?

Those are, some of the things pleases God.

The most Religion and faith is. How much, we are able to be our brother's keeper ? That is, what pleases God.

His demands are, to take care of others. No matter who they are, what they are, where they came from, and what they look like. That is, unconditionally. The goodness, we show, toward each other. Puts evil to shame, and he's conquered.

The goodness, we show each other this is how, God takes pride in us. and we become his children.

Chapter 1

GOD Love

In the Bible, story of the creation. In the beginning, when God created the heaven and the earth the light, the sky, the sun, the moon, the stars. God said let the water teem up with an abundance of living creatures on the earth. God said let the birds fly. God made all kind of wild animals. God created everything that is living on the face of the earth. All kind of living creatures. Genesis 1:1-26.

God created man in his Image, In the divine Image he created him, male and female he created them. God blessed them, saying; "Be fertile and multiply; fill the earth and subdue it Genesis 1:27-28.

When God created Adam, and Eve. They were, given long life so they could multiply, and fill the earth. Genesis 2:7, 21- 22.

The LORD God then took the man and settled him in the garden of Eden to care for it. Out of his one rib. The LORD God. Then built up into woman. Genesis 2:15,21.

The fall of man. When Adam and Eve ate from the for bidden fruit tree. They were cast out of garden of Eden. The man called his wife Eve, because she became the mother of all the living Genesis 3:6,20.

Adam and Eve begotten Cain and Abel. When Cain killed his brother Abel, Adam again had relation with his wife, and she gave birth to a son whom she called Seth. Genesis 4:1, 8,17,25.

Generations; Adam to Noah. When Lamech was one hundred and eighty two years old,he begot a son and named him Noah. When Noah was five hundred years old, he became the father of Shem, ham and Japheth. Genesis 5:6, 28, 32.

People began to multiply. They did not know God, any more. Therefore, people became very wicked. Evil was, continuously in their hearts. God was very sorry; he had made many people on earth. Noah was, found favor in Gods eyes. Revealing to Noah saying. He is about, to flood the earth in order to destroy life, and things on it Except, Noah his family, and animal. Genesis 6:1-6, 8. 14-22.

After the flood. Sons of Noah, they became a nation, and spread abroad on entire earth Genesis10:32.

I believe, long after that. There was some people, who believed in God he is the creator. But they did not care any, or at least wanting to know. How to worship him?

God always has a unique way, and special way of knowing, who to reveal himself to He is able to read our hearts minds, and souls.

When Terah was seventy years old, he became the father of Abram, Nahor and Haran. Genesis 11:26.

God made Abram, father of entire human being. Abram wife was Sara, Terah took Abram his son, and lot the son of Haran and brought them out of Ur-Chaldeans. Genesis17:4.

God said to Abram go forth out of thy country. Together they all moved to Canaan they settled there, with all theirs. Genesis 11:26-28.

Lord God said, to Abram ; go from your country, and your kindred, and your father's house The land I will show you. God said to Abram I will make you great nation. I will bless you, and make your name great. Genesis 12:1-2.

Because of, human free will. It was not easy, for Jewish people to build relationship, with God Throughout, Old Testament. God worked, with Jewish people. So he can make them his people He made Abraham to be the father. Not only, of Jewish people. But also father, of entire world.

God guided, Jewish people. Moses, became their leader.

God gave his rules, and commandments to Moses. To pass it out, to the Jewish people and entire world. Exodus 20:1-17Deuteronomy.

With God's help Jewish people became powerful people. They had kings rule over them 1 Kings.

Judaism became their religion. Throughout history, and from time to time Jewish people face some, or massive persecution. The holocaust, was plan to wipe out, entire Jewish people, off face, of Europe. It was, Nazi government of Germany, and allies. Millions of Jewish people were murdered during holocaust. Around 6 million to be exact.

I believe just, because Jewish people, they are profound prove existing, of God. Therefore evil is after the Jewish people. Thinking if they vanish, off face of the earth, no one would know God any more.

Evil also is after the Christian. Where millions of them throughout history, were murdered Evil trying to make people, forget about God. So he can own entire earth. Everyday people they are forgetting God. God he is, the creator. He did inspire people, to write down what he had planned for us. From beginning of the time.

Many predictions. Profits who claimed they spoke to God. God give, us in the Bible. Instruction For our safety, happiness, and prosperity.

God give us a solution. For all of our problems, and issues. We may face, in our life time.

In the holy scripture. God is saying. Let me do it for you. Let me serve you. So you can serve each other, he's saying.

God telling us, I am the all knowledge, a philosopher therapist, scientists. Through the Bible We know, God made all knowledge.

Myself I believe in the God, not only of all the, love blessing, and miracles. He grant it for me. Without them, I would love God, for all the great things. I received, and the life he granted for me.

Proving existing of God, it is very simple just look around you. Who made all that ? Nothing comes from nothing.

People all the time debating, whether there is God or not? I say yes, there is God, and he is the light. Over the world. He is, the sunshine will never end.

An answer. I had explain, what God is like. For all the, knowledgeable people, scientists philosophers, therapist and all the talented, and atheists movement, who don't only acknowledge God Beside they are also trying, to stop others, from believing In God.

I have news for the people who don't believe in God. Besides all people in the world who believes in God. If we don't love, and do for each other first. Won't do God, any favors. God measures how much good we do.

God gives everyone work, according to their ability. God also given us. What we need, and how much, we are able to handle.

God he is about teaching us, moral value. For our safety, and happiness.

For all the people of the world. Who are knowledgeable, genius's, philosophers, talented scientists, judges. Who don't believe in God, and the ones whom are debating whether there is God, or not? The reason behind is. They don't want to know. If there is, any power above them. They want to remain, the most highest power. People with highest power. They out to know, they received theirs. From God.

Because when they die. They become powerless. We all become powerless, when we die While the only one, who is always the highest, and above all powers of the world is God. The one, who will never die that is God. We all die. God live. How many of us still alive ?. Therefore God made the power. God made us all.

Actually to be specific. Somehow, we are ungrateful to God. We can be. Because God is our suppliers, with all the things. We need, and to go by. The gift that we received from God Pointing out to people, who are capable of protecting. The less fortunate, of this world today. Also knowing what other's needs. Still they choose not to do anything, or they do very little. Even the most faith full. Especially, when they are able to do, so much more.

God made it very simple. He gave us instructions how to defeat, and overcome evil with good. We should never give up. God know, if he helps us, conquer evil with good. Evil will vanish off face of earth. We need to keep going, and never give up. Because, when we give up pleases Evil and displease God.

God made it easy, and very simple to understand him, and to know him through holy bible. If you please study it ?. You will be inspired, by wisdom of God. It will be, immediately known to you. If you received the holy spirit of God ? There is no way anyone, will be able to hurt you ever.

God gave us at any costs, the path to the truth, leading us, to the light, the true light. God did guarantee. For all of us, salvation through our lord Jesus.

From our first parents. Adam, and Eve, God he's our speaker, and defender against evil. Genesis 12:1-2.

To remind ourselves, and the people around us to be obedient,to God always to be ready to do what's good, and not to speak evil against anyone. Titus 3:1-2,7.

We should always be gentle, show true humility, by doing right, that is how, we justify grace of God's that had being given to us. He wants, every single human being. To fully please him God wishes are. To share with us eternal life.

Our body is Temple of the Holy Spirit. 1 Corinthians 3:16-17.

This is why, we must glorify God. With all of our minds, hearts and souls. God made it very simple to understand him. He have solution for all the problems, we may face throughout, our life time on earth. Both old, and new Testaments, are guidance for humanity. They were also, called books of our life. Every question, you have form A to Z.

God always know, what we need, God doesn't, need to read our minds. Because he Is, our mind. He made our heads brain, and body. God know, how everything works. He know what we are thinking 24/ seven. If you don't believe me? Pray silently. God still hears. You will know when your prayer, gets answer. I did so many times, and my prayers were answered. Give it a try. Unfortunately for you, and I There is, a special way we pray. No one know. Not even one single living human being. Except, God knows. The exact time. When our prayers are answered. The only thing, we can do Is Continue to pray, and we can be fortunate enough ? Without knowing, what we done. So special, for our God, that when he answers. He is a divine.

God is spirit, and worshipers must worship, in spirit and truth John 4:24.

God is our joy, and happiness. He is teacher philosopher therapist, healer, counselor. We find comfort in him. He is about teaching us to be happy, safe and prospective Fully free to do whatever, we please. As long, as we don't hurt ourselves, or anyone else. Therefore, he is all about us.

Many who claim, to be Christian, never, or hardly read the Bible. They only know about what they hear. From church's and others.

Example - If you were critical having, many issues. Stopping you from moving forward in life. Of course, first thing you would want to do is, to seek help of therapist, philosopher, or someone who generally put you, on the right path. For long, or short time. If you were getting, all the help you need it? He or she, really changes your life. Especially, if you were struggling with, many issues, and problems. May be in short, or long time you got, all the help you needed. Suddenly you became different person. You were happy. Every - thing was going well for you. Finally, he or she helps it, changing your life for good. My question for you is ? What, you would do for that person. You received all the help you needed, to make your life better ? More likely you will appreciate him, or her. If you know, how to be grateful, for all the good things you received Myself if I had, any problems. If I recovered with help of some one. I would idle, the person, who helped me putting my life on the right track. See bible.

Example - If you have parents. Who raised you up very well, and you become great, and successful young man, or woman. Can you imagine how much you would love, honor respect those parents. Especially, If you are grateful, thoughtful appreciative person.

That what God is. He about teaching us. If we listen to him, we will be taking. The right path, directly to him. God also takes our problems, and issues to him self.

Through the bible, God fixing everything for us.

For the word of God is living, and active. Hebrews 4:12.

Blessed are, those who hears word of God, and keep it Luke 11:28.

Bible is word of God, Being revealed to us. Bible is the greatest book. Ever being written. God made it clear and simple, for us to understand. What he is saying to us.

Bible is knowledge, wisdom, and ethics. Of God.

For anyone, who is seeking answers? About life's, profound question. So many who are wise enough, to be committed to the truth of the Bible.

Through the Bible, God wishes of us are, to stay focused on our lives, and life of people around us. Simply, God want us to be our brother's keeper.

He wants us, to be his soldiers. Under, his orders, and command, here on earth. God create us, with free will. He will never change that.

This is why he gave the bible. So we can make our will to seek him always, and choose him.

With honor, and respect to those who are debating whether, there is God, or not? They are being deceived by the evil. While busy wondering, if God exists, or not? At mean time. They are not giving them self -much time to think About how much, we need to fix, in our world today? In order to make, entire world better place to live for us, and generation to come. We should make this one. Our number one goal. That what would truly please God. He want, our wish, and calling to be focusing on making this, entire earth great place to live.

We need, to pay attention to what's happening around us abuse, greed, diseases, Wars, and hate We need to, focus on making this world save place to live in it, for us, and for generations to come. We need to stop hunger, in this world together. One person, out of the time. We can really do it. We need to spread mercy, and peace in the world.

So many innocent victims dying, for any cost, for any reason. They don't need to die tragically We need to spread peace. Hate,and wars are both distress. If someone's father, mother, child, brother sister, or relatives, or even one of their friends, get killed for any reasons. People, don't forget. It is hard to forget. This is how people, become enemies, and spread hate. So many, who seek vengeance therefore, there is no end to it. taking vengeance won't be the best solution. The best thing, to do would be, to reach those people, who are in great need, to mourn with them, to be there for them. To reach, their hearts. Letting them, know they are not alone and we care. We can, make things better for them. Surely, no one can bring their loved ones back. But we can guarantee their security. We can also guarantee them to live. In peace, and harmony.

God give us grace, love, mercy, taught us how to be compassionate. God favors the ones who are always motivate, and those who never give up. Giving up, pleases evil, and displease God.

God always want, what best for us. He also intervenes in our life for our own good.

Always, to be confident, he will answer Matthew 7:11.

If we ever, become critical. We should call on spirit of God to come and live with us to rescue us from all the danger.

God is love.

Nothing can, or will separate us from, the love of God. Romans 8:11.

In Christ Jesus, our Lord. Power of God, was revealed. God reached to us. God made it possible to touch him to reach him. To see him, face, to face through Jesus Christ. See, New Testament. God wished to be with us, as divine human. Flesh, and blood. To suffer, and die for the sake, of humanity. To open the door, and the way to heaven. Giving us chance, so we can be able to repent.

Jesus Christ, put evil to shame.

Because of God, unconditional love for us. He became, the son. He put him self- down for us

To suffer, and died, on the cross. So we can be saved Mark 15:24.

When we do good, we are asking for God rewards. We get great things. Also good, and happy rewards. When we sine, we are asking, for evil reward. What kind of reward evil will give us? That is when we sin. Evil rewards are making us suffer more. When we sin, we open the door for the Evil to put us through more temptations.

God is our refuge; he is our savior always, on his way to rescue us. God is, the father, who is too, over protective over his children. Psalms 4:17.

We became, children of God. Through, our Lord Jesus Christ.1John3:1.

We must stay holy, with our Lord Jesus Christ. Jesus said I will take you, to the father. John 14:2.

At the end, of our journey here. On earth. He would

We take. All of our goodness, and challenges, we may face through our lifetime. Even all of our wrong doing, and hard times take it to him. By simply repenting, he is ready to forgive us.

God is holy

Merciful he is. He always, do what he promised.1 King 8:56.

All community, of Israel praise God. Through Moses God granted them miracles, and gave them instruction.

God always ready to serve us. God often say let me do it for you. God humbled himself through Jesus Christ.

Jesus washed feet of his disciple John 13:1-17.

Jesus gave, freedom to the poor, he fed the hungry, he healed the sick, he did all that, and much more So he can teach us to do, for each other John 15:9-10.

If we continue, to go by word of God. His love will remain with us. John 14:23.

Jesus is, unconditional love, of the father, for humanity. If we have like heart, of Jesus, to be like him, to do what he commands us to do. Which is, to love each other, as he loves us We will have greater chance to see, and be with God someday.

The mighty God, the Lord has spoken he summoned all humanity from east to west. Psalms 50:1.

God will bring, all faithful people to him, and the ones who made covenant with himself By giving, all the sacrifice. Along with all the suffering, abuse, persecution, we face. To put it in perspective. We give to God. He knows how to fix everything. God will wipe the tears off our eyes. At the end. We will be comforted.

Lord is, a warrior Lord, his name. Israelites song praising, God for saving them from pharaohs. God show Israelites, his abundant lasting power of love, to his people Exodus 15:3.

Just like all humanity, when we have it all goods in our lives, we praise God, but for one little bad thing happened to us. We immediately lose our patient, and we blame God That's what Israelite **did** too.

Understand then, that the lord, your God indeed. He who keep his covenant down to thousands of years, and generations to come, toward those who love him, and keep his commandments. Deuteronomy7:19

If we obey God, and do what he commands us faithfully? The lord God, will keep his love with us. As he promised. Faith without work is not enough. I mean doing charities for our spirituals enrichment. Doing for the less fortunate. We need, to train ourselves to do what God command us to do. We need to do what is best for our spiritual being. God want our spirit to be pure.

The suffering, we indoor in this life, It is the road that lead us to the truth, and hope, in the living God. If those among us, who strongly believed.

God said he, is the beginning. There is no end to him. This is a revelation from Jesus Christ which **God give**. Revelation 1:8.

John concerning, about the events that will happen Toward the end of times. Angel was sent to John. So he can share revelation.

With God's other servants, which is, all of us human being John faithfully reported, word of God, and the testimony of Jesus Christ, and everything,he saw in the vision.

This will be made, manifest at proper time the blessed and that only sovereign, the King, of Kings, and the Lord of Lords. Timothy 6:15.

If we all become the living word of God. Obeying his commandments, so we can be ready at the return. Of our Lord **Jesus Christ, from heaven with the power, of Almighty God to claim us**

We will live, with God forever.

At end of days, people who trust, in God will be saved. Isaiah25:8.

Salvation was given to us, through Jesus. God want everyone to be committed to him, every moment we live.

We must love God, with all of our soul's hearts, and minds Deuteronomy 6:4-5.

God is love. John 4:16

If we only believe, in the love, God has for us. He will give us, unconditional love If we just, love each other His love, will be perfectly, pure for us. If we, always have love in our hearts. God will be with us.

Our faith in God, comes from the bible. He is rich, with wisdom, knowledge. He is, fair judge Romans 11:5

God he is, a mystery. No one can ever, or figure out exactly. God has, his own way of dealing with us.

We should always, examine ourselves;

Judging, ourselves first. This is our only chance While we are alive. So we have the chance to correct our self. If we, know we are doing wrong. Before we face God at, final judgment of God. It might be too late. If we don't live repented life according. Therefore, with the God nothing will be imposing.

Mother of Jesus, when she was told, the good news by the angel. That child will be born. He will be called holy son of God The highest Luke 1:37.

Merely trusting God, because of her faith, and belief. She was full of grace She said the hand maid of the Lord, be it done to me according, to thy word, and the angel departed from her. Luke 1:38

He will swallow up, death forever, and the Lord God will wipe away tears, from all faces, and the reproach of his people he will take away. From all earth; for the Lord has spoken Isaiah 25:8.

God said, if we come to him, we find comfort God know the past, and the future before it happens.

God want us always to focus on him. So the evil will never come near us If we only trust, in him, and live according to his work, and the words. He had spoken to us, through his prophets messengers, and spirituals. Nehemiah 9:38.

He will always be with us. God made our minds This is why, he doesn't have to read it. Because he is our minds.

Therefore, he knows our, thoughts 24 seven This is, the way God knows what, we want, and need 24/7. We don't, even have to ask, all we have to do is to think about what we need. He will give it to us. God hears our mind. He also, read our hearts God

will always, grant our wishes. If we trust, in him. He would never let any harm comes to us.

And now, our God, the greatest, the mighty also awesome God, who keeps his covenant, of unfailing love for us. Nehemiah 9:38.

Nothing, from earth can be compared to the love God give us. He never leaves our side, even when we sin. He walks along our site, waiting for us to repent, and return back to him. God is merciful, and gracious.

He's got unlimited patient. God assured, Moses of his love mercy, and full of grace, he is. Exodus 34:6.

Salvation was made possible, through Jesus Christ. In him we have redemption and forgiveness of sins. Jesus Christ. He is the son of the living God Ephesians 1:7-8.

We put our hope fully, in Jesus Christ. We must, think clearly. With open hearts exercise self – control. To look forward for all the blessings we will receive, at return of our Lord Jesus Christ from heaven.1 Peter 1:13.

We were called children of God. John 2:28

whoever, do will of God will be called his child. We continue asking for God's protection.

He will definitely, be with us, and as we do will of God. What can we ever possibly be afraid of Psalms 18:30.

If we know God is with us. What possibly, can go wrong? God is good. If we continue to do his will ? For sure Goods will come, always.

Abraham rewards, were great. He had of great faith in God. Genesis 15:1

we can never succeed, without faith, in God Eternal Faith, is fulfillment word of God.

Jesus answered. I am the way, and the truth and the life John 14:6.

Jesus is, the way the truth, to the eternal light leading us to the father, to true life. God is everything he is worthy of our trust. God is love, just fair merciful gracious. And full of grace.

We worship him in spirit, and truth. John 4:24 Jesus said, we must worship God in spirit, and truth.

By his word, he created the heaven, and earth the seas, and ocean. Psalms 33:4

God made us, to be his own children. Now we received, not the spirit of the world. But the spirit which is from God. That may understand the gift best owed, by God 1Corinthians 2:12-16

He has, actually, given us his spirits. So we can know the wonderful things God has freely given to us so we can speak wisdom. With words that they were given to us, by the holy spirit of God. We speak the truth. Spiritual truths.

It is clear that, no one can ever be right with God. By only trying to keep the law For Scripture say. It is through faith, we become righteous people Galatians 3:10

If we wish to find life. It is by obeying all the law, and must obey, all the Commandments, and to live according, and go by it.

God watch over the ones, who do his will. When he hear them calling for help he come down and rescued them. Psalms 34:6-18.

We turn, all our problems to God, and all our complaints, he will solve it for us. We turn to God whenever we are in bondage.

Fear of the Lord, is the beginning of knowledge Only fools despise wisdom an instruction. Fearing God it is loving him, and it is beginning of wisdom. Proverbs 1:7

Accepting, word of God. We receive, the Holy Spirit. God give us the knowledge wisdom and understanding. He grants, us treasure of good sense Proverbs 2:6.

If we walk with, integrity ? He will guard our path, and protects it. When we are faithful to him. If we take advice of the wise. We will succeed. Who don't listen to good advice, and who despise advice they will find themselves in trouble all the time.

To those who, you give advice. And they don't listen don't give it, unless they accept it. Proverbs 2:10.

If we give advice. If they don't accept it, don't give it no more. But pray for them.

God came to Abraham. Because, he recognized his faith, and believes. He was also righteous man.

Because, of his faith. God declare, Abraham righteousness by choosing him Genesis 15:6.

We do will of God, by keeping his commandments by doing that. We are, accepting his terms, and conditions. Deuteronomy 27:10.

Jesus Christ. He is the fulfillment of the scripture. He said. I did not come, to abolish the laws. But to full fill them. Matthew 5:17-20

He is, the good news. Being delivered, from heaven Jesus Christ, asked people to believe, in the gospel Asking, people to turn away from their, sinful ways and come back to God. Jesus was, heaven here on earth. He revealed to us heart, of God.

Through Jesus, God showed us, how much, he wished to heal us, feed us Also lived among us. To forgive us. He gave his son to die for us. and to lay himself down us. Died for our sins. So we could be forgiven Can you imagine how awesome this one God is?

God gave, his only son. John 3:16

Abrahams, faith was active along, with his work. His faith was completed. Romans 2:22

Abraham, trusting in God. So much that. He was willing, to do whatever, it takes to please God.

Faith with action, and hard work charity is a strong faith.

At the temptation. Jesus Christ told evil. God will give us our daily supply. But it is more important to focus on, our spirit. You're not to live by bread alone. But by, every word that proceed, from mouth of God. Matthew 4:4.

Jesus told, the evil. I am bread of life that comes from heaven. Jesus Christ alone we needed.

Evil tried to figure out, if this is really Jesus son of God. Descended from God Jesus always put evil, to shame. Jesus conquered evil with good. So we can do the same thing. We should be evils, disappointments. That is, when we do will of God.

God will always give us, food to live. We should focus on enriching our spirits To live according.

Just like earthly fathers. God always, forgives.

Generation comes, and generation go, season will come another will go away.

But not one word of God, will go away. It will stay forever. Isaiah 40:8.

The truth, will never go away. We all die. But God live. Glory to God is forever Jesus said. The old was never lost, but it is accomplished, and is stronger, and more permanents Luke 16:16-17.

Jesus showed us. He is the living, word of God. He was heaven, here on earth He wants us to have hearts like his.

Faith in God is good, and spiritual. We receive Holy Spirit of God, through devotions, and prayers God is the shining light on every corner of earth.

God always extends his unlimited love, to all the generations Acts 12:24 Holy Spirit of God, is the author. Bible, it is word of truth. The truth that defeated and Conqueror the evil. Ephesians 6:17.

All goodness in the world, came out of the Bible.

The light of God makes the darkened on earth. Turn into the light that shines forever. Psalms 18:28

With prayer, and devotion, for the Holy Spirit of God. Trusts in God. We would never fail. We will always succeed. If we do will of God, all the time. Where would evil fit ?

In faith, and love. Which is In Christ Jesus Guard the truth, has been entrusted to you. By the Holy Spirit who dwell within us the gift we receive from the Holy Spirit 2 Timothy 1:13-14.

Holy spirit is the gift was given to us. We need to share it with others. Therefore if we can be trusted little. Will be given to us twice more.

We practice our faith. By putting it into good work. Therefore, we were made temple of God.

God will dwell in us, and make us holy.

If we don't obey, the commandment. We will bring destruction, into our lives and the people around us.

By obeying, the commandment. We will have, moral values peace mercy, and happiness. Wise people, think before they act.

People who follow, and obey the commandments, They will be reworded. If we know the Commandments. God want us to, put it into practice, and teach it to others That would really, pleases him.

The word of God, from heaven. It is promise ready for everyone here on earth Psalms 119:89.

God, will never put us down. Word of God will remain forever.

The predictions of Prophets, and the Commandments of the Lord, and Savior Jesus Christ, through his disciple's. Peter 3:2.

God through his prophets, prepared his coming for our solution. The way was prepared. The good news and testimony, of Jesus Christ our redeemer Jesus spoke with power, of the holy spirit of God Self -tests reveal.

Jesus told, the crowd. I am not, teaching you on my own But from God within me. John7:16-17

We need to practice, what we preach. Because, when we preach. We don't look for praise from the once we preach to. But trying to express to them. There's no power above God.

Gospel must be, first taught, to all nations Toward end, of the day's. People will need to know the truth Mark 13:10

Because, of so much hate, greed. abuse persecution, destructions, hunger People, will be disparate. Hope. For an

answer. Toward end of the days. They will find hope. In the gospel. Holy Gospel will guide them, to God.

The gospel, is capable of leading, the entire world out, of the darkness, into the light of the truth. It is unlimited, power of God. World will discover. They do need God.

We need, Jesus alone. For our Salvation. He is unconditional, love of the father Peace mercy compassion, and full of goodness.

Do your best, to present yourself, to God, as a man, a worker. That cannot be a shamed rightly handling. The word of the truth 2 Timothy 2:15.

If we want know the truth about God. That is, Wisdom of God it is truth about God. If we are a shame, to teach it, to others. God will be a shame to know us.

We improve our faith, by working hard on it. By love, charities. To live life of grace, virtue, peace, and mercy. We should be like. Army to defend God here on earth.

Paul said, cannot be a shame. I do not be a shamed of testify to our Lord 2Timothy2:8

Paul was prisoner, suffering for the gospel. By power of the Holy Spirit. He spoke, word of God without fear, or shame. Because he knew, he was on mission from God, he had to accomplish word of God here on earth. Paul knew, the suffering he endured, it was only temporarily.

We all can, become pure by guarding our life. So we can go according to the word of God. Psalms 119:9

In God, we find peace, and happiness. God want us, to have safe journey, to heaven. God called us to know him, to understand him, and to obey him.

We must humble our self. Because we are sinner. God always forgive. Because he know we are human being, and weak. When it comes to sin.

Jesus Christ revealed, to us face, and heart of God. Love of God, who wanted to heal us, feed us Protect us, watch over us, and even die for us. So we can have a chance to repent, and the door of paradise to open for us.

So we can be with, God in, his heavenly kingdom forever Romans 10:16

We are not supposed, to make, any money preaching the gospel, it is free of charge from God 1Cornthians 9:16, 18.

Especially, we are not, supposed to have any personal gain from preaching the gospel. It is important preaching of the gospel because, it is word of God.

Gospel lead everyone, from dark to the light. Be at rest, in God alone, comes our hope. God alone is, our rock, and salvation. He is, our security Psalms 62:6-7.

We never fail. When we find our refuge in God. Especially, when we put our trust in him. We are letting him take control, of our lives.

If we trust in God, and resist evil. God will always be with goodness, he will come to us James 4:7-8.

If we are good, hundred percent of time, or even, if we keep trying. Where would the evil fit. When, evil see we are not about to give up, he stay away.

We are free, to approach. God for all our needs For the needy, shall not always be forgotten, and the hope of the poor, shall not perish ever Psalms 9:18

God gives hope to the needy. They will not be dismissed by God. His gives freedom to the poor. God put in other people's hearts to rescue, the poor and the hungry.

When hope, and mercy accomplished. It makes the less fortunate. Humble, and they continue to trust in God. Bible gives us hope. It is the word of, the truth. Psalms 119:43-44.

Therefore, we ask the Holy Spirit, to inspire us to be devoted, to the words of God, which is the Commandments and the laws.

Jesus answered him, why you call me good ? No one is good, but God alone Luke18: There is, no end to God's holiness, and goodness. God created us. So we can share with him the goodness he offered, to us.

Jesus said, be perfect, as your heavenly father is perfect. Matthew 5:48

Everybody in the world make mistakes, we all sin. But it is, in our power to be hundred percent good, people. By having unconditionally love, mercy, and forgiveness toward everyone around us.

Always to defend the less fortunate, to be fair hundred percent of the time Protect the abused, and the neglected. Also the orphans. Try our best, to feed the poor, and the hungry. To seek justice for the ones who, desperately needed.

Whom are innocent. To defend persecuted. So they can live in peace, and harmony, with everyone we have the free will. We can always try to do what's best for our self, and the people around us. God called us to be our brother's keeper, and obey the commandment.

Anyone who, has this hope, passed on, to others, and makes himself pure, as he is pure.1 John 3:2-3.

God promised, we will one day be with him in heaven, so we can, praise him face-to-face. For now we worship God in spirit

Love is God

God is love. Whoever loves, is begotten of God and know God.1 John 4:7-8.

If any has no love, in their hearts. Does not know God.

For God so loved the world that. He gave his only son, so that everyone who believes in him, might not perish. But might have everlasting life. John 3:16

God send his son, not to judge the world but to save it. Jesus came, into this world, to take us to God. Jesus Christ, put the evil to shame. He truly showed us, what heaven Is like. He touched our hearts, and souls. Jesus called us to walk into his footsteps. So we never trip. He said, I will take you, to the father. If we do what he commands us to do. Which is to love each other as he loved us?

Jesus died for us. Jesus wants us, to love our enemies, and always, conquer evil, with good. Matthew 5:43-48.

King David he praised God, he trusted in God, he prayed, and said. Stand firm through the love, of the most high. Psalms 21:1-13.

The truth about God is. He wants to give us un-conditionally. He wants us, to put our life, under his control, and command. We should never be afraid when it comes to God. God wants us, to be courageous, confidence that he will answer our prayers.

Furthermore, when we pray to God, we transform ourselves, by receiving the Holy Spirit of God. We speak to God just like. If we were talking to our earthly father, he is there. When we need him.

Jesus said, believe. Matthew 21:21.

God will give, what our hearts desire. We can give God, our requests, and struggles, in this life. So he can, prepare us for next life with him.

God blessed them, and said to them, be fruitful, and increase in number, and fill the earth. Genesis 1:28.

God, will always bless us, and multiply us. The fulfillment, well of God promised for, all human beings to fill in the earth. Deuteronomy 7:13.

God gives, us freedom to do what we want. As long, as we don't hurt our self and others.

God wants us, to be happy. He knows if we are happy. Everyone around us, will be happy. God also give us freedom to prospect. The most profound thing. It is God wishes, to gain every single person living, on the face of earth.

The gospel, must first, be preached to all nations Mark 13:10.

God depends on good, and faithful people. Who are capable of teaching, and explaining to people. What God call us to do. Luke 10:17-18.

God want us, not to judge anyone. But to reach, to them, letting them know how much God is concerning. About our moral values, happiness, and safety.

God wants us to know, how much, we could benefit, by doing, following, and going by his Commandments.

Fortunately, there is God. Because no one lived forever here on earth. We all die. God lives forever.

Unfortunately, we are so deceived. Because we are not able to debate. People who have doubts. If there is God or not ? People

who don't believe. In God are more deceived then the ones, who do believe, in God.

Evil making us so, busy wondering When at the meantime. There's so much needed to be done for our world today.

We need to focus, on our life, our children, our neighbors relatives, and friends Mainly, all people around us to make this world, of ours. Safe, and peaceful world So we can enjoy, what God have entrusted in us.

Blessed are they, who maintain justice, for who constantly do, what is right Psalms106:3

We need, to concentrate, and focus on stopping the wars, hate, abuse persecution killing, and greed.

Make sure everyone, makes meaning, to their living. Treating each other equally and fair. Defend the less fortunate. To bring justice, to the abused. We need to bring, cheers, and happiness into hearts of the lonely. Stop the suffering in the world We can do it, one out of time, or one, on one.

Killing of innocent's. Need it, to stop. We need to spread peace, and mercy of God around. The world desperately, needed.

Letting people, know that. God love them, and want them back. So he can call them his children.

Our faith can inspire us, to be good, holy. To live according all the teaching.

We received from **God. Greet every saint, in Jesus Christ Philippians 4:21 4:21.**

Saints in heaven, they pray, for the living. We can prepare people, to become saints. When they get to heaven. There is, no saints living, on earth. Only when they get to heaven. They become saints. Saint are the ones. Who pleases God in every way here on earth.

It is great, and spiritual, rewarding, for every person who pleases God fully. But it is not enough for God.

God still, wants us to look at bigger picture. Which is, the world around us (The people) to see what is wrong to fix it. To take

care of anyone who's in need. It don't matter. Who they are, what they are. Or what they look like.

Unfortunately many of us. In the event that we die. Before we enter into the gates of heaven. More likely. We will be pause So we can be reminded. There was Someone, who when, we were able to feed, and we didn't feed him, or her. Someone was sick; we did not go to him, or her, to comfort them, and a lot more. We neglected to do for others. When we were alive.

God is holy.1John 1:5-7.

We are called, to be holy. We are all being reminded. Especially, of all of our obligation, and responsibilities toward each other. So much, we can do. God want us to be our brother's keeper.

Authority comes from the bible. Romans 11:2.

So many who don't understand the meaning, of their faith besides being moral.

Religion, is rules regulations, and laws, we put over our self's. So we can, control the way we behave. We learn all that, from the bible.

It is great, to attend church, or holy institution. If we don't think God will be present anywhere ? For sure 100% He will be in the church, and holy institution This is why? We go to church, for spiritual healing, and purification.

Word of God is living, and active Hebrews 4:12.

The authority, comes from the bible. That's word of God. Religion is. How much, we are pleasing God?

By the way, we treat others.

Which is, how much we love? how much we forgive ? How much we give into society? How loyal, we are.

Jesus. He is the living word of God. John 1:1-2.

We often hear about some people. Being called, God's people. Those are, the people who do everything to please God. All their teachings, and knowledge comes from the holy bible. They believe, and practice word of God accordingly. They also, put everything that comes, from the bible into perspective. They believe. They have great faith. Because for some reason always

things work for them. They trust God, in the most profound way. They have, the calling.

They believe in miracles. Jesus said. Believe. Everything, is possible, with God Mark 9; 23.

Jesus washing, his Disciples feet, they called him teacher, and LORD; He told them. If I am your LORD, and teacher have washed your feet. You also ought to wash each other feet, and serve. John 13:15.

Jesus said to them. I am given you an example. God call us, to serve each other. Because he is always willing to serve us.

All the people, who lives on earth today, and also the ones, who is, about to be born, in the world. They are, descendant of the ones. Who saw, Gods face. Over two thousand years ago. In the person, of our lord Jesus Christ.

Now among us, who chooses to be, like Jesus. Everyone, who look, at them.

They will, see face of God.

Chapter 2

Charities

Throughout the bible. God is very concern about the poor, hungry the less fortunate, and orphans. Widows, victims the abused, and persecuted. Doing charity, helping the poor and feeding the hungry. It is our key to heaven.

Jesus said, love your neighbor, as yourself. Mark 12:31 Matthew 22:35.

Neighbor is, not only the person, who live next door to you. It is your family, friend mainly stranger.

We could say, to anyone. I love you until we turn blue. For sure, will please them, some – what But how much good would do her, or him. If they are, lonely, depressed sick poor hungry have no one, to lean on. Having many problems. With no job. How much, the word, love would help them.

God want us to, reach to anyone, to see what, need to be done. That what, will please God. His demand are, to reach to everyone to make sure, they have what they need. If we do so, were would, evil fit.

Blessed is he, who considers to the poor. The Lord delivering him, in the day of trouble Psalms 41:1-2.

He is, ever giving liberally, and lending, and his children become a blessing. Psalms 41:1-2. But when you give, a feast invite, the poor, the maimed the blind. Luke 14:13-14.

Share your bread with the hungry, and bring the homeless Into your house. Isaiah 58: 7.

Sell your possessions, and alms, provide your selves with purses that do not grow old, with a treasurer, in the heaven that does not fail Luke 12:33.

He who despises, his neighbor, is a sinner. But happy is he who is kind to the poor. Proverbs 14:21 He who, has distributed freely. He has given to the poor, his righteousness endures forever, his horn is exalted in honor Psalms 112:91.

Be merciful, even as your father, in heaven, is merciful Luke 6:38.

He who gives, to the poor will not want. Proverbs 28:27.

For God loves a cheerful giver. He scatters abroad, he gives to the poor, his righteousness endure forever. 2 Corinthians 9:7.

One man gives freely, yet grows, all the richer another with holds what he should give, and only suffer want Proverbs 11:24, 25.

For the rich, of the world, not to get their hopes, on uncertain riches but on God, who richly furnishes us, with everything to enjoy 1Timothy 6:17- 18.

If you pour yourself, out for the hungry, and satisfy the desire of the afflicted, your light shall rise in the darkness,and your gloom is, as the noon day. Isaiah 58:10.

Blessed is, who considers, to the poor the Lord delivers him in the day of trouble. Psalms41:1-2

He is ever, giving liberally, and lending and his children becoming a blessing. Psalms 37:25-26.

Do not go, over your vineyard, a second time, or pick up the grapes that have fallen leave them for the poor I am the LORD your God. Leviticus 19:9-11.

There will always, be poor people in the land. Therefore I command you, to be open hand, toward your brothers and toward the poor, and needy Deuteronomy 15:11.

Defend the cause of the weak, and fatherless, maintain the right of, the poor, and oppressed rescue the weak, and needy. Psalms 82:3-4.

He who oppresses, the poor show contempt to their maker but whoever is kind to the needy honors God. Proverbs 14:31.

If I publish this book. I would like, to start charity foundation to help the poor, homeless hungry. I will try to find people, with no jobs, or having a hard time finding one. May be I can help. Even if I can help one, out the time, or few. I will be able to make some different. The only profits. I want to make, out of this book, to live financially comfortable. I don't care, if I am not, very healthy, as long, as my bills are, paid in time, and I have roof over my head. I also like to help, the refugees, no matter what they are, or who they are. Or were they came from. In particular I like to help my people. Many of them, escaped persecution from Iraq Because of their Christian beliefs.

My people, they are ancient Chaldean's, from 5000 years ago. Many spread all over the world. Especially, some came to America; most of them live in very terrible condition. It is hard, to imagine, or believe that someone who's, with children have nothing. No food, no clothes, no roof over their head. Many generous people, are taking responsibilities to care for them but that Is not enough.

Here in America, many needs our help. I will like to team with other, charity foundations Together we can, make a different.

Here in America we, have many people, who always help the needy feed the hungry give away clothes to the ones who need it. It is great, and blessing.

If we feed someone, who is hungry. Will need, food the next day, for. People need to eat. If we give shelter. Will need shelter, the next day. If we give clothes, will need clothes again, and many other things, the needy need.

Fortunately, many are, generous givers. But unfortunately there's no end to it. In order for us, to reduce the poverty.

We need to find people, with no jobs. We can try, to find them jobs. So we can, put them to work. The ones who are not healthy, we can try to bring them to health, so they be able to work.

Because, of all the statements. Jesus made, all the charity were created. Feeding the poor It is our key to heaven.

Chapter 3

The Ten Commandment

God came to Moses, on the top of Mount Sinai. Moses was given the commandment, and was written by God, on two stone tablet. Exodus 32:19. Ex24:12. Ex34:1,14.

God gave Moses stone tablets on It. Was written the commandments, and intended for the people at that time, and for entire human being today,and beyond For all the time instruction.

The purpose of the 10 commandments. For God to instruct the humanity. How to deal, and go by with a life, and how to get along with each other. How to live happy, and to prevent our self from suffering. It is not only sinning against God. But it is true to be his children.

The 10 commandments. Were first. to worship him only, no other God. Exodus20:1-17.

To need acknowledge, God is creator of heaven, and earth and whatever is seen, and not seen

God he is, a jealous God Exodus20:4-6

He wants nothing to come before him. He created as his own image Genesis 1:27

God don't want, to lose not even one of us to Evil. God love for humanity is love at first side; This is why he created us. So we can enjoy, and share his heavenly kingdom.

The moment, that God created Adam, and eve he was very pleased. He put our first parents into the paradise, to enjoy, and control entire earth from A, to Z. Even after they sin See (Genesis).

God created man, to his own image. Like image of God, in spirit he created us. Genesis1:27.

At first,in the beginning he created them male, and female. God made Adams flesh out of the earth. See (Genesis).

God give us part of his spirits to give us life. God is awesome, wonderful and beyond our imagination. God love for us is beyond our knowledge, and Imagination. He made us part of him in spirit.

Even when Adam and eve committed first sin, and offends God by disobeying God(Genesis). Still promised them salvation. God create things in the most unique ways Therefore, he made us part of him. He made us so we can never depart from him. God's love for us is great. He gave us the opportunity to be fruitful and multiply.

Because all of our continuously falling he gave us the commandments for our moral values. To put in laws, rules, regulation over our self's. So we can live by for our own being and safety. Also to control the way we behave.

First the Laws began with, what it a human is being duties toward God. Also concluded with our obligations toward one and another. Also the knowledge, and wisdom we receive from God, they are for us to, practice,and to put it into perspective. See Exodus.

When people heard what God command them to do they kept it they went by according. It became their understanding, site of people. Surely great and wise nation Deuteronomy 4:6-8 people seek God, and whenever, we call upon him by praying. We receive the Holy Spirit. He is merciful God. We don't have to search for God because he is everywhere he's a light of the world. He is our hearts and minds because he made us. Therefore, he's part of our spirit. He is God with us, and present among us

The values, we learn from the 10 commandments. Evil trying to wipe it away.

Evil trying to block, our children minds from understanding, and knowing what moral values is about. I mean it is sad unfortunate, that always trying to remove the 10 commandments display, from court house, and judiciary buildings.

People in major, and especially our children, and future generations more likely or eventually Will become normal to kill, murder. Will be OK to steal. Will be fine if they commit adultery Children will think it is OK to dishonor their mothers and fathers, and even the Elders. Everyone will think, it is fine to bear false witness against their neighbor. Especially in court, where the law, and justice are practiced Our kids will also think it is fine to covet their neighbor's goods, and murder them They would not know any better. Our children, would not understand the consequences. They are about to face. Many don't know anything about the 10 commandments.

The ones who, are trying to remove of the 10 commandments, more likely they do not want to know, or care about moral values. Any person with moral values, it should not matter what their beliefs are. They should respect, and protect human dignity. Only the ones with no moral, or family values Hates God. The truth, and the people around them.

For the sake, of humanity. We have the Laws. Includes the commandments. They are about every single human being living, on the face of earth. They are about our happiness. And safety.

People who hate God they don't want to be the only ones who do. Therefore they want everyone around them to hate God also. That is taking every one freedom.

One of the things, we need to remind ourselves. One of the biggest things other happening all around us. It is families are falling a parts. Divorce rates, are very high. Truly, getting divorce becoming common thing. Marriages being destroyed, and falling apart.

The ones who fought against moral values. By wanting to remove, the 10 commandments, they are in the dark, and being misled by the evil. They may be have, best and highest education in the entire world. But they could never, be able to come inch close. To what had being given to us in the, bible Wisdom, grace, love, mercy, peace.

There are many People, who hate God, and others trying to take people's freedom. If they think they have any values. By basing their morals values, on taking others freedom. That is not values. Also they don't know how to be moral. The way I look at it, if someone tries to take my freedom. It is act of; Evil hate. That is great terrorism against me.

There's so much we need, to accomplish in our world today. When at the meantime people are trying, to destroy what God put together for us.

Stupider we got, when it comes to values.

We are losing our pride, and destroying our dignity, our freedom. We have no more common sense. There are so many are too, ashamed to look at 10 commandments, because they think it is only about religion purpose. I don't understand where they got this information from. Even a little child if we explain to him, or her consequences. If they do wrong they will understand. How much more adult who should know the consequences.

The Ten Commandments, are so we can understand. How to live a life Also to understand that no one can judge us, if they don't give anyone reason. No one can judge except God. Therefore the fair the just, and the honest judges, are descended from God.

For all of the people the powers is not ours. God give us power, and strength.

Anti-God and religion they are deceived. Otherwise, they will be able to distinguish between good, and evil. How is it in the world would anyone want to be against love, peace, mercy, grace. Or against people who are united together to do, what best for everyone.

The ones who hate, they also try to stop what it is beneficial to humanity. God's intention is not to hurt us, but carry us to the end.

God want us to be happy and comfortable. Our comfort is God's peace of mind. From 10 commandments. We learn goodness charity. How to become honorable to act proper to get along with everyone. To be positive, and moral. We learn about the things, we should do, and thing we should not do God mainly, want us acknowledge him, as our creator.

First. commandment to maintaining, and keep personal relationship with God. It must be our main and first priority. God want us to depend on. Him every second of our life.

Second. commandment it is only, to love, and worship true God, and that is our creator.

Third. commandment meant, for us to praise God. We also need to represent him, to each other, and throughout entire world. To express his mercy, peace, love, compassion grace. Extending it through us and the entire world. Stay on guard. Also to remember the Sabbath. On this day we remember what God had given us enough wisdom to love, and to get together with our families,and friends so we can receive more blessings, and joy. This day, we reserve to draw closer to God.

Fourth. commandment it is very important to God. To love, and respect especially, our parents they brought us into this world, and give us life.

Fifth. commandment is to respect human life, only God takes life.

Sixth. commandment to respect your spouse not to put our marriage down.

Seventh. commandment is not fair, trying to get what does not belong to us. Everyone works hard for what they own. It belong to them. Only them

Eighth. commandment, always speak the truth. Especially, what is against the innocent. Never speak about any one falsely. Like making up things, about others, or rumors, and gossiping behind someone's back

Ninth. commandment. Keeps praying so you don't tempt, or desire anyone else. We pray, only to desire our spouse. Never covets a married woman. God gives us our own spouse, to have, and keep

Tenth. commandment. We should always pray for others. For God to give them everything they need. Especially the poor. Not to be jealous of others.

About the old law and the new.

Jesus said do not think, that I have come to destroy the law, or the prophets, Jesus said did not come to destroy but fulfill. Matthew 5:17, 19.

If we ignore the commandment. We could get punished, and if we know the commandments We are obligated. To teach it. Prefect love, cast out fear.

Jesus said beloved, let us love, one another for God is love.1 John 4:17-19.

Would be wonderful, if we could use consent definition of love especially when we are speaking about the love God has for us, and the love we should have for each other.

It is very sad, to some point the world is lacking of love, and mercy. Most people will acknowledge love, as to some degree is, to respect. Love should be meaningful cannot be accurately defined, and understood.

Gods goal, and purpose, of the Law to destroy, the power of evil. When we walk, into right path.

The more we learn about God, the more knowledge, we get, and understand the fundamental of the truth; We also, learn how accurate the bible is. I mean it is word of God.

The scriptures old, and New Testament teach us how to love. In the most profound way.

Jesus said, is to love each other, as he loved us. John 13:34.

Jesus knows true love. Because, he laid down himself for us, and for the sake of humanity.

Love should be, even if, we have to risk our lives for others. Jesus said our true love to God, is when we love each other.

But first love God, above everything. To love God with all of our heart, with our entire mind with all of our soul, and love your neighbor, as yourself Matthew 22:35-40.

Moses wrote to the people of Israel. To fear God is to love him, and to walk in all of his ways and to serve him. Proverbs 1:7.

Commandments are to protect us from evil. Never less, every commandment God given us. It is for our own good. The commandments. defined love. As the foundation. For Godly relationship with us. God want us all, to live forever gaining eternal life with him one day after life, on earth.

In order for us to attain the eternal life. We must be protected from evil.

God want us to unite together not to be divided. Never give chance, to evil, to squeezes him between us, to pull us apart, far away from each other.

When we have, any problems. We needs to do will of God unconditionally. That's fixing it on the spot or we will lose, touch with God.

Evil always, jealous of humanity. Because us human being, God give us a chance. I don't know If evil have, any chance. Just the way. God wants us all for himself. So the evil.

Evil is great hate, anger, lust, greed, killing, wars persecution.

The bible define sin as lawful; breaking commandments that God had given us. We need to put everything into practice Deuteronomy 10:12.

Make holiness perfect in fear of God. Holy is not deceiving. 2 Corinthians 7:1.

Jesus said, that your lights shine before men that, they may see your good work and give Glory to your father who is in heaven. Matthew 5:16.

The way, we love, and express ourselves, and feelings for all the people, the goodness mercy charity, caring for others, being compassioned toward others. That is how people see God through us.

Just the way, people say often. When someone is good to them. They thank God. This is how; we truly become children of God.

The lord is with me; and not afraid; what can be against me? The lord with me, as my help Better to take refuge in the lord. Psalms 118:6-8.

As long, as we know that God he is with us. Who can be against us? Trust in, the lord with all your heart, trust in God and not on earthly things Proverbs 3:5.

The, Ten Commandments Exodus 20:1-17

First commandment. I am the lord your God. You shall not have strange Gods before me; you shall not make for your self's, graven image Exodus 20:3.

God said I am the lord your God. Brought you, out of Egypt you shall have no other Gods before me.

When Jesus was asked, which of all the law of scripture is the greatest. Matthew 22:36-40.

Jesus respond, was with the commandments, emphasizing the supreme importance, of our personal relationship with God.

Many people tried to do away, without God. That just doesn't work. World without God, will be a disaster. Worshiping the true God.

making him our supreme. It is the most important thing to him This is, how in the way Acknowledge him, as our creator.

We also pray for the conversion of others to God. The only true God. Is the lord true God. The creator. Jeremiah10:10.

He is the living God, who called us his beloved. Therefore he gets jealous, very easily because He wants us all for himself. He want us, to be his children. We are, his joy. By prayer, Marcy, love peace, charity, adoration, sacrifice, and promises vows. We will definitely feel, and know of God.

Second commandment- You shall not take the name of the lord God in vain.

For the lord will not leave unpunished, him who takes his name in vain. Exodus 20:4

We must honor God, not only with our lips but, also with our hearts Our entire life should be and must be praising God. Matthew 15:8

To be holy, it is being spiritual, and spiritual means doing always Godly, and heavenly things Blasphemy, cursing and perjury are for bid.

Jesus said, about swearing. Not to swear falsely but fulfill the oath to the lord.

Jesus concludes. I say to you not to swear at all; neither by the heaven, for it is the throne of God, and not by the earth for it is his foot stool. Matthew 5:33

Cursing, and blasphemy against God, people who do that,they are facing severe consequences' I don't believe this from God. Evil love, to see us putting God down. Evil rewards for us is punishment. When we sin, Evil take our life over,and control it.

Evil vengeance, against God. Is taking our life over from God. This is why, the more we sin, the more we suffer.

I advise people not to use God's name in vain. Usually consequences are severe, and not very good at all. In the small town I grew up whenever something used to happen Rumor, spread quick People immediately find out.

Once upon time someone died. The news spread of quickly some people goes there. Because they were concerned. Others wanted to be nosy. Well at one occasion, when I was very young Tragically someone died, couple streets from my house. Just like everyone else, I went to see. I got there Fortunately, I was always being good listener.

While there. I heard people saying one of the relative of that dead person was cussing, and cursing God, while doing that he had a stroke, in his mouth, he was not able to talk any more I do not remember if he ever healed. I hope he did. I am not sure, if it was true, or only rumor. I don't know. I only know what I heard. I could not judge, then or now. The only thing I can tell you I was witness to that event. People who offend, God very often they struggle a lot more than. Others.

Third commandment - Remember the Sabbath day, to keep it holy Exodus 20:7

When God finished creating the heaven, and the earth and the rest of the work he had done He blessed the seven day and called it holy. God he is truly our creator. Genesis 2:1-2

God wanted to remind us, to make this one day to worship him, as will, as defining who we are Also to make a proper relationship with him, and how to be relate to him.

On this day, is to spend some time with our loved ones. To know that God loves us all bunch Just because we have each other, and not to be all alone God. He is telling us, yes we do need to work prospect so we can make a living. But we keep our self-busy all week long away, from our loved ones away from our personal duties toward God, and our family.

Our rest should be, *when we are spending some time with our family. The day of resting it is the day we have the chance to develop a spiritual relationship with God. As well. It shapes the way we perceive with God, and worship him. It is vital to our relationship with God. To put our family together We are obligated.*

Fourth commandment. honors your father, and mother Exodus 20:8

Honor your father, and your mother that your days may belong here on earth Deuteronomy 5:16

If we honor our parents. God will bless our life. Yes we could have a long life. But God is talking about how fortunate we can be. How much more blessing we can have throughout our lives.

We might not be rich with money. But we could be very rich with love and peace of mind.

Good people who struggle more in this life. Would seem too short for them. They always think it is the end of their life. Often they don't think of the treasure they have in their life. That's all the blessing.

Jesus, said let him who curses father or mother be put to death. Matthew15:4.

Jesus trying to say because of your parents, you exist. He also meant we are the image of our parents.

When God said honor her mother and father. He did not have question mark. Next to the commandment.

God did not mention if your parents were not so great not to love them. We should be proud of our parents. Never to be a shame, of them. God also commanded us to respect, honor love, and to be obedience, not only to them. But also to any parental figure. As aunts, uncles.

Even older people even if they were strangers to us. Among our family, and friends. Because they are some ones else parents.

We need to keep it, in our mind. Our mothers carried us for nine months give them us. Be grateful if would've being for women none of us would be in this existence.

To me is a joke, when people often talk about women's rights. I say your mother gave you right to live, and be free. To be born.

Our parents, they get hurt, when we are hurting. They cry when we are crying. They weep when, we are weeping. They nourish us; support us for many years. Until we became matured enough to go on our own.

Even after that, they still help take care of our kids. Parents are, very valuable to God. He made them as his associate here on earth. To help us grow with faith, and to know God.

God created man, like his of image, and out the man God create a woman. So they can be male, and female out of the woman will produce, and multiply Genesis 1:27

Because we are made, like image of God, our parents are part of him in spirit.

God takes image of our parent's image, and give them us. He takes spirit of their spirit gives us a spirit (Life). This is why children, they look like their parents, and image Children resemble, their parents also, their sibling.

Grandparents deserve the honor, and respect Because of them, our parents came into the world. They are our original.

All parents, are qualified. They carried us, through everything. When we were younger.

When they grow old. We supposed to carry them People who neglect dishonor, their parents more likely their life will be cursed. Unfortunately some people are blinded to see that.

About obey the commandments. Helps children establish a lifetime of honoring, and respect rules that were given to them.1Peter2:17.

All of the parents are obligated, to take all responsibilities, from God, to teach their children the basic principle to go by it. To have moral values.

Parents need to teach children concept of life. Parent must teach their kids how, and in which way, they need to love God.

Honoring parents does not end, when kids become adults. Kids are obligated by God, to be committed to their parent's life. Even if they become, physically disabled. Supposed to care for them Children are also obligated to help the parents financially, if they are able to. Because they were fed, by their parents, and supported. Kids were being care for, by their parents. Children are, to honor their grandparents, because they were parents to their parents too.

Children are not allowed, to neglect their grandparents. Many grandparents contribute significantly, to grandchildren. I mean helping raising them, along with their parents.

I know this touching story. I learned how blessing it is to do for older parent, or older person Friend of mine once upon a time told me a story. He had no proof if it was true. But it meant something I believed because of my faith. I also believe in miracles, understanding how the holy spirit of God works.

Story goes as following. Once upon a time this one monk, who was continually pray for many years. One day he decided to ask, the holy spirit of God. How close, he had gotten to him spiritually.

One day the holy spirit of God, finally answered him, and told him your deeds are not close to me, as much as,certain butcher in certain butcher shop. When the monk heard that, he went back in his room. Prayed even harder. Asking the Holy Spirit, what the meaning of that.

He finally, got his answer. It was, to go, to the butcher shop, and ask the butcher to take him home with him, at the end of his working day. He did exactly that. When he was there, he asks the butcher if he can go home with him, at the end of his working day. It was OK with a butcher

When was, the end of the day. He follow him, to his house. As Soon, as the butcher walked in the house Before he did anything, for himself.

He immediately, went into one of the bedrooms. Where was disable old man, more likely he was his father?

He immediately begins, to care for his father, helping him sitting on a chair, clean his father bed Shaving him, and feed his father.

When the butcher got done doing, all he need it to do. That's when he went, to do with personal things. During all that the monk watched everything in detail. He was amazed, and discovered that is not by praying. But also doing, helping the less fortunate. Because God hear, their prayers through us. Especially, our parents

God he is a spirit, and works his miracles through us. We honor our parents because we are part of them We're made, like their image.

Then God said, let us make man in our image, after our likeness God created man in his own image. Genesis 1:26-28

The lord God built up woman, from rib that he had taken from, Adam flash then; she became bone of his bone flesh of his flesh. God blessed Adam and eve saying; be fertile, and multiply fill the earth. Genesis 2:22-23

God still, at creation. It began when he creates, our first parents, Adam, and eve. Genesis God continues creation. At fertilization all human chromosomes our present. That is God's creating human being. That is when unique human being, life began. It is a flesh. God taking out of our parents flesh, and give them us. Is being proved. In many ways, we get our parents both genes.

That is our spirit. When embryo begin implantation, in the uterus, and the heart begins to beat the child own blood, is the spirit that gave the new human being. Baby to be born. Therefore we don't only have flesh of our parents.

We also have their spirit. It is blasphemy against God. If we hate our parents ?. Because they were made like Gods image that's in the spirit.

Also if we hate our parents, we are also hating, ourselves. Nevertheless, we are created by God from their flesh, and their spirits.

Our spirit goes through their blood, to our blood to reside into our hearts, to give us life. Before we were born.

When we die, the reason our heart stopped, because our spirit time to leave, and depart from our heart.

God said honor your mother, and father, he did not have, question mark Next to it.

We must, no way out.

Even if they were very difficult, to honor. Not all parents can be good, and honorable Therefore, it is not easy to respect them. Some time.

There are, out there. Some abusive parent. It is hard to honor, or even to love. I believe God demands of us, to work with them. Hoping they change by, repenting.

Jesus commands us. To reach everyone. We also needed to change our attitude toward each other.

This is why Jesus said, love your enemies Luke 6:27-28

Jesus said, do good to those who hate you, bless those, who curse you. Pray for those who mistreat you.

If Jesus want us to love even our enemies. How much more important for him to love, the same way our parents?

Hating anyone. Is giving evil control, of our lives.

Maybe we disapprove, the way our parents live, and the way their life is. We still must respect them, as human being.

We will be blessed, when we stay, on the right side of God. And look good in his eyes. Those who dishonor their parents, they sufferers, and struggle more than others.

Fifth commandment -You shall not kill [murder). Ex 20:12

Jesus said if you want enter life, keep the commandment Matthew19:16-19

Yes we will when we die. We will find true life. If we do what God command us to do.

Jesus was asked which commandment, 'he answered you shall not kill. You shall not commit adultery. You shall not steal, you shall not bear false witness. Honor your father, and mother and you shall love your neighbor as you self.

Human life is precious. God is the only one who takes life. We must respect life. God give this life to every human being to live on earth to prospect, to be happy, to be free

God forbid abortion, and to respect the unborn dignity. Abortion is murder.

Also, Suicide, battery, and justified, anger, scandal, hurting each other as human being, it is wrong.

Whose ever shall shed men blood his blood is shed Genesis 9:6

God permit self-defense of individual, and all entire nation of the world.

Just war is permitted. Capital punishment is permitted.

No one is, allowed to murder anyone.

Exodus?

This commandment means, you shall not murder, and that is deliberately killed. Not even in stage of anger.

We must control our tempers. We have no right, to decide, to take another person's life. We believe God, only, give life and take it.

He gives it, when we were born, and take it, when it is our time to die.

So many unborn babies, are being murdered, by millions

It is very sad. It is blasphemy against God.

If we know abortion is being performed, and we don't do something, to stop it. We become conspiracies to sin.

Babies are the most precious gift from God. Genesis 9:6

God told Jeremiah, I formed you in your mother's womb I knew you before you were born Jeremiah 1:1.

All babies are spirits alive with God. Every baby born Have calling. And reason to come into this world. For Jeremiah was born to be a messenger of God. Prophet to represent God.

Every time another baby gets murdered, by abortion. More likely that baby could being very important, and valuable.

To contributes, somehow.

Sixth commandment. You shall not commit adultery. Ex 20:13

The lord God said, it is not good that men should be alone. I will make him companion Genesis 2:18

God made, for Adam a woman out, of his rib called her eve. To be his wife. That was, the first marriage.

The way God designed eve, so she can be part of her husband Adam This is why on the moment we are getting married. God is at the creation. When the two say, I do to each other that when they become one. But first into their heart, they say I do God.

They are not supposed, to break that promise. From the beginning God designed man, and woman to be together. Marriage was established by God.

God only intended for humanity to have sex for that to exist, and multiply.

Sexual relationship, only allowed within marriage. We pray. We don't desire anybody else but our spouse, any sexual relationship outside marriage, is committing adultery, and it is the violation of marriage covenant. By lawful participation in sexual relationship with someone else, other than one's spouse.

Committing adultery is the way evil want to divide, and break apart what God put together.

Evil also want to take our joy, and happiness. That God give us. In the marriage.

God worn us, of consequences of adultery.

Many marriages ended in divorce, because of adultery. Kids become victims of divorce. Many times the couple uses, the kids to take revenge.

The couple also gets affected plus, they struggle a lot. If they have children.

Unfortunately people, they just don't get divorce, and the problem is over with. There's a chance, may last a lifetime.

Divorce also affects the people around the couple. Because while they were in process building a relationship during marriage. They're also doing the same thing with everyone around them.

Because of the divorce all what, they accomplished falls apart

God intention is to protect us, and to let us know, how miserable. Evil will make us, if we commit adultery. God know the price we pay.

In the beginning of a relationship. We meet and fall in love. God dwell with us, because he is love. All heaven rejoice. When the couple, get engage to each other, also their friends and family have the joy.

As they prepare for the wedding party relatives friends all give them the full support, and the meantime. They share the couple love, and happiness.

Most of their loved ones, get involved somehow to make sure, the couple gets to their blessing day.

The moment they become one, in marriage, they become the new Adam and eve. To live happy and full of joy to bring children into this world to know God.

Getting married, is the final step to heaven. Because we don't need to sin anymore.

Through marriage the couple,get adapt, by large family from both sides.

Mostly surrounded. By love, and happiness.

It is the most profound way, of building great relationship. To be built on base of love, and happiness.

Things can become very close to perfect.

Just imagine living with someone, who has only the joy, love, peace, and happiness.

Faithful people, whenever they have children, they say that this gift from God.

Unfortunately for the mistake of adultery. If it ended in divorce. Can also affect, the people around the couple.

Especially the feelings, and emotions, of those were who shared, with couple. The way life was supposed to be.

God gave us commandment, about adultery to be directed, on defining sexual roles, that brings lasting happiness, and stability. To be within marriage only.

In a marriage. Committing adultery is violation of marriage. We should always pray, we don't attempt, or desire anyone else. But our spouse. To have any, sexual desire, with someone other than our spouse. It is blasphemy, against God

When we were, created by God, he also gives us freedom within marriage. To have sex when having children. Also the privilege to enjoy, and have pleasure of sexual relationship within marriage Any sex outside marriage will be pre marriage sex. It is evil.

Sexual relationship with our spouse shows devotion, and love we have for our made.

There is many warning, about adultery in the bible.

Why then, my son, should you go stray for another woman, and accept embraces of an Adulteress? Because, by his own iniquities. The wicked man, will be caught in the meshes of his own sin Proverbs 5:20-22.

God does not punish anyone. The evil does. Because whenever we get tempted, and sin. Is giving chance to evil, to make our temptations, bigger and bigger. Evil is all hate. God is all love.

Evil always take pleasure of punishing, us human being . Whenever we sin, we are asking for evils rewards, and what kind of reward we get? Bad.

If we ask for, God's rewards, will be good. Because God is good. Society, is suffering because of adultery, and premarital sex.

Seventh commandment- You shall not steal. Ex 20:1.

God forbid theft. Because, it is taking what does not belong to us. Taking advantage of the poor, it is stealing.

God demand for us, to respect possession of others, and pay poor people, enough to live

God also for bid greed, abuse, doing injustice. Especially to the poor.

Many companies go out of business, because of theft. Not only, the owner of the company get affected. Also the workers loses their jobs, and source of living. Each worker has bills to pay children to support, and they need to eat. It will be in workers best interest to take care, and maintain their place of work like their own. So they can make a good living.

It is one of the keys to success. And the secret of success number one is be Honest.

I apologize if I offend anyone. Suggesting, or a theory only assuming. That is so many or a few companies. Sale their merchandise, percent or two higher because of theft.

Insurance companies raise, their rates because of so many claims, they lose so much, they need to make up. To stay in business. Only because of few people fault, insurance company takes it out, on everybody else.

When insurance prices, rise up. It effect every one. This is the consequences, we face. Because of others mistake.

A friend of mine once owned a pizza place, he trusted employees. For while he was shown no profit, he end up closing down his pizza place. I believe his, own employees, were stealing the profit Maybe they were happy, when they're stealing, and enjoy what they were doing.

When my friend closed down. They lost, and affected their life, for sure. They also lost the security they could've had working there.

I am not supposed to judge any one. But their reputation can affect when trying to find, another job in future.

Once upon a time, it was early one morning. I stop at the bank to go through drive through window to make a deposit. As soon as I opened the box to send my deposit to the taller. I found envelop. I knew was money in it. I immediately send it back to the bank Taller, she thank me for being honest. After I did my deposit, and went to my work in convenience store. Little while later around midday. While I was busy working behind the counter, doing my job. Older woman struggling, walking with a cane trying to approach the check - out, counter. She pointed to lifting up her cane saying to me with tears in her eyes. Are you the young man who found my money ?. I answered: yes.

She immediately came behind the counter, and give me big hug. She said that was her check she cashed, so she can make a living throughout the month.

I felt very humble; I found her money, and no one else. Because I return it back to her. So she doesn't suffer financially I'm sure. She needs It to pay her bills, buy food, and medicine, and other necessities of life. For being older woman, more likely that was her retirement income, and only income If she was to lose it. What she was to do. Maybe get sicker, if she did not take the medication, if she does not have the money to buy it.

People don't care, or understand. Why the commandments ? They are all about, self-safety moral values to show us how, connected we are to each other. Usually people lose, or gain together. No one is left out. Especially, when so many are associated together in any field.

In the olden day's people knew how to work honest way, and why.

God fortunate, and blessed, our fathers Abraham, Isaac and Jacob because they put, their trust, and walked with God. Their faith helps them know, and understand God so they can show, love to him In the process they learn. It would be in their best interest to obey God, and follow his commandments.

It is crying shame, what money does. I say love of the money, and greed makes people blind from doing enough for others, and them self.

I often say if I was hungry, and did not have any money to buy food. I would rather beg for food, or stand by the church begging hoping someone would help me. Eventually someone will feel sorry for me, and will give me some food. But if I Steal, and get caught I will be a shame, and in trouble with law Is it worth it?

Everyone has the right to protect their own property. Especially when they work so hard for it God save guard the ones who work hard, and honest.

He who want to steal, let him steal no longer but rather let him labor working with his hand at what is good. The thief not to steal any more in order to make an honest living to work for it Ephesians 4:28.

Jesus said, give to the one who asks of you, and do not turn your back on one, who wants to borrow. Matthew 5:42.

If or whenever, we are able to help, is good to help. We take the stress, off someone. Because people do crazy things if they don't get the help. No one, under any circumstances have the right to steal, no exception. It was about, the widow got her way by being persistent The Godless was the judge who did not believe or fear God. Luke 18:1-8

The widow kept coming to him saying do me justice against my adversary, after begging for a long time. The judge said to himself. I don't fear God I don't respect, any human being because this widow keeps bothering me I shall deliver a just decision. For her lest she finally come and strike me. If we humble our self be persistent, in begging we bring compassion out of people hearts.

Jesus also said, that dishonest judge, helped the widow. How much more, your heavenly father would do for you, and securely your life.

God always, chooses the faithful. He is waiting for others to repent. Do not delay not to give to the needy. A beggar in distress do not reject. Do not turn your back away your face from poor Sirach 4:3-4

If someone needs help, we must help. God hears prayer of the needy. God hears, who have hope in him.

Most of my life worked in convenience stores, whenever I catch someone stealing especially younger people I told them all they have to do is ask. I normally give them something so they don't steal no more. If I embarrass any one they, things could` get worse.

I have news for you hunger is for real, becoming homeless is real.

Once upon a time, there was this juvenile, who was being prosecuted because he was caught stealing. The sentence was to stand out site, holding sign showing he is a thief. So he can be embarrassed.

No exception, for the people who do wrong. Everyone should pay the price. But if I was the judge who gave, the juvenile the sentence. I would also try to get him some help.

God told Adam because he sin by not obeying him. Cursed is the ground, because of you in toil you shall eat of it, all the days of your life. Also God said to Adam, in the sweat of your face you shall eat bread till you return to the ground. Genesis 3:17, 19.

The only we are allowed to make money to live, by working hard. No one can ever, make something, from nothing.

Stealing is making, nothing from, and nothing.

People who steal, they have something do not belong to them. It is only temporary, and is nothing to be proud of.

Jesus said love your enemies. Luke6:27, 30.

Jesus said do well, to those who hate you. Give to ever one who has asked. Jesus speaking of assisting, the less fortunate, and the ones, who can never return the favor. Our reward will be bigger and greater. God favorite the merciful, and generous. God serve us, so we can serve others.

I know a story I have no proof how true it is but it means something.

This story about people, who gather their fortune, at the dishonest way how they lose greatly They either lose profit, or gets in trouble with the law. Or sufferers, and struggle more than others Maybe they continue, to raise the millions. But still their life could be trouble always. No way out Cheating and stealing is evil.

My father told a story, about this merchant, and the monkey. In the olden days people went, by the ship's to take their merchandise, to trade, or sell from city to city, or from country to another.

Once upon a time, a merchant aboard ship to sail, on the sea when nightfall he was ready to go sleep, he had bag of money, he put it under his pillow, so no one can steal It.

He did not know there was a monkey, with another merchant watching.

As soon as the merchant, owner of the monkey fell asleep holding the leash, of his monkey. The monkey had a chance to get away, went straight to the bag of money, quietly pulled out the bag he opened it, and spread it on the floor. Holding the bag open, he began putting one coin in the bag, and one, he threw over board to go into the sea.

When he got done doing that, he put the bag back under the pillow Then went back to his owner When the morning was. When the merchants with the bag, woke up first thing he did, was check on his bag, upon finding it about half gone, he notice it because it was light, he became furious,and mad trying to find out what happened to his money. Luckily another merchant, not the monkey's owner Watched what the monkey had done.

He immediately came, to the merchant who lost some of his money comforting him told him. I would tell you what happen to your money, if I can ask a question first. The first merchant, reply that's fine. The question was. How did you make, your money? The answer was, my mother make yogurt we sell. I guess she mix water with milk, and make yogurt. That merchant give the, first merchant answer. What the monkey did he threw the money that came, from the water back to the water, and the money came from milk, want it back to you The merchant lost what he gathered, at the dishonest way, and the honest, he got to keep. What came from milk and labor only? This story is about us, to learn how to be moral. Writers, and philosophers wrote wisdom, they used animals.

That each one gives according. 2 Corinthian 9:7

Forsake of God, we should help, and give, as much as we can.

A cheerful giver, give whenever is necessary. God love cheer full giver Corinthians 9:7

Give because, we want to not, If we have to. Giving, and charity comes from the heart

Any type of stealing, is greed.

It is evil temptation against, anyone who their stuff gets stolen Especially, the poor. It is not fair, they already don't have. Poor people, they barely earn a living.

I wish If people, have deeper understanding. How deceived they could be. I mean people don't see. How connected we are. That is how much people gain, and lose together.

That is why will be in our best interest, to be a team and work with each other, to make sure, everyone around us make it. It is our keys, to the success. (Team-Work).

Years ago, I purchased auto insurance from out of the state. I was their client for many years Rates were very comfortable to me at yearly policy During all the time I had the insurance with the company. I never had a claim or a ticket.

I figured because of my records. I should have good, and reasonable rate Unfortunately at the end of one of the final year,with that company. I received renewal by mail. I immediately opened it. Because, I knew it was important. When I open the envelope first thing I did looked, at the statement

I was in shock, premium went up almost 50%. I immediately called the company Speaking to an agent, explaining, to him saying, I never had a claim or any ticket. Why did my premium, gone up?

The agent put me on hold, to find out why. When he finally returned back, his answer was. The company had so many claims. In the state I lived in. I told him it wasn't fair, for me, and many others.

Anyway later, I canceled that insurance, found cheaper insurance. The point is I was a victim along with me, so many other people, who were with the same insurance, who never had a claim or ticket.

All that, it happened because of other people's fault mistakes, and more likely frauds.

Every time one of your relatives, or friends steals, cheats or make others lose. One of you, or more could be paying, the price.

Another tragic thing happened, to the local dealers Located next to a family business. I happen to open every morning.

One of the mornings my first customer came in. First thing he told me the bad news, about the dealer next door it was vandalized. I told the customer. It is crying shame; the dealer will have to make up somehow. For the lost. They just might go up in prices. So they can make up for the lost.

I added who ever done that. It may be their friends Cousins, relatives or people, who want to buy car, they will end up paying a higher price. Can you imagine? How many people will get effect it?

By the sweat of your face you shall get bread to eat. Genesis3:19

God from the beginning. Informed Adam, he must work to make a living Many for long time work, so hard to make their money. At the honest way They should be, able of keeping. What they earn.

There's no exception to stealing. Thief's they need, to be disciplined The way I see things. There are at least, four tapes of theft, and the reason people steal.

1- Some people steal, because they are hungry they have no jobs, no money, and no one to help them and they are too persistent, by not asking anyone. They become very desperate. Stealing becomes a habit.

2-Some people steal, because they are lazy, they choose not to work. They wanted to get their money at easy way, also they want everything to be hand it out to them. They think, every-one owe them a living.

3-Some people steal because, they are affected, and addicted to drugs. To the point where they cannot work anymore. They try to steal to meet their demand for drugs. And fulfill their other habits. Being addicted usually hurt themselves, and the people around them.

4- Some people steal, for greed. One thing, they have on their mind is to get rich fest. A lot of these people are not, trust worthy. Eventually all, the above get caught.

Let the thief no longer steal, but rather let him labor doing honest work with his hand, so that he may be able to give to those in need. Ephesians 4:28.

We need to work with everyone, to make our world safer place for ourselves and our, children.

We often hear things on, TV, in the news tragic, and alarming sometimes horrible news. True and real life tragic.

The things that affects others life, Nothing hardly, any good anymore. People who do stupid things, hurting others they need, to be disciplined, maybe jailed.

But the best to do is be wise to help them, work with them. So they can become, good, and better citizen That's, the first right thing to do. The second right thing to do. We should reach to their hearts and mind to see what is going, through their minds hoping, to correct them leading them, to the right direction.

Hoping they become, better people.

Before they hurt anybody else, no more. And their self.

If we don't do something immediately, things can, and will get worse. Someday most of our cities. Will become, one big prison surrounded by big security fence.

It is into our power, the choice we make. Which is, to have saved, and peaceful world around us. Or danger, and corrupt it world. The choice is ours.

Eighth commandment-You shall not bear false witness against your neighbored Exodus 20:15.

Owe nothing to anyone except to love one another, for the one who loves another has fulfilled the law. Love does no evil to the neighbor, you shall love your neighbor as yourself Romans13:8, 10

If all we do, is love. Evil will shy away. God is the truth. We can speak of nothing, but the truth about our neighbor. When we love God from, our entire mind, and keep our focus on God. We belong to him 100%.

When we love God, from all our souls. That would give us life. When we love God with all of our spirits. We return back to him. At the end, of our life on earth.

Therefore, putting a way false hood. Speak the truth, each one to his neighbor. We are members of each other be angry but do not sin. Ephesians 4:25-27.

Getting angry for what's right. Only to bring justice, mercy, and peace. To anyone, who is seeking it. Beyond that is from evil. Speaking falsely of others is evil.

Rather it is your crimes that separate you from God. It is our sins what separate us from God Isaiah 59:2, 4

Many lay even if they don't have to or to get away with things Isaiah59:2, 4

Absent of God, is evil doing bad things. Is pushing God out of our lives. It is wrong to see others faults, and don't look, at our own faults. Also we need to respect others reputation. Everyone deserves to protect their own privacy.

Speaking behind someone's back falsely is sin. But if you speak about anyone you must speak face, to face.

Everyone has the right, to defend themselves, and their reputation. At the court, both defended and plaintiff has to be present, for the judge to hear both sides' stories. In order for the judge to pass fair judgment. There's no way the judge's able to de side which is, right, or wrong. It not right and fair, to hear only one, and not both.

Scripture speaks about God, and that's the truth, and he is pure love. We need to be example and fullness of the truth. That's when people will know Gods according to our action, and the way we behave.

Sometime people have trusts in you. They feel comfortable, and free to talk to you about their private things they are very confident you will not,reveal it to anyone else. You should keep it in your heart. Because everyone entitled to have private matters. They only speak about it to a special people into their lives. Misuse their trust in you. You are sinning against them.

Ninth commandment - You shall not desire your neighbors wife Exodus 20:16

Desiring someone else spouse you are trying to steal her, or him and also the love, they have for each other's.

Once we vow of marriage we become one. And our life do not belong to us anymore it belong to God. Because that's how God's creating us in the beginning. It began with Adam, and eve. Obeying God is to live life of virtue. and purity. To love each other. Through our good times, and bad times. To raise children, teaching them how to grow with God's love, and under God's protection.

Jesus said anyone who looks with lust, at woman has already committed adultery, with her in his heart It will best for our spirit to desire God only, so we can live with him forever.

Enjoyment of our body will not last, but our spiritual body will last forever. Some people ignore what could become of them.

They are, not worried about consequence of Sin. Lust is evil, we must pray, we don't desire anybody else. Only our spouse, we desire. Watching porn it is disrespect, and dishonoring your partner Is not fair for either one.

Because both couple only have the right, to each other body 100% within marriage only. Once we, joined together, and becoming one.

The reason God forbid desiring somebody else wife Because sexual thoughts, and fantasies inconsistent with one's marital status, we are departing ourselves from our spouse, and it is giving chance, For the evil to squeeze in between us to divide us spiritually, and physically from each other That, what could destroy marriage.

Focus on God 24/7 so we don't get into temptation. Matthew5:28

Jesus said for where your treasures there also will be our hearts. Matthew 5:28

Purity from, our hearts, and mind that is the biggest treasure ever. We pray, for God to make us pure, at heart holy in mind.

Chastity it is God's reward, and it is God's special calling. So we can belong to him. Matthew 6:21.

Jesus said out of man are, what defiling a man. Mark 8:21

It depend what comes out of our mouths what can make us or break us. Mark 8:21

With faith, and trust in God's will always, speak, the truth, and do good things.

Without faith, out of hearts comes evil thoughts adulterers, immorality, murders, thefts covetousness, desist shame fullness, wickedness, jealousy. That this all evil. Many thinks, there's nothing wrong with what they are doing. Is wrong.

They become Idolatry. They put greed, and lust, and all the earthly things about God.

Put to death then, the parts of you that are earthly immorality impurity, passion, evil desire and the greed that is idolatry. Mark 8:21

Because of those, the wrath of God we will come upon the disobedient. All the sins can prevent us from entering kingdom of God passion, evil desires that is disobedience to God. Without faith nothing can and will work ever. Colossians 3:5-6

Tenth commandment -You shall not covet your neighbors wealth Exodus 20:16

This commandments are about, our relationship with God. And that is all about each other. God wants us to be our brother's keeper.

To make sure everyone, has everything. So they don't, need to desire, what people have. Our goal should be for each other, to set our goals together, to reach our dreams, as one people.

Loving our neighbor. It is defining our love to God.

We ought to focus, on doing, away with evil

We don't allow ourselves to be tempted. Therefore, don't stray, and far away from Gods love and his mercy.

God is telling us. When we desire anything that belongs to our neighbor. We do more harm to our self, then good.

When we become very excessive, with someone else belongings. We hurt our mind. We suffer mentally. Getting jealous, at people comes out of hate. IF we love those who have everything. We should be happy for them. Or maybe will be in, our best interests to joined them. It could be rewarding People who hate, and never forgive. They become alone, and miserable.

If you are ever, jealous of someone.

You are doing, yourself worse in your precious time While that person may be getting richer happier. A lot more advanced. Then you, when at the meantime. You are yourself going down.

Chapter 4

Faith, Religion, and God

The Lord, my shepherd. Psalms 23:1- 6

God lead us, to the path of righteous, and he gives us comfort. Very simple examples, of defining. What God is He is also, our counselor.

I understand God. First as creator, of everything. We see, and don't see. He is, also teacher philosopher, therapist, protector, healer, and counselor. Mainly our savior. He gave us instruction in the perfect way. To guide, our self. Because if we have rules over our self. It will be, very small chance. We get into trouble.

By reading, the bible. We understand God, and appreciate him.

Just the way, we become very grateful when someone do something great for us, putting our life back, on track.

Example - If you have lots of problems, seeking help. By going canceling, or psychology Whoever might be, given you good advice, in order for you, to get all the help you need. Might take short, or long time, then one day. You got all the help you needed, to put your life back on right the track Of course you will be, very grateful, showing appreciation for the person, who really helped you. If you are considered person. For sure, you would. Appreciate the person who helped you.

Example – If you have a father, who raised you very well, gave you great childhood, and happy one, growing up having successful life. Can you imagine, how much you will love your father and appreciated him ?.

That what, God doing for us. Through, the Holy Scripture. He is, putting us on right track. For our, safety happiness, and successes. Mainly, to help us overcome temptation, and to conquer evil with good.

God figured, if we have strong belief in him, and take his advice. We will become, holy in him. Trusting in God, we fear nothing no more. Therefore, evil will never be able to come near us.

God is not only the author of our existence. Genesis 1:1.

God is also the relationship that makes, all thing meaning full.

Atheism, with respect to their beliefs. They Keep themselves busy debating whether there's God or not ? When at the meantime, there's so much we need to pay attention to. Starvation abuse, wars, greed, and so much more needed to get fixed. Suffering, and horrible events, and real life stories.

By faith, we understand that. The world was, created by the word of God Genesis 1:1.

Without faith, we can do nothing.

By faith Abel offered, to God more acceptable sacrifice then Cain. Abel received approval from God, as much, as righteous, because He offered, to God a sacrifice, more exclusion, then Cain Hebrews 11:3-4.

God is, divine author. He is, our spiritual LORD, and master. He rules over the universe Everything in heaven, and earth belongs to him. Psalm 103:19.

He is far above. All rules, authority, power, and dominion.

We are not sure, when the angels were created. Some obeyed God. Some did not. Those who disobey were fixed evil, and became the devils. Ezekiel 28:17

When we sin, our intelligence limited by the material part, of our intellect. The brain in, our heads, for a mater brain is much less powerful, than the spiritual intelligence our souls have this mean. We seldom, see things, as fully, as possible at once.

Angels sees everything, as fully. It is possible, all at once. So he cannot go back on his, and still keep the great power natural. To a pure spirit. So they can do things that they, seem like miracles to us.

Good angels, are pure light, and power of God. They are sent to guide, and protect us.

Every human being, has a guardian angel.

Angels, for tell birth of Isaac. They were, three angels. But Abraham saw them, as one Chronicles 29:11, 12. Ephesians 1:21-23. Genesis 18:1-3

Vision of Jacob's ladder, he saw in his sleep, touching heaven angels of God ascending, and descending by it. Genesis 28:12,13

Behold, an angel, of the Lord appeared, and light shined, in the sell, and he struck peter on the side, and woke him,saying, "Get up quickly" And The chains fell off, his hands Acts 12 :7

Peter was delivered, from the prison. By the angel Acts 12:7

It said, he will command his angels, in all your ways, at time of protection, and temptation They can give us both light and they present our prayers before God.

The bad, and wicked angels, because of disobedience to God They were, condemned, to eternal punishment. Psalms 91:11

When some, of the angels sinned. God did not spare them, but consigned them, to the pit of hell, and fire to be kept, for judgment.

It said will, of the devil is fixed. Therefore, he tries to seduce people, and harm them even to bring them to hell.2 Peter 2:4.

Be sober, be watchful, your adversary. The devil prowls around like, a roaring lion, seeking someone to devour 1 Peter 5:8

Evil is enemy, of all humanity, he circle around the earth looking for victims. We are weak spiritually. Easily we can get into temptation. We are to be awake, and always be ready. We need continue praying, and remain on guard. Devotion makes us spiritually strong.

God permit evil, as result of our decision, to create spiritual being having the will. God draw good, out of evil. Temptation gives us, the opportunity, to show our faith, and trust in God Also give us, the chance to grow up in virtue. Through our troubles, and struggles.

If we disobey God. His Laws, commandment, and rejected. It is possible we can live in the eternal domination.

The soul of, the righteous people, will rest in peace with God and will never suffer, the ones who always judge others are dead. They are only fooling themselves. Isaiah 32:17-18.

The ones who, don't believe in God. Their hearts is full of immortality.

Each human soul, is directly created, by God himself. It is not produced, by or delivered from parents.

Parents only produce human body. Even that only with help of, Gods power. Unity of soul, and body called in fusion. We are made of image of God in spirit.

Therefore, God takes spirit out of our parent's spirit, and give them us. Soul gives us life. You see, all the children resemble their siblings, and parents. Nothing, can be, or will happen without Gods help.

God had gave Adam, and Eve, our first parents, three level of gifts.

1 - basic humanity consisting of body, and soul, with mind, and will each has within 1/2 creation natural drives, and needs no one, of these is alivilen itself, but without help of some added gifts, to coordinate they tend to get, out of order, to rebel.

2-God gave to our first parent's gift, which is, such a coordinating gift which made it easy to keep each drive in its place. It is sometime called the gift of integrity.

When Adam, and eve sinned. (Genesis) The lower flesh began to get out of line, rebel Adam felt the need to cover. Before the fall, he did not feel that, for the flesh was easily docile. God given them, also exemption from physical death. Which, otherwise would, be natural to being composed of parts body, and soul. Which can come apart, and so die.

3 - God give them, the life of grace, to share in his own life. Which made the, soul basically capable of, see the vision of God in life to come. Also the original sin, result in a darkening of the mind, and weakening of the will. In comparison to what it might have been. Being us humanity.

God made man, from earth, and gave him soul, to become the first living human being, he called him Adam Out of his rip. God form, Adam a woman, and he called her Eve That was first holy marriage. Eve is mother of all living human being. Genesis 2:7, 22.

God did not want Adam, to be alone, God made eve as Adams wife Genesis 2:22

First marriage.

God unconditionally, loved all creation. God blessed our first parents. He made them as one.

Unfortunately, evil was there, before creation of Adam, and eve. When evil saw, the reward God, had given them. He was too furious, and jealous. He is, a miserable being, and lives in burning hell forever. He hates, the idea that human being, are loved by God. Evil want to gain, every single human being for self him. Evil want us to live life of torment with him in hell. He is deceiver, he acts very friendly at the meantime, he is full of temptation.

We are very weak when it comes to sin. God made, Adam, and eve like his image in spirit; His plan was to live with him in paradise forever. (Genesis)

When Adam, and eve disobey God. They were fooled by evil. He took, form of serpent and cost, the fall of both Adam, and eve. Genesis 3:15

They ate, from the tree, the one, God forbid them to eat. That is when original sin Acer God sent Adam, and eve, out of a paradise of pleasure, to till the earth which he was taken from. After the fall of Adam, and eve. Genesis.

God promised, he will send a redeemer. He said to the serpent. I will put, enmity between you, and the woman between his descendant, and yours. He will strike, at your head you will strike at her heel. Genesis 3:15.

This Ben Interprets, as a prophecy, of coming of messiah. For both Jews, and Christian.

God still love them, he remains with them in spirit. He promised, he will send them a redeemer to teach, and save them from evil power. Genesis

God promised human being, kingdom of heaven.

God also like to live in each, and every one of us. That is, If we wish him to remain into our hearts, and souls.

God, always one call away.

Evil roam around the earth, and every inch of earth, it is full of evil traps. We can make evil powerless, with our goodness. Evil cost us losing paradise, and the Joy.

Then the first killing ever, was when Cain murders his brother Abel Genesis 2:7, 21

God love sinners. They put, evil to shame. When they repent. We are Gods, favored children God's extreme goal is, to save, and deliver every human being, to himself.

From the beginning, human being, continue to multiply. They forgot, about God he is the creator. They were. Empty shell, not knowing God's mercy. With no moral values Therefore, they were easy to sin.

When people, don't know God anymore. Evil has, full authority, over human being life's With full, command without, any jurisdiction also, and with no competition to compete with him.

God often look down on earth, and see how wicked people can be. God reform them

He gives us, human being too many chances.

God has so much patient, for us human being. He loves us very much. God know, we could go out of the control.

God destroyed people so they don't sin anymore. Only Noah found grace before God and his wife, and kids they were saved. Genesis 6:5-6.

God blessed Noah, and his sons said, to them increase, and multiply fill the earth Genesis 9:1-15.

God established, his covenant with, all the people that will not destroy earth by flood any more.

When our first parents sinned. Genesis 3: 1-15.

God cursed the earth. Therefore, evil took over. God always know, what would be like for us, to live without him on earth. God know the earth will be like living hell, without him.

That's why makes sense. If we live here, on earth according, to his commandment We could be living, like paradise here, on earth. Before we, get to the true, and real one with God.

We need to pray for our children's guardian angel for protection. Guardian angel, has the power, to protect every single human being. That what God want.

All descendent of Adam, and eve, were conceived with Original sin, without sanctifying grace, the soul is not capable of seen the vision of God in heaven.

Except Jesus, and his Mother Mary, were conceived without, the original sin, and with sanctify grace. Pope John Paul 11. Said Original sin, also resulted, in a darkening of the mind and weakening of the will, in comparison to what might have been. Each new baby arrive without the grace God willed it. Adults who sin mortally also lack grace, they should have Except that adults, it is our own faults, also decisions, we may make because, of our free will.

In the beginning, generations after Adam, and Eve the world spoke same tongue, and same speech. They tried to build a tower, to reach heaven. All earth spoke same language. Genesis 2:7, 21.

God scatter, them upon face of all countries. I am able to imagine, how all that happened. During that time people who worked at building. The tower were standing next to each other, handing material, from the bottom to top. They were handing different things.

But eventually, meaning of words change. People were not able to understand each other Therefore, they were not able to get along any more. Every group of people who understand each other went their way.

Back up the story. True, and fact is that, if and when- ever something said to one person as past to different people. More likely, the story changes people add, or take some words off Especially, when it comes to gossiping.

This is, why whenever I say something, I try to memorize it this way no one, can change it. That's why people begin, putting everything in writing.

After tower Babel, many generations. People did not know God, any more. Then God came down to check on his creation.

God found one man, he favored that was Abram. Lord God visit Sara told her she was to bore son that was Isaac. God told Abraham, I will make you father, of all nations. Faith, and obedience of Abraham, to God. He was chosen to be, the father of the nation.

After Abraham death God blessed Isaac, he Begotten Esau, and Jacob. (Genesis).

In Old Testament. Exodus, is the second book of Moses Signifies getting out, children of Israel whom received. The 10 commandments, on Mount Sinai after, he led the Israelites on. Exodus. Out of bondage in Egypt

Moses was born in Egypt; he was hidden. After pharaoh ordered, the slaughter of all male of Israel babies. Moses he was discovered, by pharaoh's daughter who raised him in luxury as her Son. (Exodus).

Moses lived his life as an adopted prince. When Moses grew up, he went to check, on his people, and saw how they were treat it by Egyptian. (Exodus)

He saw, one striking one of his, Hebrews brother. Moses slew the Egyptian, and hid him in the sand. Moses fled, and stayed in the land of Median. Took to himself wife.

God heard, cry children of Israel. He remembered the covenant, which he made with Abraham, Isaac, and Jacob. (Genesis)

God, appeared to Moses, as flame of fire, he saw the bush was, on fire but not burnt gave very bright light. God spoke to Moses, commanding him to lead the Israelites out of Egypt.

Pharaoh, finally after the entire miracles God did through Moses. Egypt suffered under his hand. He let the people out.

But getting out. Pharaoh was, sorry he let them go, he send Army to pursued them God miraculously, and parted the water of red sea. So the Israelites can cross into dry land God gave Moses the go by. (Exodus)

For forty years, Moses led the Israelites, through wilderness. Moses was only able, to get to the edge of the land, that was promised by God to Abraham descendant, and he died, he was 120 years old.

God also promised, of savior to save us, from evil sin, and bring us to God Genesis 3:15. Genesis 12:7. Genesis 21:1-3. genesis 25:5, 25-26. Exodus 1:10

Because, God loved the world. He gave, torah is which is term teaching in Hebrew, refers to Jewish laws also called. Hebrew bible. It is the highest testimony. The gospels, and Gods power. For Christianity refers, to the Old Testament, and then the New Testament.

Jesus said. Truly, Truly, I say to you he who believes has eternal life. He also said I am bread of life. John 6:47-48.

Jesus Christ, testimony. Has reshaped, and reformed the world through the Old Testament.

God revealed his power, and prediction, promising salvation, for humanity. (Jesus) bible

Old, and new testament, are entirely without mistakes, or error entirely.

Not only an ethics, and theology But also the history geography, and science, were proved, the bible is inspired by God.

Every word, and dot from the beginning to the end, from first page to last page. Mercy Love, and peace for humanity. Bible is, our guidance how to be protected, from wicked evil.

We need to read, and study the bible, and teach others. Especially, young children, so they can have, and grow with the moral values. We are obligated, to teach our children.

Judaism is, the major religion, of the world. It is the most profound prove existence of God. Jewish people present. It is actuality, and reality of God. Because Of Jewish Christian have Jesus, and they are strong back, of Christianity.

For God so, loved the world that, he gave his only son God did not send his son to judge the world. But to save it from evil sin. John 3:16-17

God choose, to be the son. Christian we put our hope, confidence faith, and full trust in God. He send us his only begotten, son to die, and suffer for us so we can be saved. See Jesus (New testament)

The ten commandments, are human being duties toward, God Conclude, with our obligations to one, and another along the way. Exodus20:1-17

God inspired writers, and help them write all the books. Especially the old, and new- testament The two, makes bible.

God revealed us, as holy Psalms 77:13.

God he is holy, and just. Full of faith, grace, peace, mercy, and love Overall. We ask God by prayer, for wisdom. So we can live life, of virtue to walk along the way. Knowing we've God.

If we have God, on our side. Evil will never be able to come near us. It is critical that. We don't realize how much hunger in the world, for the truth. There is, so many are starving for God's Love.

In every corner of earth, so many problems. Many blame, God for their own actions So many natural things, bond to happen. Things every, person goes through naturally. But so much more happenings, to allot of people. Others cost to happen to them. That's unnatural Need to stop.

Because of, our free will. Evil hate me, and you. Therefore, he wants to steal our happenss and freedom. God grant it for us.

God called human being his beloved. Romans 1:7.

We are indeed. His beloved. Evil cost all hate, greed, wars, materialism, selfishness, deceit deceiving problems deception, murdering, killing, adultery poverty, hunger. Separation from each other, and famine anxiety starvation, and oppress people. Offence, and being racial toward others, abuse. Let alone unthinkable, and unimaginable. Millions of crimes, all wickedness around, the world.

We are losing our freedom. It is just the beginning, of the doom days.

Evil he is the tempter anger. Evil betray, God. When he mislead, and deceiving us. Evil confuse power of our mind. He cloud our heart. So nothing would it seem. Too rewarding to us.

Evil main goal, is for humanity, is to hate God. Therefore, he cost hate anguish, and divorce Especially what God put together.

Adultery, envy, jealousy, sloth, lust gluttony, voracity, sorrows, sadness negativity and many other horrible things. Those are, only some of bad things, gives pleasure to the evil.

Would be, great disappointment for evil. If we begin to do, what takes to please God. We are very weak, when it comes to temptation. Evil know that.

In the beginning evil tempt it, Adam, and eve. Got Cain to become envious, and jealous, of his brother able, he end up murdering able. Genesis 4:8.

Evil tempts it People at the time of Noah. God destroyed them by flood. So they don't sin no more. Also during Sodom, and Gomorrah, when their sin become exceedingly grievous. God destroyed them.

Then the, lord God rained down fire, and burning sulfur, and dust from heaven. On Sodom, and Gomorrah. Genesis 6:1-22, Genesis 19:1-38.

Also at time, when Moses brought, the Israelites from land of Egypt, in Sinai desert They were always tempt it complaining, and being very ungrateful, to God.

Throughout the old, and new testament. People, were tempted, tested, and they were put under trial. Especially the faithful, because they are closer to God. Exodus 1:

God allowed evil, to test job, so he hates God. But job, disappointed evil. Because of his loyalty, and faith in God. Job 1:1-22. Jesus was tested, and tempted, by the devil. When he was led into desert by the spirit. Matthew 4:1

Because, evil wasn't sure, if Jesus was son of living God. Jesus taught us, how to win over evil. When we, trust in God One word comes, out mouth of God, and the devil disappears

Jesus said, I did not come to destroy, what was said by the prophets but to fulfill. Matthew 5:17-27.

Jesus also said, I assure you, until heaven, and earth disappear. Not one dot, or one title shall be lost, from the law. Till all things, have been accomplished.

Jesus said, do not be afraid. Just believe. Luke 8:50

Teaching the bible, is very powerful. Jesus is heart of the living God. He taught us, mercy love, and charity. It is, not right to pretend loving others. But we don't.

We should, always live, by the word, speaking the truth Romans12:9-21.

Faith is not only, pleasing others by, smooth talking them. Romans 16:18

Faith should be. Sincere. Love should come, from our hearts. Some people, they express to you, how they, love you But. behind you, they speak badly about you. They say anything just to please anyone for time being. But never accomplish, what they promise.

Especially, they are very nice. When they are, about to gain, from you. Some people if they don't need, or have any business with you. They won't care about you.

Hate is evil. Evil holds to what it is good. Romans 12:9

Hate is wrong. Love must be sincere. We most rejoice, and hope in God. He is, patient in tribulation. Persevering in prayer. We prays, for the ones who persecute us, and blesses them.

We do not curse. Because, cursing comes out of hate. cursing any one, it is asking Evil to do harm to that person.

If we do well. Good will comes to us.

God teach us, how to be obedience, to him, by being subject to his high authorities.

There's no higher authorities, except from him, and those who exist, have been appointed by God.

Those who resists, the ordinance of God. They bring in themselves. condemnation. Romans 13:1-5

We have, social duty toward God. To live life, of charity, and love. We are obligated to be our brother's keeper.

Once upon a time, lady, and I we were talking how important prayers are. She said I only pray for my children. I answered her, and said. Do you like, to have better, and safer world for your kids to live in ? She said of course. I said then, you should also pray for the entire world. She agreed.

True faith reveals, happiness in God, and we become positive. If we only trust in God. We will not have anything to worry about. I pray, and then. I finds peace with God.

Jesus said, in (New Testament). We need to pray, for Gods heavenly kingdom, then everything, will be grand it to us. Praying is starting from the top, bringing heaven down on Earth. We need, to pray for faith, grace, and wisdom.

Our heavenly father, he is unlike our earthly father's. God never refuse requests Because. God loves to spoil us. So we continue seeking him. God he is like our parents if they spoil us. We go back for more. If you spoil your own child, and never say no. He, or she will keep coming to you.

Our children, they keep coming to us. When we never say no. That is, how they get spoiled. Therefore, God knows, if he never tells us no. We will become, spoiled, and we continue to go back to him, for more. That's what exactly God want. Us to continue to go back to him. Same way, our children continue, to come to us.

Our prayer should be, unconditional with certainty.

Jesus taught us, how to pray to God. How to please and promise him to be loyal. LORD prayer Jesus said, that when you pray, do not multiply words, as gentile does for your father knows, what you need. For you shall pray.

Our father, who art in heaven hollowed be thy name thy kingdom come, thy will be done on earth, as it in heaven give us this day, our daily bread, and forgive us our debt, as we also for give our debtors. Matthew 6:7-12

First. We acknowledge, admit, and appreciate, confess and confirm, our believe in God

Second. We acknowledge, his name, the most holy. There is, no name above his name and we are waiting for his kingdom, to come down here, on earth so, God will put perfect justice on earth. Just the way, it is in heaven.

Third. we ask him, to forgive us, our sins we already for gave whoever, sinned against us and we are telling, and pleading with God telling. Promising him we are not lying.

So many, prays this prayer daily, still they don't forgive. So many, pray daily hoping God would answer. God never come directly to anyone. But he put his mercy, in others hearts. So they come for rescue. God put his mercy through us, so we can pass it to others who are seeking it. Some give up, and lose their faith.

We can, easily increase. Others faith, by showing them mercy, compassion, kindness They will, truly know God

So much need to be done. Hunger is real. I did not understand hunger until, I begin to feed, the homeless. You can see, how fast they eat. So many are, almost starved, to death Starvation is real.

Once upon time, I stopped at the gas station, there was beggar begging, for some money to, buy something to eat. I was glad; I helped because, he run inside. I was watching him coming out, with food in his hand, and drink. Praising God. I give him encouragement letting him know there's God, and he loves him. We need to find, a solution to every issue. We need to face life knowing that, everything is possible.

Never give our self-chance to feel guilty, about anything. People move away, or pass away. I mean you have a friend, or relative, having dispute with anyone. You should always make peace. Especially your loved ones. Otherwise you could feel guilty. If you did, not get a chance to make up.

Decent people, always fix their mistakes, and make up the different.

Therefore, if we try to make peace, and others refuse. At least we, have clear conscience. But continue, to be merciful toward them.

If they refuse, to make peace. That will be the guilt they have, to live In their hearts.

If we have, the smallest problem. If we don't fix immediately, can get bigger, and bigger Like having a big gap between us, and others, who we have a problem with. That is evil squeezing in the middle, to make a gap wider. Putting us, further apart from each other.

God will never, give us more than, we can take. We need to have a long conversation with God. Like if, we were sitting next to him. God love it, when we beg.

Just the way, we speak to our earthly father face to face. With God we acknowledged, his spirit is present. When we speak to him.

Why even have, to worry about anything. When we know he's our creator, and he has the greatest power

God is ruler, of universe, and he owned. In order for us, to grow in the faith. Is to love, everyone also to help the needy, poor, the neglected, the persecuted And heal the sick Always spread peace, and mercy. For the living spirit of God to live among us

Jesus said, resist the evil doer. If someone strikes you on the cheek turn to him, the other. Also who, want to borrow don't turn away. Love your enemies. Do well to those who hate you, and pray for those, who persecuted you, and calumniate you. Matthew 5:38-42, 44

People who, always do evil. They have no good conscience, to bother them. They feel no guilt, or remorse.

If we continue to take care of the poor, and hungry. To make sure everyone have what they want. No one will have, any reason to hurt anyone. No one, will have any reason to steal If we love, the one who loves us, we are already both of us, pleasing God. Will be greater in God's eyes. If we love the ones, who hate us. By doing that, we will be conquering evil, with good. Also by doing good for the ones, who hate us. They will be in shock. We also put them to shame, they would not know. Where, to turn, or either look at you. Knowing that. They, don't know how to be good.

Jesus said, by doing all what's good, we become children, of our father in heaven

God he is light, of those shines, which rise, on good, and evil, and sends rain, on the just, and unjust. Matthew 5:45.

God already, have the good people. He will never give up on bad ones. He loves sinners, to come his way so he heals them.

Jesus said, our heavenly father (God) is perfect. He knows we, can never be perfect If we only follow, his commandments, and laws. That what will truly, please him

We should be persistent, in helping others, never think evil. By showing mercy, and compassion. Toward everyone around us. Brings hope, peace, and freedom to the people. Who are pressed for?

There is, always someone one among us, who is capable, and have what takes to help the less fortunate, and the needy.

We don't, need to figure out, what's happening, or wonder about. Everywhere, bad and horrible things, happening around us. We either see it, or hear about it, every single day Instead of worrying about it. We should, do something about it. It does not take a lot, to take care of the Poor homeless, less fortunate, and persecuted.

Our job should be, bringing justice to all. Forgiving, is the only way we get, evil out of our life. For giving, it is the key to success.

The reason we have, no choice but to forgive. God forgive us, before we sin. How could, we ask God to forgive us. If we haven't, forgiven someone else yet. Read lord prayer

We need to get used, to forgive, any one. Any dispute, we have with others. Always we have no choice.

In the event, we hold anything, against anyone. That individual, more likely, he, or she make peace with, God. If we don't, make peace immediately. We remain, guilty with God never looks, in the past, he only care about today, and beyond.

Jesus said, but I say to you that everyone, who is angry with his brother, shall be liable to judgment. Matthew 5:21-22.

Instead, of being angry with anyone. Why lose a sleep over it ? It is healthier to fix everything, on the spot. Myself, whenever I have dispute with anyone. I don't rest until I make peace. If I am wrong, or right, I go to that individual if is my friend, or relative I speak my heart, and mind until, I make peace.

Sometime, people they can be very persistent.

Mercy, and compassion, reduce suffering. We should, always be at peace with everyone Especially, with our neighbor. Because, if you have, any problems, and become critical your neighbor, can get to you faster, then any of your friends, or relatives. Who lives, so far away from you ?.

God forgiveness, is beyond our beliefs. When, we sin he doesn't make it his choice not to forgive. Because, usually say to himself. I must forgive them. What do, I expect, they are human being, they are weak when it, comes to sin.

God focus always, on sinners first. This is why. God love us, to plead for specification cancellation. He listen hears, perceive.

It is good, to be positive, decisive. Especially, when we pray.

Billions people around, the world know God, from the bible, and the miracles. For Christian they know God because of Jesus. He is heart of God, for others they know him in spirit.

No one ever, seen God. Still, we welcome him into our hearts, and minds, and life. If we find that, so easy to believe in God. How much easier to, fix all the problems that comes ahead.

All earthly things, can be explainable almost.100% of the time. We must be tolerant Our number, one goal should be fixing everything, always.

Love for God form all of our heart, and mind. We need to respect others emotion, as well as ours. No matter what situation, we are into. We must make time to fix, and put it behind us. God only cares about today, and beyond. He forgives, and forgets always.

Then peter asks Jesus lord, how often shall my brother sin against me, and I forgive him? Up to seven time ?. Jesus said to him, I don't say to you seventh times, but 70 seven times seven. Matthew 18:21-22.

Jesus saying we are obligated, to forgive not 100% of the time but a lot more. If we forgive unconditionally. Love will always, take place. Where can evil fit ?.

Jesus explains. about master, and wicked servant. Matthew 18:23-35.

How critical, and necessary is to forgive for our own good. Jesus explained, the way kingdom of heaven work. The servant begs his master, to forgive his debt. His master, had compassion, and forgave him his debt. But as the servant went out, he met one, of his fellow servants, who owed him some money. He refused, to forgive him. he put him, in prison.

When his master found out, what first servant, did to his fellow servant. He told wicked servant; I forgive you, all that you owe me. Why couldn't, have pity on your fellow servant ?. And his master, being angry. Handed him over to the torture until he should pay all his debt. God saying, If they are, able to pay you, make sure you get your money. But if they are, not able to pay you must forgive them. How do we, expect God to forgive us. If we don't forgive first, and the must.

There are, lots of people who, go up, and down financially some, loses everything. When they are, not able to pay they file, for bankruptcy.

I believe because of this parable bankruptcy court, came about, to forgive people their debt. Giving them, second chances to the ones, who lose everything. Discharging their debt giving them the chance to start all over.

God bless, America.

I believe four, of many; will be hard, to be forgiving, by God

1. Any types, of greed in huge way, to hurt others.

2. If we do not, for give anybody for, any reason, any condition.

3- For persecution toward any one.

4. Judging others. Because, color of their skin (Being. Racial)

Smooth talk from, an evil heart like glaze, on cracked pottery your enemy shake hand, and greet like an old friend all the while conniving you. Proverbs 26:23-26

We need to be careful. Who we deal with, now these days. There's a lot. Who are, very smooth talker. There are, a lot of people, who are very. A very nice. They have, those people. They are, only nice to, just for time being. Not because they care. But for their own gain. They don't care about others feelings. They are selfish. They act nice to people so they can, great them. They persecute people, and justify that. They refuse to, acknowledge What they are, doing is wrong doing. They think, they are perfect, sometime they make themselves. Believe they are saints, descended from heaven oh yes. They don't practice, what they preach. They take advantage of others, and they think. It is, strictly business.

They have, no consideration, for others. Only think of them self's that is about it. People with no, good conscious they don't know how, to have mercy on others. They don't know how to practice compassion. Because yet none of it, into their hearts. Yes they go to church only Because, they are scared, and feels guilty. But they don't know how to find themselves, how truly to get in touch with true God.

I define as following, there are, some people who have two groups of people. They deal with, on daily basis.

First group. They always treated them very well. Always get all the help they need They get, golden treatment dine together, and ensure each other's happiness moments they never cheat each other. Because they have big business, with each other. They are kind, and merciful, toward each other. They think, their relationship is made in heaven. This first group They think, and confirmed them, well, and such great people. But something they don't know. If are they fair to the second group of people, they are dealing with.

Some who don't care, as long, as they are getting what they need. Unfortunately, this group admire, those people not knowing. They are, not treating other people the same, I mean fair, and equal. They know they are very selfish they don't care, as long they get what they want They have, no consideration for others, as long, as they are treated very good. First group Only was being treated, very well. Because, they had the power, and the money.

Second group. At the meantime, in another hand. Because they are poor, and those who are less fortunate. They take their advantage, use them charge them more, and pay them less. Poor people, always put up with it. Because, they are desperate and needed the help. They are, persecute every day, being humiliated. Almost their freedom is taken. People put up with it, because they are despaired. They also, make them believe, they are less. They don't realize that. Nothing can make anyone better, than anybody else ever. They are, treated very unfairly unjust. Just because they are poor.

One hundred percent, good person. I defined him, or her fair, and Just. Never takes advantage of anyone never steal, or cheat anyone, or put any anyone down, and respect everyone. Treat everyone, the same regardless, if they were poor, or rich who, and If they are, young or old. Rich or poor, as long, as they do same work. They should, get exactly the same pay. No one should get, any special treatment, because they are any better, or richer.

Good person, value everyone one the same. Good person, should be sincere, virtual merciful, thoughtful, considered, and compassionate. Always seeking justice for others, holy and Faithful. Always practice what he, or she preaches Great conscience, forward. Always speaks the truth. Never deceive anyone. Fearing God. Love everyone the same. Never hold grudges always forgetting, and forgiving. Never take advantage of anyone. Good person, should be pure, at heart Kind persons. Always pleasing God. Good people are sensitive. Especially, If one of them owned business to think, of their workers, they need to make, a living too. Good people, are always fair, and they have enough to live, always look around them to see. What needs to be done for others. Good persons know. What's right, and what is wrong. Often judge them self to see how well, or bad they are doing. They know, themselves every one of us sin. Every one of us knows, and could be 100% Good person.

Finally good person, follow, and obey all the commandments, and laws of God. Have good conscience. Whenever, they make a mistake, or wrong to anyone they go, and apologize and makeup.

Everybody have life need, to take care of it. Every one needed to make a living. If you, or I think we are better than others. We are not, because we all have one thing in common. That is, at the end we all become dust when we die.

We are not, allowed to judge anyone, but we can help others become good people like us Because many are bad, and always do bad things. They feel locked, and they don't know how to be free, and to become better people. Some people, all they know is only to do bad things. We can, always work with them. If we can help, one of the time. We can make, some different that will please God, very much.

There are, so many different ways we can help. We need to build better`society. If we think, we're considered thoughtful, charitable, merciful, and many more good things. We can teach people around us. To become like us.

So many have no one. So they can lean on, they live abusive life. Some of these people takes good out of bad, they change their life. Some others thinks, this is what life, is about, and they continue to you live through it.

Before we, past judgment at anyone. We needs to judge our self-first. If I treat certain person very good. Then treat someone else. Less, or different, is not fair. There's no way I could call myself, good person.

We can't say, to our self. It is OK to do, 99% good. And we do only 1% bad. God want us, to be good always.

Everyone, was born with mercy of God. Therefore, our heart full of God's mercy. When people try to reach, and touch our hearts. We feel the mercy, coming out of our hearts. Especially when they beg, for mercy, they we will find it in us. We can teach everyone, how to be merciful.

Good persons, lives life of holiness, genuine, Full of goodness, spectacle. Full of empathy.

A relative her son got killed-murdered, in Iraq, because of his Christian faith, and beliefs In my old country Iraq. Murdering, Christian become common thing. To some point They think all American are Christian, and invaded their country. Anyway, she was very sorrowful, sad crying, and kept saying I don't understand. Why this, happened to me I've never, hurt anyone I always help, any one she Said. She does charities. Never bother anyone. She always, took care of sick, and needy, and the poor, she was wondering why. I answered with comforting voice, what happened to you is a tragedy. But you are lucky, God made you good person I add it I am sorry. What had happened, to your son. It was meant to be. If something destines to happen will. Only God can change things, by miracle.

Jesus saying about good, moral and generous person In the laborers in vineyard Matthew 20: 1-16.

Jesus Christ explained, what heaven is like for the kingdom of heaven is like, a house holder. Hired laborer. For his vine yard. Early in the morning. He agreed with laborer for a denarius a day. In the third hour, he went out to the market saw others standing, he also send them to his vine yard. He said to them you go also, I will give you whatever is Just.

He went again on sixth, and, on ninth hour, and the last ones were standing there all day ? They said, to him because no one hires them. When the, evening came. Every one receives same pay. The first ones, were complaining. Because, they thought they were getting more Complaining talking to each other, against the owner saying, we worked longer. He answered to one of them, and said to him. I did you no injustice. I did agree with you for a denarius have I not have a right what. I choose Or are you, envious because I am generous.

Jesus said even so, the last shall be first, and the first shall be last. For many are called, but fewer are chosen.

During Jesus time, until these days some places. There are, people who needed job every day. There for, they stand in market places waiting, to be hired for a day of work. They did not have a steady job. That is how, they made their living. They got hired by merchants. Farmers also still goes on, at some part of Middle East.

That particular vine yard owner. He was good, generous, thoughtful, considered, and fair man. He knew, those laborers depended on that day of work. More likely he was just thinking exactly He pays them for, a full day of work anyway. Because he knew, they needed to feed, their children or pay their bills, and whatever, they needed, for the day. To get by.

This parable, also means, that the ones who had a strong faith for little problems in their lives, or step back. They lose their faith. The ones who do not have, any faith, and lived in Sin they repent it, and they came, to believe in God.

Jesus meant, to say in this parable. To God it does not matter, which comes first, or last to God. We are all number one, and his favored.

Every one of us, is important to God. We are all first, in his heavenly eyes. Good persons, they are the ones who feel, hearts, aches, and minds of others around them, and run to them, to see what need to be done. Also try to learn. What needs to be done for other. Not only, to fix things. But also to make it better.

We need to help, reduce people's suffering. Especially our loved ones. Because when one of us is suffering. Evil takes pride, in himself. Because evil know. God plan for us to have, a happy life here on earth. Therefore evil hate us. His enjoyment is huge. When we, are miserable. We need to encourage everyone, to have mercy un-conditionally. Not only, to explain to them how, to be merciful, also, to show them Good persons, are the ones, who have good character. Who is very charitable, generous, fair, and honest. Never, deceive anyone. Philanthropic, forgiving. Always happy and joy full, pleasant, grateful. Always cherish, every good thing he or she gets.

Good person, has strong faith in God. Believes in the salvation of the soul, and sacrifice of the body for the sake of the truth.

Good, and morals, are the ones who respond, to the cry of the less fortunate. They are good, and devoted, angelic, Godly, humble, saintly, just, and prefaced in God's eyes, spiritual honest, frank Fair, and homologous, equivalent, and associated with. Whom is fault less.

Good persons, have virtues, and always devoted. Helps the sick, and needy. Gives hopes to the once, who are seeking it Good, and moral, they are merciful, faithful, spectacle, side rate reliable, genuine.

Selfish, and inconsiderate, and who don't care about others feelings. They always, struggle more than others. It does not matter, If they are, rich or poor.

I often say, if we are to wonder, or have any fear what will be, in next world when we die. I say, If you are always good. What possibly would go wrong be good.

Besides, it will be safer for us. If we judge our self-daily, to see how good, or bad we did. So we can fix we, done wrong. We have, the chance while alive. Before facing the last judgment of God. Might be too late.

Jesus, preached. How rewarding, life could be, if we can just hold on. Matthew5:3-12 Jesus said.

1- Blessed are, poor in spirit, for theirs is the kingdom of heaven, about the ones always peaceful, quiet hardly, or never have any complain. Down to earth. Never think big, and holy.

2-Blessed are, the meek. For they, shall possess the earth. All the ones who never offended anyone always cheerful very nice pleasing everyone. They will not only own the earth they will also inherited the heaven. To be with God. The new earth at the last judgment. The are chosen by God will enjoy the new paradise.

3 - Blessed are, they who mourn, for they shall be comforted. People who always, suffer the most, and excepted with faith, and patient. They will be relieved, at the end. God will wipe the tears from, their eyes, and remember their cries, and heart aches.

4 - Blessed, are they who hunger, and thirst for justice for they shall be satisfied. About the ones. Who were hardly treated fairly. Always cheated, and being taken advantage of People always put them down, and treat them like if they were less. At the end they will be satisfied. God will never leave us alone. He will always be here, to rescue us. Especially when we call him.

5- Blessed are the clean of hearts, for they shall see God. He love us. He will bless us, and remain into, our hearts.

6- Blessed are, the peacemakers. For they shall be called children of God. For many peace bring safety, and relieve. Whenever, and were ever peace resume. If there's no peace there's no mercy. Also when there's no peace. There's wars. Many innocent, becomes victims. Will be peace on earth. When word of God, and his well will be done. because God love will be living among us. The holy spirit of God is always, were peace is. Out of peace, comes mercy Peace bring safety, and comfort into the world. Mercy bring, relieve into our mind, soul,and hearts.

7- Blessed are they, who suffer persecution, for the sake of justice, for theirs the kingdom of heaven. God he is fair and powerful. He sees, all the things, the less fortunate go through in life. God also, see all the evil had done to them. God said the people, who mistreat you in any bad ways. They will, get their own punishment. God said, that you suffered, with patient, and strong faith. You will get your own rewards.

8-Blessed are you, when men reproach you, and persecute you, and speaking falsely, all manner of evil against you for my sake.

Jesus he is, the truth that lead, to the true light. So many Christians, who died for their faith, and believe. In Jesus Christ.

Gossiping, and spreading rumors about others, is evil. Especially, talking behind someone else back. When they are not present. It is not fair, and just. Everyone deserve, and have freedom, to be present, to defend him, or her selves.

Evil always, work through people, to stop them from speaking the truth. Especially about God. Many through history, got murdered because of their beliefs. God always mention. If we suffer, for the sake of the truth. We should rejoice, and exult be joy full, and the reward we'll be giving us In the heaven. That will be great.

Jesus said, Even the prophets were persecuted. Matthew 5:12

Jesus Christ, our lord praising. The good, and moral. The ones, who always do will of God He is, also describing goodness, come out of bad. Our goodness, what really, and truly makes us children of God.

When we continue, to over com evil with good. That's how we control our temptations We should ask God, to continue, having mercy, on all of us always.

Sometime people, find it difficult to acknowledge God. So they can do, whatever they please, at the same time. They stop believing In God. So they don't feel guilty, or shame. For all greed, lusting, abuse, selfishness, inconvertie, and much more. They become very immoral They often, feel free to do whatever they please. Without feeling, any guilt.

God is showing us, the price we have to pay spiritually in order for us, to over com evil With good.

God said, be joy full, and happy, your reward will be great, in the Heaven. Jesus said for they persecute the prophets before us. Matthew 5:12, 1Kings 18:1.

Jesus also he is, praising the good, and moral, and the ones who always do will of God Jesus Christ describing. How much good, comes out of bad things.

Goodness, we show others. Will make us, children of God. He will, always give us mercy. So we give. The same to others.

It is difficult to not sin. This is why we have the 10 commandments, to teach us what's right. Also what we need to do In order to put end, to the wicked.

Noah, and his family survived the, flood because of his faith. (Genesis).

By faith Abraham obeyed, and he wasn't afraid of anything. Because he knew. God was with him, and as long, as he do will of God. (Genesis).

God told Abraham. Why are, you afraid if you know I am with you ? Also by faith, Sara she believe she will have baby, at her old age.

She knew with God. everything is possible. By faith Isaac blessed Jacob, and Esau. Even regarding things.

God gave a blessing to Isaac. Because, his faith that, and beliefs. He gave his blessing to his son Jacob because, knew he will be father of the nation.

By faith, when Jacob was dying. He blessed each of the sons of Joseph (Genesis) Hebrews 11:6-10

We are also able to give, blessing to our children. To grow up with faith, and whatever needed.

By faith Moses, was not afraid of the kings, because he knew God protect him, and gave Moses power to lead nation of Jewish, the chosen people out of Egypt. God always know what best for us. See. Exodus.

Paul said, Christ had been. Minister of circumcision, in order to show God's fidelity, in confirming, the promises, was made to our fathers. Romans 15:8-13.

God promised, our fathers, the savior to save us from. Evil sin. Jesus Christ is for the conversion of hearts.

Also Paul said, now you may know, God of hope full with joy, and peace in believing, you may abound in hope and in the power of the holy spirit. Ask to have unshakable faith, and trust in God. Romans 15:8-13

Paul said, if God is for us, who is against us ? So much we worry, and concern about Christian gives all that to Jesus Christ, to help us, and give guidance. If we love our neighbor were evil fit, if we do, unconditionally good. Where would evil fit.

Greed, and selfishness bring end, to all good things. Greed, and love of the money, makes us blind from doing what is right. Too much money it shuts out our hearts, and minds. Love of the money makes us, forget about, the most important things, into our lives To Some, money becomes, there God.

My father told me, a simple story how greed, and selfishness. Dishonesty brings relationships to the end, or sometime to catastrophe.

In my country where, I came from. Some people before breakfast. They boil egg, just for a few seconds. Before getting completely hard, I mean over -easy. They pull it out of the hot water, and let it cool then the crock small hole, on the top, used some salt, and stir with small spoon then they drink it. They thought it gave them energy.

Once upon a time, there were two merchants. Owned business together for long time First few years, everything was great. Everything was built, on Mutual Trust. Usually one of them open business first, and prepare two eggs one for him, and one his partner. To treat each other equally, always prepared same size two eggs in the morning. Waiting for the partner to get to work so, can eat the eggs together. One day the older partner becomes, suspicious of the younger partner things were not going very well. Unfortunately, someone was being dishonest. Before, the older partner confirms, he want to make sure. He was very wise. He made, sure he made it to work first, and immediately prepared two eggs. Only that one time, he prepared one extra large egg, one small, and wait it for his partner. So they eat it together Only to see, how selfish his younger partner he can be. When he arrived, he took the extra large egg he was not humble. He was only thinking of himself. He could be more, thoughtful, respect full, and take extra large egg.

The older partner, he was disappoint to find out. How really selfish, and in consider the younger partner is, and not very thoughtful.

The older, things kept going through his mind, all day long thinking. If his younger partner like that, in small ways. Can get bigger. He just could not trust, the younger partner loyalty. Therefore, at the end of that working day. He decided not be, in business with that partner no more. They each took their share, and went their separate way The wise, and the older partner, did not want, to take a risk of losing, any more.

Paul said, if I have prophecy, and know all mysteries knowledge, and if I have all the faith to move, all the mountains. Yet without charity are not enough, and I am nothing 1 Corinthians 13:2-5.

If we give everything for poor, and we don't love is not enough for God. If we have faith to move mountains. Without charity, is not enough faith. So much charity, we can do don't cause us anything. Like act of love compassion toward the sick, needy, and less fortunate Mercy, peace, and bring happiness into lonely hearts will please God.

Some people can be misled, not understanding concept of charity. Often saying they don't have, any money to give. The fact is, there is many things. We are able to do, act of love It is number one. Helping someone, who is disabled, to do for themselves. The most effective, acts of charity it is praying for others. Serving others. Also spreading love, mercy and peace.

Friend of mine. Once upon a time, told me a story I don't have proven how true it is. But it mean, something I believe, because of my faith.

The story goes, as following. There was, a monk continuously praying. He Did that for many years. One day he began to wonder. How close he was to God. while praying, he began to ask the holy spirit, how close he became to God. Also how please, God was with him One day, finally the holy spirit answered him, and told him. Your deeds is not close to me, as much to me, as butcher, pointing to the monk. The butcher shop in town.

The monk, went back, to prayer asking. What he most do. The answer was, to go to that butcher shop, and ask him to take you with him home. He did, exactly that. He went and ask the butcher, if he can be guest, at his home at the end of the day. The butcher agreed, and saying to the monk, if you wait here, and follow me home, at the end of the day. Just as, working day was over. The monk follows the butcher, returning home. First thing the butcher did. When he got home, took care of his old, and disable father Who was, in the bed room ? He helped, his father shaving, and cleaned him. Then fed him. All that time the monk was watching the butcher, what he was doing.

That is, when monk understood the message he received. From the Holy Spirit. Act of love, and charity, and prayer. Puts our faith to work.

Our parents are, valuable to God. Also all older people because, they are, parents most of them.

So many older people are in nursing homes. They have, no one to visit them, and to comfort them. Each of these older people has their own story to tell.

The biggest, and the most important charity. It is for to pray for others. We could get, unconditional guidance. If we let, the Holy Spirit have complete power, over our life.

Faith is giving others, example. To what life should be about, and not to judge anyone. Also to be great example for everyone. True faith, is when we practice, what we preach. That what faith is about.

Jesus said, stop judging, that may not be judged. For as you judge, so will you be judged and the measure. With which you measure, will be measured out to you. Matthew 7:1-2.

Just the way, we want to be treated. We treat everyone the same. When people judge others, they act like. They never make, any mistakes. We all make mistakes.

Controlling others, by passing judgment to them. Is not fair. We need to respect Every one freedom. Every one, have right, to defend them self.

While Jesus, was at table with many tax collectors, and sinners came, and sat with Jesus and his disciples, the Pharisees saw that, said to his disciples. Why, your teacher sit does with tax collectors, and sinners. Matthew 9:9-13.

When, Jesus heard what was said. Those who are well, do not need a physician. But the sick. Jesus said. I desire mercy, not sacrifice. He basically said. Christ came, to call us to the true home.

Those sinners, Jesus was able to judge them. By simply telling them, your sin is forgiven, and send them away. Instead he reached for their hearts, and mind. He made them feel, the same like everyone else, and not, any less. Or worse than others.

We all sin. No one was, better than them. They were important, and valuable to God as well. Jesus always calling sinners. Most of those people, became Jesus followers.

Jesus saying, about Isaiah prophesy of saying,this people honor, me with lips, but their hearts, far from me. Matthew 15:7-8

Some who are, only smooth talk. But they are different in heart. God always, concern and thinking of us only. If we all love God, will not do him, any good. If we don't, love our neighbor, friends, strangers, and family.

For every good thing we do. People will see, and know God. We often noticed, on people face, when we do well toward them. Many who appreciated us. But first they thank God and they feel humbled.

In the beginning, of Christianity, they share everything (Book of Act).

It is harder, to do that now. Because, they are billions, in the world today. Therefore, we can do it, one on one. So we can extend, Jesus love toward each other. And others. To spread peace, mercy. To take care the poor, needy and, the negligent, persecuted,orphans, widows, and to put end, to the poverty around the world.

Jesus said, let your light shine before man, in order that they may see your, good work and give glory to your father in heaven Matthew 5:16.

No one ever see God. But the charity we do. Mercy, and compassion we show others They will know what God is like, and about. We are temple of God. Therefore, all his goodness comes, through us to show others.

If we think we have enough faith. We need to see how strong it is. Just by the way we reach others. We need to examine our faith.

Story of act of love, generosity, mercy, and thought fullness. Older and wise used to say stories, so we learn.

In small town tilkepe, in middle north of Iraq. It is located about eleven miles north east, of the city of Mosel along, long time ago farmers, used a very small equipment to harvest their farm. Agricultures in town. Harvesting follows a particular order. Farmers harvest, barley first, then wheat. Typically farmers, will early in the morning go, to the market place to find workers, to help harvest the crop. Everybody in the family helps with the harvesting, even woman and children After they finish. They take the wheat, close to the town where the ground was wormers, so that can dry. Then, they use old fashion machine called " Gargera to crash, and separate the wheat, and the barley from its shat.

Any way one of the times they happen, to be two brothers, whom had set their harvest next to each other waiting to dry. Both of those, two brother behind each other back.

One brother was married. The second brother was single.

The married one, was saying to himself. My brother, he need more money than me. Because, he need to get married he is going, to have some expense. Therefore, he was taking off some wheat, of his pile, and put it on his single brothers pile.

The single brother was doing same thing, and saying, to himself my brother need more Because he has kids, and wife to support.

They both continued, doing until one time. The two brothers run into each other. They each drop what we're carrying, in their hands. Both of them. Dropped, what they had in their hand, and hug each other. Telling sharing, their story. Example of kindness, and generosity.

God want us, to be like him. Merci full. Because, we are his children. He want to be like, any earthly fathers. Who want their children to like them. Therefore, if the children, are good. Everyone will praise the father, for raising such good children. If we are, good everyone will praise God. Because we are, his children.

Jesus said be merciful. Therefore, even as your father is merciful. Do Not Judge, and you shall not be judged. Do not condemn, you shall be not being condemned. Forgive, and you shall be forgiven. Luke 6:36-38

God he is fair, and good. He reward who are fair. If we judge any one. God will judge us more. God create us, and made, to be equal. He do not favored, any one more, then other How could we, expect God to forgive us, if we do not forgive others. At the end. We will be judged according.

Jesus said, he who would save his life will lose it. But he who loses his life for my sake will save it. For what it profit a man, if he gain the whole world. But lose himself. Luke 9:24-25

If we own everything, all the martial, and things which is for our fiscal body. Will not help, our spirit, or can buy us ball with God. Love, mercy, love, charity, and much more goodness will in rich our spirit.

Jesus saying, about poor widow. She put so, little money in the treasury. She did not have much. and helped anyway. Mark 12:42-44

It mean allot to God, if it comes from our heart. No matter how much we give. We give not because,we have to. But if we want to. Romans 12:1-6

Jesus Christ said, it is more blessed, to give then to receive. Charity, compassion for the poor, and less fortunate will enrich our spirit. Jesus want it everything to be perfect. Therefore, the devil can, never take control over our lives. Living holy life. By giving God your spiritual service.

If we don't have the sick, the poor, and the hungry, homeless. We will not have the chance, to do any goodness, or either having to do, any deeds. In order for us, to please God

The poor are the reason for the rich. To do good deeds. Toward God.

Feeding the poor. Becomes, one more step toward heaven. Poor people, are excess to our salvation. Poor are, our key to heaven. Ask Jesus Christ, he will tell you.

Therefore, God said. I commend you, to open your hands, to the needy, and the poor Deuteronomy 15:11

We need, to run to the land. Where, does not grow any food. Try to make it fertile. So they can, grow food to eat and survive. Deuteronomy 15:11

Around the world, there is places, it is impossible to grow, any food. But with, our technology, we can make it possible.

God he is, lord of the truth. Psalms 30:6-

God, we will be rejoicing in his love, and mercy. Especially, if we put our spirits into his hand always.

Each one, give according as, he has determined in his heart. Not only because the compassion. Also because God loves a cheerful giver. God is able to make, all grace abound in every good work we do. 2 Corinthians 9:7- 8.

God he is just, and fair judge. Psalms 7:9-13

He is God of love, Compassion, and mercy. He wants every human being, to himself. At the final judgment, he will judge us according to our doing.

God said, I am the lord your God, and the jealous God. Who shall not take the name of the lord your God in vain, for he shall not be unpunished, whoever takes God's name in vain Deuteronomy 5:8-11

Jesus Christ appeared, for the destruction of sin, by sacrifices himself. For God did not send his son, into the world, in order to judge the world but that the world might be saved through him. Hebrews 9:26-27. John 3:17,19,21

Jesus, he is, the true light came, into the world. Yet people love the darkness, rather than the light. For their work were evil. John 3:17

Many refuse to know the truth. There for, they continue doing wrong without feeling guilt, or shame.

Jesus said. For everyone who, does evil hates, the light and does not come to light, that his deeds may not be exposed John 3:20.

People who always, do wrong they don't want to admit it, because, they don't want to be ashamed. Or know there is doing wrong.

A stone, which the builder rejected, the same stone became the head of the corner Acts 4:11.

Jesus Christ, he is pointing to himself. He was rejected, and also crucified. Then he became to billions, who believe in him. Became their salvation.

Jesus said, to them, to my food is, to do will, of the one who sent me. Will of the father is to save us from evil sin, and left us up with him to heaven. John 4: 34-35.

Jesus spoke, of the last judgment, and end of the world. He said no one knew the day, or hour, neither the angels in heaven, or the son only the father.

But Jesus said; need to be ready to keep praying. They will be like thief of the night. If we know the thief is coming. We will be ready. Mark 13:32-33.

Jesus said, to them. Go into whole world, and preach the gospel to every creature He who believes, and baptized shall be saved. But he does not believe shall be condemned Mark 16:15-16.

It is impossible, to know God. Unless we know Jesus Christ first because through him Made everything, possible.

We are obligated from God, to give the good news to the world. let the world know Jesus Christ. So they can be saved too. Even if it means, losing our life for the sake of the truth.

We serve God by, spreading, and teaching the gospel God heals us. Through Jesus Christ God gave us the freedom.

This is why, we must keep good things into our lives, and always fix the bad things We stay ahead in life in order for us to remain happy.

Jesus give us peace, for all of, our hearts not to be troubled, no more Mark 16:15-16.

Jesus taught us, to put our hope in God. Always continuously, fixing things, as they come along through our lifetime, in order for us, to be on God site. In our life time.

We all sin; we make mistakes, and bad decisions. At meantime. We should be, careful Always, try to do things leading us to heaven.

Blessed are, the peacemakers. For they shall be called children of God Matthew 5:9. Our obligations toward God. To keep peace among people, and to helping them, to do away with evil. Jesus peace will remain with us forever.

Jesus Christ, also said peace. I give to you. Don't let your hearts be troubled. John 14:27-28.

He said he's, going away, but he is coming to get us. Jesus saying don't be alarmed Believed in me, your problems will be fixed. He is going to the father. He will back to get us, he said. If we have the love Jesus has for us ? We should rejoice that he is going to the father We must let, God take control of our lives 100% of the time.

Bear with one, and another, and forgive one another. To you must make allowance for each other fault, and forgive. The person who offends you. Colossians 3:13-15

We need to remember, Jesus always for gave us. Therefore, we must forgive others Above all these things have charity. Which is the bond of perfection ? And the peace of Christ is in our hearts.

We have peace with God, if our hearts, and minds. Come to term with God. When obeying him, and following his commandments.

Paul said, having been justified. Therefore, by faith let us have peace with God through our lord Jesus Christ. Because of Jesus the access to the true life by faith. Romans 5:1

We receive, grace from our Lord Jesus Christ, and Glory was given to him by God the father. Without God everything, in the world will be reduced to nothing.

But the fruit, of the spirit it is charity, joy, peace, patience, kindness, and goodness Galatians 5:22.

It said faith in God is, by our work we produce. Which is the goodness. If we truly want to experience God love, we continue, to do work of charity, mercy, goodness and forgiveness. To reach who, are in need of comfort. To morn with mourners. Feed, clothes the poor.

Pray for the, ones who hate us maybe. They find mercy, into their hearts. Pray for who persecute us.

God favored, the meek, the humble the pure at heart, and the ones whom are fair and just. The generous, the considered, and the thoughtful. Who have always, have hope in God. Must love our neighbor, as our self.

One of the best deed we can do,toward God is help someone find a job. For someone who is very desperate.

And endurance, tried virtue, and hope does not disappoint. Romans 5:4-5.

Because, of charity God is poured forth into our heart by holy spirit. Trusting in God we keep him In our life. He became our guidance.

Rejoicing, in hope be patient in tribulation, persevering in prayer share the need of the saints practicing, hospitality. Romans 12:12-15.

Jesus Christ said, bless those who persecute you and bless, and do not curse. Rejoice with those who rejoice with you. Weep with those who weep with you. Matthew 5:11.

Happiness should be, our number one goal through our life, as long, as we have each other's, at the end of the day.

You shall not, hate your brother, in your heart, but approach him openly. So you, don't commit sin against him Lying and deceiving others. Leviticus19:17-18

The truth, always comes out. When people lies eventually. We see it on their face, and we don't believe them anymore. Also nothing stay in hiding always uncovers.

Jesus said, don't be afraid of them, there is nothing concealed that will not be disclosed. And nothing in hidden will not be known Matthew 10:26-27.

Jesus Christ always spoke the truth, and said to his disciples you out to teach all nations. What you hear. So they will come out the darkness. To light of the truth, and the truth will set us free.

Jesus Christ said, but let you speech yes, yes; no, no and whatever is beyond that comes from evil. Matthew 5:37.

If we lie, we are making evil proud. Because, we are hurting someone else. Allot who believes, their own lies, so they can get someone else, to believe their lies. like story of pinnnocus whenever, he lies his nose got longer. That when his mother knew he was laying ultimately people will see it on liar person's face.

Most of my life. I learned whenever, I am dealing with someone. If they are liars, always thinks everyone is liars. If they are cheaters. Thieves so on, and on. Because, they don't trust anyone. Always feeling guilty. They just don't trust anyone. Because, they have whole kind of things wrong in them.

If we tell something to someone, if they are willing to believe. All we have to do is say it once. If they want to believe they will. If they don't want to. They never will

Deceiving others, it is act of evil. Failure from telling, the truth. People lose always In fact they lose. Love of people around them.

We should not be faints. When speaking the truth. There will, be always someone. Who will love our honesty, and they will always be there for help.

We need, to be sincere, when it comes to the truth because, that is what God is. When speaking the truth, we can walk tall, and never afraid of anything. Always goodness win, and the bad loses.

I used to believe in white lies. There are, no such thing white lies Sometimes use term white lies. We used, with small children. It is almost like a promise, we don't keep. That is still deceiving. Some time we tell someone we care about any - thing. So they don't get upset, or worry. It will better to say whatever it is on the spot, or thing could get worse.

That makes things worse.

White lies gives false hope, and promise. Will be in our best interest always to keep our word. In the long run we will be honored, and respected.

Almost everyone, of us sometime says something. We are not sure of or exaggerate about something. We don't know of it, or for sure. Once we find out. We apologize, and correct ourselves.

Everyone somehow lies. Evil lying would be if we lie, to gain. Or If we become false witness, against anyone.

People who lies all they do, is hurting themselves, and others. Saying the truth, will always help us, during the most critical time.

Especially, if we did not do anything wrong. If we were, accuse of something. Many decent people. Who will hear us, understands us, and feel our hearts, and believe, we are saying the truth. So many wise people. Will automatically know we are honest. Jesus said. All you need is to say simply Yes, yes, or, no, no. Matthew 5:37

Jesus said, for is nothing hidden that, will not be made manifest. Not anything concealed that will not be known, and come to light Luke.8:16-17

The walls has ear, soon, or later people catch you, in the act and just the way we do, and express our self's. This is how. we gets revealed to others.

As Christian, we should always say the truth, to be, and have mind heart, and spirit of our lord Jesus Christ. There is, no other way, he will be able To represent us, and take us to father. Jesus Christ said, be aware of false prophets Who comes to you, in sheep clothing, but in their heart they are like wild wolves. By their fruits, we will know them. Matthew 7:15-17.

A lot only smooth talking, just to get their ways. Also there are some only help us. When they need us, but otherwise, if we go to them for help some other times, they would not help.

A story I heard before.

Once upon time, was this young person. One day he was out in the field suddenly decided to scream help wolf coming, to get him. Some people in town, run out to rescue him. But he was lying; people did, not see a wolf. Then they went the second time, he did the same thing, and there was no wolf. The third time, he did that unfortunately, this time there was a wolf and no one came out. People thought. He was lying again. This time wolf hurt him.

Real person is the one, who always focus to do what's right for himself, and all people around him, or her. To live in peace, and harmony among each other. Unconditionally, for giving. Will get evil out of our lives.

Do not let, the sun set, on your anger. Ephesians 4:24-27.

Getting angry for justice. It is being angry, with mercy into our hearts, and not hate.

Jesus Christ said, enter through the narrow gate For the gate is wide and road that lead to destruction, and those enter through it, are many How narrow, the gate constricted the road that lead to life, and those who find it, are few. Matthew 7:13-14

The wide gate is, for the people, who live, life of sin. lusting. The narrow gate is about. The human suffering. But continue to have strong faith

A generation goes, and generation comes but the earth remains forever Ecclesiastes 1:4

It said generation come, and generation go, but the earth will remain forever. At last judgment God will, renew the earth,and make it perfect. Just the way it was. Before Adam and Eve sinned.(Genesis)

Apostles asked Jesus increases, their faith. He told them, If you have faith the size of mustard seed, you would say to this mulberry tree, be uprooted and planted in the sea, and it would obey. Luke 17:5-6.

Faith is deep. It is growing with Holy Spirit. We multiply our faith in action. We increase our faith. By loving everyone unconditionally. Living life of grace, and charity.

Jesus Christ said. Believe me that, I am in the father, and the father in me John 14:11-12.

Jesus is the image of the invisible God. He is the light, that shines. He is everywhere, and all the work, Jesus Christ did was work of the father Whom dwells in him.

Jesus said, strong faith is, like a foundation for the home with build on the rock. Nothing will shake it. Luke 6:46-47.

But some, little change in their life, and suffering they lose their faith.

Faith is, the realization, of what is hoped for evidence of things not seen Hebrews 11:1, 3.

Faith is hope in God, and the miracles we received from the above We believe, and understand that universe was ordered, by word of God Genesis 1: 1. Creation.

Therefore, God, he is great. Of those fears the lord, and trust in his name will be rewarded. Malachi 3:16.

If we neglect, to acknowledge God? Catastrophe will come upon earth.

Jesus Christ, healed the sick, cleanse the lepers raise the dead, cast out devils. Matthew 10:8.

Jesus said, for free, we get the faith for free. We share and give it. Some believe that, God fortunate them with wealth. Therefore, they become humbled generous, and giving. Charitable, merciful, the more they give, twice more they receive.

There are some, who have all the wealth. Money becomes their God. Sometime they think, they are God, himself. Those tapes of people suffer more than others. They act very happy. But unfortunately allot of them are not.

He who gives unto the poor, shall not lack. but shall be rewarded with many more. Proverb 28:27.

If we give, and feed the poor. We will, never go without. God will bless us, and multiply us.

Good faith is, truthfulness. Most start from us first. To be completely honest with our self, and others.

Without speaking the truth. We could have very difficult time, solving anything, and we become very week. If we are always honest, we will not have difficult time solving anything.

Jesus Christ said, blessed are they, who hears the word of God, and keep it. Luke 11:28.

Evil always look for ways, to destroy, our faith. This is why we focus guard, and maintain, our belief in God.

Jesus said, in my father's homes there are many mansions. John 14:2. God always, busy preparing, places for the faithful, to be with him someday to enjoy his kingdom.

Jesus Christ said, I will go to prepare a place for you John 14:3.

The greater you are, the more you must humble yourself. So you find favor, in the sight of the lord. Sirach 3:18.

When you humble yourself, greater you are. You will be, found favor with God. Faith is to be Virtual, humbleness, humility, guidance, meekness and honesty. Generosity, obedient, gentle, kind, and loving. Thoughtful, truthful and forward. Serving others, attentiveness. Respect, a clear conscience, and good, devotion. Unconditionally, for giving, love, merciful, and peaceful. True faith should be always conducting all our life affairs, with humility.

We conquer evil, with good. conscientious, common sense, devotion belief, and trust in God. Faith should, never be deceiving any one.

Normal human being, are always subject to sin. God promised, he will save us if we only put, our trust in him. If we love, each other 100% of the time. We will become, invisible to the evil. When, we do good. Especially, if we are willing, and able to be unconditionally, our brother's keeper.

Human being they are at war with evil.

Faith is like, winning the war with many casualties, the fail ones, they become heroes Who died for, the sake of faith, are God heroes.

Chapter 5

America Judeo, Christian Value

President George Washington, on September 17th, 1796 Said it is impossible to rightly govern. The world, without God, and The bible. His prayer, at valley Forge.

It was as, the following ''almighty, and eternal lord God. Great creator of heaven, and earth, and the God, and father of, our lord Jesus Christ. Look down from heaven. In pity and compassion upon me, your servant. Will humbly prostrates myself before you. Bless o lord, the whole race of men kind and that the world be felt. With your knowledge, and your son, Jesus Christ' 'of all dispositions, and habits lead, to political. prosperity.

Religion, and morality are in dispensable supports. In vain would that man claim, the tribute of patriotism. Who should, Labor to subvert these great pillars of human happiness

President Washington prayer, asking God, to do justice to love, and have mercy. He acknowledges God, as divine author of our blessed religion.

By miracle, Washington, believed he won the revolution. With God's help, made United States of America. The law of land came from God.

Our fore fathers, plant America our country always to remain the greatest nation, on the face of earth, and still is, and will. If we only continue to strengthen in God. We will remain under God's protection.

Therefore, America is bless it. In God we trust, and under his protection we are. So many wonderful people living in America.

God made it powerful, to lead many nations. God give the wisdom, and knowledge to our leaders, whether they use it or not.

Our government has power to help many nations. To gain their freedom.

God give power, and courage. To those who fought, to make our country what out to be, and what it is today. I mean great.

Many lives have being lost. To preserve, and maintain our freedom.

There's no country, in the world who gives, and pure out its heart out for others, like America does.

Our country, feed the poor, and hungry, take care of less fortunate.

There is, no country, on the face of earth, who has so many charity foundations. Like America has.

Our country helps other nations, restore their economy, and help them gain their democracy.

From the day, America was discovered. People from, almost every spot of the earth people came here to live. and make it their home. Today wherever we travel, or go anywhere into the world. Somehow these people, are part of us. Because more likely. Some of us came from their world. This is, why we run, and rescue other people, around the world. Because we feel it. When we hear crying of others. From any, spot of the world. Because somehow they are, part of us.

So many came, to America, seeking freedom, taking advantage of the opportunities, that offers. Freedom of speech, and religion.

I believe, America is a miracle. God planned to give human being second chance after we were divided, at the time of Babylon.

Before tower of Babylon time, people were, as one, and spoke same language. They were able to understand each other.

In old testament. Tower of Babel. The word Babel means confuse. It is an ancient Babylonian, word language of Babylon, it was called Chaldean, during some period of time.

During, Jesus Christ time, it was called Aramaic language. Now it is being called, Chaldean language. The people who speak it, they are Christian. Their native country is Iraq. They are the minority. So many of them, escape persecution. Mainly, because of their Christian faith and beliefs. Nearly half of them flee Iraq. Many immigrated, to United States Late, 19th century, all the way through 20th century, and 21st century during the war, they came, as the refugees Because, they were being murdered, because of their faith they also scatter all over the world.

The story about prideful people, who tried to build a tower to reach the heaven When people, of Babylon begin Their construction of the tower because of their pride Genesis 11:1-8.

At that time whole world, spoke one language. They use same words. When they begin, to talk about the construction. when they begin the construction. God came down to see the city, and tower. People were building.

The lord said if they can accomplish this. When they have just begun to take advantage of their common language, and political unity. Just think of what they will do later. Nothing will be impossible for them. Then God came down, and give them different languages.

Therefore, they won't be able to understand each other. God came down, and confused their language. They all spoke different languages. So they won't understand each other Therefore, they scattered all over the face of the earth.

They were not able to communicate with each other. So they can finish the tower. They banded their tower, and scatter across, the globe. Carrying their languages with them.

Here in America, ever since was discovered. People from all over the world. Have being coming until this day. They come here, along with their own language, culture, and nationality Once they are, here in America, they adapt to the English begin to understand each other's They also are adept. To American culture. Many times, they keep their own language.

My point is, that. The world became one language. I mean, here in America. As one nation, to understand each other, and get along together. Just the way it was at the time of Babylon. Until this day many languages the words it sound the same. But it mean something else.

America made us, one people, all over again. That is American,and all united. People bring all their languages here. But they speak same language.

America is a miracle. God given us, second chance, to be one people, once again The language of united states, should be always English, the official language. Because, everyone is free, to use, or speak their own language. That's, what makes America, so beautiful.

America, our country is one great nation, under God It is bless indeed.

There are, so many, wonderful people in America. God made America, so powerful to lead the nation's.

Since that time, of mass immigration. Our country has opened, it arms for many. Who brought with them, their culture, tradition, and nationality. Desperately, so many wanted to make, America their home. Because, of their sacrifices, and struggle. They found joy here.

Many immigrants, came here, to escape persecution. Many as well came here, for the opportunities, our country can offers.

America messenger of peace, and mercy. God loves all his children the same. But he favors those who spread, mercy, love,and peace. Here in our country we have, the step back economy So many are, losing hope. But don't be afraid. We will succeed. We made it before, and we can do it now also. There's no time to blame each other, or anyone else. We have no time to judge each other. Because all we going do is, wasting our time valuable time.

Now these days, there are majority of people. who are confuse, and about to lose their hope.

In our country, there's a majority of people. Who are waiting for the government to do something, about the economy, and our society problems. Also a lot more wasting their time listening to the news hoping, to hear the good news.

Our government, have enough responsibilities. They are here, to make sure, we are safe Help creating jobs, make laws to please everyone.

Our president he is only, one person, he cannot do it alone. The rest of government are, just a minority. We're the people, the majority. We need to back up, our president, and our entire government.

We need, to be a team, we need to help each other fine jobs. We need to have the, moral value, we had, in olden times. Back then, people communicate. They welcomed immigrants Neighbor, helping, neighbor. If someone did not have a job, may be a friend, or neighbor need a worker, at their job.

in olden days people, were close, and found more time, to do things together. They back up, each other. They were more sociable. Now these days, everyone too busy. They don't have enough time partly, or hardly for themselves.

We need to, slow down, and look around us, to see what we need it, to be done. We need to, team together. In order to accomplish our goals.

American give, help, feed, clothes. Not too many people understands. What happening around us. We are living in denial. I mean trying to lose hope.

We need to be strong. We need, to back up our government, in order to stay strong and to remain, the most powerful, and successful government in the world.

We can really do it. We have, what takes, to make it happen.

So many, who lost faith in God, and stopping others from practicing their faith, and belief People are ignoring God, and his commandments. Evil is absent of God. Spiritually, I feel good, and happy. When I read, on our money "in God we trust. If we do so?. Our moral values, should come from God old, and new testament. If we trust in God. What or who, we should be afraid of.

Christian, Jewish. All who believe, in one God Should unite together, and make it their duties. To teach, our children to know God, and what he is calling us to do.

In olden days was not, only that parents raised their children. Everyone helped uncles aunts, friends, and even neighbors. If someone was, to see anybody doing anything wrong ? They did not judge, that person. But gave advice. If someone did not have, anyone to lean on. Always someone run to, him, or her. People were, not as much lonely, or alone like, they are now mostly. There was always someone would help, and be comforted by.

Now these days, people growing, apart. They don't understand, how much they need each other. Many are under, so much pressure.

Our country began, and based, on religious values. That is Judeo - Christian values That mean. We believe in freedom,for every individual.

What God call us to do ? To close our eyes, and hear cries, of the people around us No matter who they are. What they are. What they look like. Or were they came from. To love care and help. If we able to see, what needs to be done for them. That what will, truly please God What made America, so unique, and different from the rest of world. Welcomed people, from many nations, and give them a chance.

Christians who, discovered, America. Broad, with them the old, and new testament. Our founding father, were religious. knew they received their power, from the above.

Our constitution,and decoration of independence are based on bible.

People who don't believe in God, and stopping others from believe in God, or practice their religion. They are deceived.

There are, so many who say we believe in God. They say don't belong to any religion. I say if all the world believe in God ? Every single person. Will not do God, any favor. If we don't love each other first.

Religion, and faith in God it is. How much, we help ? How much, we take care of all of those, who need help. Faith, and religion is. How much, we bring hope into someone's else heart ? How much we feed, and Clothes ?. How much we love, and forgive ?. How much considerate we are.

Religion is, to be our brother's keeper, and not to judge anyone. If you think you are lot better person, then your friend, or any of your relatives. You can always train, and teach them, how to be good like you,and me. There is always, someone who don't know how to be good. That what, will please God.

Our government, borrowing money, from different countries of the world, we are in debt to them. Unfortunately, we pay them interest, for a long time. We make our selves obligated under their control. When at the meantime, here in our country, we have enough money to cover the world. If all, or some of our corporations, and banks. Become, wise enough maybe. They should, cover our government's debt, and charge interest. From profit the companies can expand, and create more jobs. Also the government's, charges the corporation taxes on interest the corporation, are making. This would be, a great opportunity for everyone to make it. All the money stays here in our country. We will never be in debt to another country. We need to begin to see America, as one big house hold. To be a team, so we can work together. Moral house hold never leave any one behind. God calling. Especially, the faithful. We are the only true democratic government, in the world will never, ever change that, or let it slip from under our feet.

We are, free to do what we want, as long, as we don't hurt anyone, or ourselves. Gods hope is in our country. God, need America. We have, the true equality. Means everyone's entitled, to their own opinion.

Everyone's, opinion counts. Does not make a difference of any of us race, gender, age ethnic or religion. We are, **all American.** As a member of our community. We have the right to our freedom, and treat everyone equally. Under the law. It is our civil right. As a citizen of United States of America.

We have documents, of the constitution, and lays out the rules for the American. System of the government. The first leaders of the united State believed, that individual freedom, was one of the most. Important, principle of government. They want to be sure that, the new government there were created, to protect the right of freedom of it is citizens.

At first, the constitution, did not specifically missed all of these freedoms this concerned many people. There for, new laws, called amendment, were added.

The first amendments, to the construction are known, as the bill of rights. Every single person in our government, had the most profound duty to fulfill. Everyone do, the most profound job. The dishonest they are usually revealed, and they are cast away.

Our government began. First with our commander in chief. The president, and the executive branch enforce the laws of the country, and the office of the president, and vice president.

The White House staff 14 to zero departments and hundreds of independent agency the most important things are, departments are, manage it by securities, who form the president's cabinet.

The president is the leader of a state, and commander in chief of the military. The vice president, presides over the senate. If for some reason the president un able to perform his duty. Vice president must take over, and independent agency helped to enforce laws carry out policies, and provide special services. Candidate, from a political party run for presidency, vice presidency. Together on, the same ticket. Entire, nation chooses the next president.

Congress create laws, and the president signed it. Or if he chooses not to signed it. Then, this is called the veto. If the president veto the bill, it is impossible for the Congress to overwrite the veto. But in order to override a veto, at least two thirds of Congress most vote against it.

The president. Besides, his duties to press, and enforce the laws. The president has number of other duties. The president, he the head of the state. Which, means that, he must meet with the leaders of other countries, and he is able to make treaties with them.

However, the senate must approve, any treaty the president negotiate with support of colors; the president can manage. And order, American forces, into military action overseas.

Along the president, the vice president, and a different departments of government Work together, to protect the rights, and interest of citizens. The president, establishes the directions, of the nation domestic, and foreign policies, also you prepares, the government's budget deciding, how tax money is to be spent.

Congress in, government, is an important part of government in United States Congress do a lot for the country, and for many schools, hospitals Parks are controlled or built by the government. The government also support the police, and other public services.

Our government is, a Federal government. It spreads all duties between two parts; one part is the national government. They deal with matters about the whole country. The other part is made of all state government, and it handles matters within each state.

In government, we also have the senate, and the house. That is the Congress is made up of two parts, called chambers. These chambers are the senate's hand the house representative; which is, also called the house. The power between the house, and the senate is the same Each can make name, and change or get rid of laws.

Politician officials, who hold high offices, to run the country, are just a small percentage compared to the millions of people in the America. I mean we are able to have more advantage of doing huge amount of work. For our self's, and others. If we can be a team, and work together. We can really bring up our country. We have to have some self - motivation we never give up. They common saying, the more the merrier.

Short story on my mind.

My friend, and I,one day were driving. By a very rich neighborhood. He mentioned how wonderfully, those homes looked, and they were very expensive. I said to him how happy, to see others make it in life in fact. I pray for God, to give the ones who seek.

Myself, I been most of life I've being poor. But I managed to live good. I live simple life. I replied to him saying that believe me. I am more, concerned about these people, then myself. Because, I don't need much, to pay my bills. For them they need, to make thousands of dollars every month in order to make a living and keep up with their payments.

God forbid, if they don't make that kind of money, for only a short period of time. Chances are, they could become very critical. Some of these people, can lose everything. In such a short time. If you live rich life, you must continue to work, very hard, and smart, in order to continue making enough money. to remain rich, and to maintain the rich style.

I told my friend. You know what ? If the, majority of people become poor, and the rich are just a minority. They will have allot less people to deal with. Therefore, their money will not worth much. Because of less, or no profit there's a chance they lose what they own. If no one have, any money to deal, or do business with them.

This is, why so many businesses, closed down, or moved to different location. Some moved, out of the state. To they were, originated from, or other states. Some to other countries.

Seems like the worse, the economy gets. The higher price of everything go. When everything, it seems to be getting higher, and higher.

These companies, not able to compete. When the economy began, to drop down, and the profit shrinks. They move out, so they hired smaller paying for labor hoping to sell for less.

One of the shames, in our country that's happening here. Which is, the more people become un employees. Retailers and grocery stores raised price on inventory.

Some companies, raise prices, because of theft that occur, or to make up for the profit they lose. So many companies in big cities closed down.

If I was to own a company, and if I was making millions, and if I was to see the neighborhood, in declined. I would invest in that neighborhood. In order to continue to rise and maintained success. It would've been essential, and necessary. In order to continue operating successful, and profitable business.

United States of America. It is the greatest nation, on the face earth. People, come from around the world to become part of this country all different people. It is such a blessing to be called an American.

People who hate, our country. They are, the ones who are envious, and jealous. Also those who are, not allowed to be here's.

As an American, when anyone around the world needs our help. We feel obligated to run for help.

Once upon a time, I was talking to a friend during the conversation I called myself a citizen of in a state. But immigrant. His respond was. I was the, first immigrants, and you are the most recent one. What he meant by that. We are all, immigrants to this country. Except the original people. Who lived here before. It was discovered.

I was so happy, and proud the day, I arrived here. I am very grateful, for the freedom and opportunities this country offers.

I came here when, I was very young. I was the minority in my own old country. In my old country. I lived under of dictator ship. I lived through few revolutions, at young age People always, desperately seeking their freedom. In the country where. I came from. Whenever there was ever a revolution. The minority went through abuse, and persecution.

Before, immigrating to America. When, I was very young. I remembered that, they came from new government into our small town kicking people around, and torturing them. A lot of bloodshed everywhere. Very disturbing sites to see. I was able to watch. Because, I was too young, and they were only out to get the adults. Incents people.

When, I arrived here in America. I Kissed the flag of United States of America. This country unite my family. We found it so much better to live here. I discovered that, I don't have to be rich, to live good. Even if I am poor, I can still live good.

One of the best things about living here, is having peace of mind. Living condition here are great compared to other parts of the world.

In many countries of the world. Especially in Middle East. Many people, living condition like they were 2000 years ago. To which poverty. So many, are very poor, and they go without.

They don't have, many charities foundation, or food banks, or so much, more help. like we have here in America. We do.

We have welfare assistance, and until late eighties to early nineties, we had the general assistance. It is if you're single with no job, you get check every two weeks. Until you get a job Here in Michigan, we had the program I don't know, about other states. Back then people who were very poor, with no income, and with children. They received rent assistance, plus cash, and food assistance.

During 1990s the alleged leaders, and the governor of Michigan. They had welfare reform. They stop the general assistant, and reshape the system without any warnings.

Many end up with no income, and no one to go to. Basically, they were not, given enough time, to find jobs.

People become very poor, could not afford to spend, any money. Businesses, were in declining. It was happening very slowly. Businesses, did not make enough money, to stay open anymore. In the big cities crime was on rise. People began, to abandon their homes. They could not afford it. Or some tried to relocate.

In very short period time, things got worse. While businesses, were still closing down in big cities. Mainly things went down.

Because of the crimes. People losing their jobs. Wasn't save any more. Many abandoned homes, become hazardous, to the people. Vacant homes were vandalized.

Poverty, can really drive someone, to do illegal things. So many were, facing economic hardship, slowly happened.

So many who, didn't have a place to stay anymore or roof over their head. Some moved, from one place to another. Many, times a year. They were, not able to keep renting, or stay into a home. Because, they don't make enough money. Therefore, they have no choice but to move out. Some who lost their motivation.

Our government, is facing very critical, economic hardship, and working very hard on stimulus, packages to bail out, corporations wanting billions of dollars. So they can help, and provide more jobs.

Our government is trying to create jobs, developed roads, and highways, or build new construction. The corporation, will need people with lots of experience. More likely with higher education, constructors, engineers, and people who are professionals.

What about jobs, for regular working class families. There's, so many people, in America who need, a job. Do not require, high education, or maybe very low education.

There was, a lot of these jobs, in our city. Especially, in Detroit, jobs in walking distance for many. Jobs only needed it simple training, to learn how to operate machine. Now lately If anyone go through Detroit will know. What I am talking about. You will see all these vacant buildings small, or large. Where so many, people had jobs, at one time. But now, there are many empty ones. Every corner, every street, every road in Detroit. That is, what you will see. So many, close down businesses. Allot of it, were jobs it did not acquire, any education.

Once upon, a time in our country. We had the rich the middle class, and the poor. Now we have the rich, and the poor.

The way, I see things, we have at least,three group of people.

First group - The poor, of the poorest, they live in the low level, of poverty. The unfortunate once. Who, aren't too lucky. It is not into their control, to stay in this condition. They don't choose to live like that. They try so many times, and they failed. Some people after trying They humble themselves. But they don't give up. Sometimes, when things happen to people if it is destined to happen. It will happen. These people, they have to move all the time Mainly they get evicted. Because, they are always, short of money. Or they don't make enough money, to keep up with place to stay.

Second group. The homeless, there are, so many reasons why they get into this predicament Everyone, has their own story. Hardly, anyone want to be homeless intentionally. Each homeless has own story to tell. We can easy get relieve of the problem. If we can reach to them. If only someone, who can try put them, on their feet, one out of the time.

Third group. The ones, who don't make enough money to make living. Even, if they are working very hard. These people come home every day tired. More likely stressed. One thing is on their mind. Which is, working so hard. But not making enough live. No matter, how much they budget the money. Still far behind, in payments. No matter how much they stretch their money It does not, help them anyway.

Our officials, in big cities are trying rebuild homes, and tear down buildings. I say for why, or for what reason people come back, to live in the city. If there is no jobs.

What we need first, to bring jobs small, or large. There for, when the builders see that companies, and businesses are being rebuilt, and people are working. Builders, will say to themselves. Workers, will need a place to live close to their job. One of the time things can be built and might take,some time. That can happen.

It would be my dream, if I was able to transform, some buildings into apartments, condos, or townhouses. Ground floor would be stores, and medical center. I would bring people Who cannot, afford a place to stay, and get them enrolled into state temporarily assistant. Until I find them a job. Once they get a job. That is when they can decide either to stay and begin to pay rent, or leave on their own. To get established some- where else. Of course after they get on their feet.

The homeless people, I would bring, to help them. The ones who needs medical attention I will get them help. The stores, and ground level. I can hire some residents. The ones who are working, but they have, no car, or either cannot afford one. I will get, a shuttle to take them people back, and forth to work.

It is unfortunate thing,when people steal, so they can eat. Stealing is wrong no exception When, anyone steals always hurts someone else. There is no exception. No one needs,to get hurt or anyone to steal from them.

We see, that every day, on the news. It is crying shame. It not fair. People, have to steal to make a living. It is in our control to do something about it.

When we see these things occur. We hear it on TV or read it in the news. We freak out feeling so critical, to what's happening around us. People who get caught, doing wrong things. It's all right to get to disciplined, for their crime. Jailed will also be the right thing to do. But that, alone does not solve the problem. How long before, we begin to help. Our prisons will get packed. If it continue, will have to make. Some of our cities, into one huge prison in order for everyone to fit in it. Would only right to pay, for their crimes. Will also be second right thing to do. Reaching for their, heart, and mind and to see, what they are up to. Felon should not go unpunished.

They are, human being. Everyone, deserves a second chance. The best thing to do try to them help. One out, of the time. Together we can, help changing their lives and to become better citizens. We need to find everyone, a permanent solution.

It is great we have so much helping hand in our country. But that it does not solve the problem. If we give someone food, for the day will need food the next day also. Someone needs clothes today will need, more once again.

What we really need to do, is creating jobs. We can really do it. But one person cannot do it alone.

If I am capable of starting a charity foundation I would love to work with other charity foundations. Once I began to establish myself. I will need hundreds, and thousands of helping hands. I will have to educated people to put my ideas to work, and to establish my goal. I will need investors, to join me.

It will be great. If I could get grant from the state to start my project. That is, to rebuild business, one out of the time. I will hire group of people to work starting with lower pay, but with profit sharing. People themselves can run it, and be responsible for it.

Once I am, done with that. I will start, with another building. and hire more people I can even make it, where they can be all owners.

We need to build, and create jobs. By building furniture stores, tools shops, manufactures whole sales. If we can build at least half of the businesses, that being closed down. We can make huge different. We go into other cities, do same thing.

Within such a short time. Everyone will have a job. People who commit themselves, to help build these businesses. They can also work, and have a job there. Many, of these businesses. They will be trading, with each other.

We can celebrate, successes. Sales, and export to other countries. People can regroup and start things, and build many things. But they need someone, to back them up.

Why import anything. When we can make it here, at home. We have all the resources knowledge, and capability.

We are not lazy. if we can have everything, in our homes, as American made. We can be the richest country. And wealthiest people in the entire world, and remain.

We need to give ourselves a chance to make it. We have nothing to lose. There isn't one thing we cannot make it happen.

The more, money we make, the more taxes we pay. The more, people have jobs, more taxes will pay, that's more revenue, for our states. People will get to keep their houses, their belongings. They could afford to go on vacations.

Our government will never go debt. Never give up. Dreams always come true.

May God bless America, and I hope my dream come true. For everyone to get a rich, and no one will go without.

I understand. We are used to high paid jobs. We needed, because cost of living is so high. The worker start with lower pay, so their company, to be able to sell their products lower. Eventually will, sell a lot more. The workers will get profit share to makeup. Another great idea would. People team together to rebuild business. May be can get a loan, or grant they can always pay back.

What makes America so unique, and blessing, is the freedom of speech freedom of religion, and the equality.

My feelings, and opinions hoping I am not offending anyone. If I do I apologize. That is if I want to be elected for, any position I would never judge anyone, or hurt their reputation I would leave the facts for people to find out, about the people. Who are in the race, with me or against me. For me the proper thing to do to be elected. Is I would, speak my heart out to people to give t hem, my agenda Ideas, and plans. Explaining, myself trying, to prove, to the people. I will be good for the job. I will also explain to people. I will work very hard to make things happen. But not empty promises anything. Not everything always. guarantee What I could do is try my best. If I see things not working. I would try different thing. I will bring people, with different ideas, hoping to accomplish, and make job well done.

Our goals, should be to have priority, to teach all children moral values. That will, give them wisdom. Of common sense. Because, that what we are missing. Our goal should be, being honest, and to serve our people.

We must respect, and obey the government, Because all governments, are placed in power,by God. Who refuse the laws of the land, are refusing to obey God. Romans 13:1

Chapter 6

MoneyRichness, And Judging Others

The rich man told Jesus, he followed all the commandments Jesus knew, he was rich, he told him to, go sale everything in order, to in rich his spirit to give it to the poor, and follow the truth that is Jesus Luke 18:23.

The rich man went away sad, because he was very rich. Jesus all we need to follow and to be like him in every way. Jesus Christ said, how hard, it is for the rich man to go to heaven, without deeds, and charity.

While, the disciple, were wondering. Who can go to heaven. Jesus answer, to them might be impossible to human. With God everything is possible.

Jesus saying, what we own here on earth ? Someday we leave behind. God is not about material.

We could not even please God. Even if we own, all the money of the world. Actually what pleases God ? Is follow all his commandments. In order for us, to be his voice here on earth, and become true his children.

Jesus explaining, that money we will make always. But first to be ethical, moral and to live life of peace, and mercy. To do all the commandments. To be a perfect persons in God's eyes. Then we, shall not have, any fear. If we only trust in God.

We worship God,in spirit,and the truth. John 4:24.

God call us to be, rich in spirit. Because, God is, spirit, we worship him. In spirit God want us to humble ourselves, and be grateful.

Jesus said, you'll gain nothing, if you have all the money. If you don't have peace, and mercy of God in your heart ?. Without, Gods love, we become very critical, and suffer the consequences.

If we only focus on God,we will then, find happiness with no fear, ever. However making money is not a sin. As long, as we gather it at the honest and Safe way. It is a blessing from God, if we do just that.

I know many, who make their money, the honest way. They feel, very bless. I over, and over hear them saying the more we give, to the charities, and feed the hungry the more God fortune us, and bless us. A lot whom are giving, they humbled themselves, they love God they do for their neighbor, and they give percentage of their money to charities.

Making money is not a sin.

From the beginning of time, human being did not know much, about money. To be civil, first they exchange things with others, with things, they don't have. People trade by exchanging items, for items, people in the town needed. In olden days, people took what they have, in their town, to exchange with other towns. With the things they did not have it, in their own. That what they had, learned in the beginning. Later somewhere in time. People invented silver and gold coins. They begin buying things from each other's.

People were very fortunate, lucky, and safer. They learned these methods, to learn how to value their goods, and to get something in return, without no hassle. By doing that gave human being peace of mind. They learned that if they need something, they have to buy it and not just take it. Fortunate enough, people learned, to be civil. About money, and trading Otherwise they wouldn't make it.

You see if we didn't advanced, and become civil. We could being like animals, attacking one and another, just to get things from each other. Especially food.

Once upon a time my wife, and I had a dog. We took in another astray dog in we had mercy on. I always, fed the dogs first before I ate. When I got back from work. Each of the dogs had, his own bowl, eat from. As I watch them eating. If one had done eating. First usually try to get some more, from the other dog bowl. But the second dog attack, the first dog did not want, to share. Animals can never be civil. Like people could. When it comes to food.

In the beginning people. Were simple, down to earth, and humble grew up, with common sense. Then later, when the world populated. Some people, their money became their Gods. So many would do anything, to get rich. So many have lost their lives. Because, of money. Some people, who have the money, they think, they have the power. Some who lives life, of Sin, and greed. Eventually, all that will go away.

Three of many, reasons why people steal. There's no exception to any of it. Stealing is evil wrong.

1 - Some people steal, because they are lazy. They think the world owe them a living

2 - Some people steal, because they are desperate. Myself I would beg for help when I need it, until I get it.

3- Some people steal, because they are, greedy they want something for nothing, and they want to get rich quick.

God forbid us, from being lazy. He want us, to prospect, and make money the honest way, and faithfully. Not the evil way. Or by hurting anyone.

People who, work dishonest way, they are critical Because evil love that,so he can make them suffer more.

People don't understand that. If they work the honest way, even if they don't get rich with lots of money. They will be rich with something greater. That is, life's full with many more blessings than others.

When people, find us trust worthy. Will be more rewarding for us. People we, deal with on our daily life. Will always depend on us, and trust us.

It is great always to have someone to hears, our cries for help unconditionally, and feel our pain.

People who, makes their money, at dishonest way. Most of the time they struggle May not be financially. But in many different things. They are, always critical, with many problems, with issues, they face. Many who gathered, their money, at the dishonest ways. They do act happy. Only to show off. But they are not.

God knows. We need, the money, so we can pay our bills. Emergency, to raise a family and for retirement. God knows that. Sometime. or maybe all the time. We need the money For emergencies, or if we get sick, and not able to work. God knows we need to be financially stable. God also know, we need money. For our safety, and freedom.

Poor people are, the reason for the rich. If we didn't have, the poor, the homeless people, the hungry, the less fortunate. Rich people would not have the chance, to give or and do good deeds toward God.

Doing charities, helping the needy. That, what pleases God. What also pleases God, to comfort the lonely, the sick,also people who mourn. So they have comfort.

When we show compassion, to someone, who is sick he, or she feels compassionate in their heart. Will easy off their pain.

Helping places, of worship financially. So they can remain open, and to continue helping the poor, and spread word of God. If you wonder, where God spirit is ? I assure you, he is in place of worship. Thank goodness for places of worship. Otherwise we could go astray. When we stay, away for a long time from place of worship. We lose, contact with God. Once we do that we go astray. Then will be a lot easier to get tempted.

Again Jesus remind us, how hard it is, for the rich to enter kingdom of God Matthew 19:24.

Jesus look, at all of us saying, don't look at money like it is your God. It will be best for you. If you focus on one God. That is, our heavenly father. It will be at our best interest if we have full trust in God, and to give him, our life fully Continually. Trying to do what pleases God. At the end of our earthly life. He will receive our spirit.

Gathering wealth, at the dishonest way. Greed lust selfishness jealousy, judging others covets somebody else is good, un fairness, lack of freedom, justice, and peace, cruelty abuse All that means absent of God, and present of evil.

Love peace mercy, and compassion. Grace hope trust justice fairness, and consideration generously, and giving, feeding the poor, and hungry. Humbleness, meekness, and all that, and more goodness, is present, of God among us. With happiness.

Our lives will be, full of celebrations. If we stay on side of God.

When money becomes, number one thing, in our life. We forgets, our loved ones. We forget about, the less fortunate. Once we, become so much in love with money. We become slaves to it Usually end up happening.

Greed, and love of the money, makes people blind from doing enough for themselves and others. People with money, they can easily do something, for the helpless. They could benefit themselves also. For instant can always figure out what type of business to make, and put in good location, hire people who need a job. They will make extra profit, and benefit others, who don't have job.

Unfortunately many, faithful who claim, to have faith Who are, very wealthy. But because, of love the money. Sometime, they could be deceived, for them not to thinking. They could easily, build things, or maybe great things, and be more creative with their money. So they, can increase their wealth, and help others live better.

Jesus he is fair, and just. He taught us how live, and give to others. His main concern is the poor. He preached the good news of God. He plead, with us for conversion, of our hearts. To be filled, with Gods abundant love, for human being. Everlasting love.

Jesus Christ, knew dangerous of the money. We do have the freedom to gather it, but we all have to be careful. Money, are very tempting.

My father, often told me. If you have, any money ? Don't let anyone know. Don't bring it out, in public. Because even if you are in front of the most honest people. Showing your money, there is a chance. Some, of those people can get tempt it, and get jealous. They could very well hurt you. Just to get your money from you. He added that's how tempting money are.

The lord had blessed Abraham in all thing. Genesis 24:1.

In olden days until now. When people became very wealthy. They did not, only think but, they knew God fortunate them. Especially, the faithful. Among those, who become very wealthy The same way, God gave wealth to Abraham, and many others, in the old testament. Beside the wealth. Many blessings, because of their faith.

Now these day, too many people, when they become very wealthy. They did not only think. They know, it is blessing from God, they do show appreciation to God they humble themselves, they became better people. They gave to the poor, feed the hungry, they clothes the naked.

Young man, once told me. Desperately want, to get rich. I did not blame him. Almost everyone, want to do the same thing. I explained saying to him, telling him. If I were you ? I won't make myself sick about it. Because life is destiny. Everything is, at write time right place.
You just, don't know. You could wake up rich, or poor. I add it the only thing you can do, is try to work smart, and hard. You never know. If is meant to be. It will happen. I told him. I also said to him. You can always live financially good. If you have good paying job. Or get education for higher paying job. Or take another part time job. Why make ourselves, suffer for money ? When everyone somehow makes a living. There is already enough suffering in the world. Because of the money. Somehow, every one suffer to make it.

Some will struggle, to make a living. Some who suffered, to get rich. Either way, there's no way out. So why even worry about the money?. If it is so much hassle.

Jesus give us insurance of salvation. We don't, need money for, our spiritual salvation All we need to, do is to be him. Jesus want us, to call, on his spirit. To guide us in every field in every way. So we can live, the way he lived.

The rich man, he was so sad, and disappointed because he loved his money Matthew 19:19:22

He did not understand, what Jesus was trying to tell him. Jesus Christ, giving the rich man advice. Which is, if he truly want to save his soul, to give his wealth, to feed the poor. By doing charities, and good deeds.

This is how, we enrich our spirit. Good deeds, goes up to the lord God, like a smoke all the way to the heaven. When it reach's God. Pleases, him very much. This is, how we become his favorite children.

Jesus said, in a true riches. He said, treasures of this world will stay behind when we die But make yourself treasure in heaven. Matthew 6:20.

What we accomplish. Here on earth. By living. life of virtue, love mercy, charity, and grace. Is the treasurers we are building in heaven. Jesus saying,no matter how much we gather and how much, we invest in this world. Will all stay behind. We should focus, on our spiritual need, that will last forever.

Everything, we own, and enjoy, is only temporarily. Money don't make anyone, any better, or beautiful. Beauty comes, with then us. What comes, outer heart. What makes the person. Or break the person.

Our spirit s reside, into our hearts. God want our heart, and soul. Our spirit give us life When we are here on earth, and there beyond. Our spirit makes it possible, for our heart to continue beating. So can we live. When our hearts stop, and we die. That mean our spirit departed from our body When, it is our time to die, that's when spirit leave our body Actually from our hearts. Because, of our spirit, our heart continue pumping, to give life. When it is, our time to die. Our spirit leave our heart, Therefore, our heart stop.

The treasure we built, in heaven. Comes from the goodness. We practice, here on earth. Matthew 7:19-21.

Charity, unconditionally love, for everyone. Many who know, what they gather here on earth, is only for short time. They still, do not care. because, love of money.

God want us to live according, to his laws, and commandments. We build our treasure in heaven.

When we love, and get along with everyone, and find the ones. Whom is gone astray When, we show them, love. They will discover, what they are missing.

God favor sinners more. Because he already, have the faithful. Maybe bad people and trouble makers. They are not capable of figuring out. Why they are bad ? If we judge this type of people. Will make matters worse. Instead. We show them love, and compassion to work with them, to help them understand. What they ought to be. As true human being.

It will be a rewarding. if everyone get rich, and have what they want. But will not help us any. If we don't have safety, peace of mind. No matter, how strong. How much more police power, we have. Will not help us much. Is it good to have a lots money ? But living in like war zone condition. Trouble, every were. It is not good, at all.

Unfortunately, things can get worse, If we don't work with people to make sure, they become good people, to be better citizens. To help them, so they make decent living. By finding them great jobs. Poverty, increases crime.

Love of the money goes, far beyond. For so many, become an issue. Some people, worry they, may run. Out of money, even if they are, financially secure. Retired. They try to find part time job, worrying might run out of money.

If you or I, were the richest people. Having the most money, and everything we want But If we have the most miserable, and terrible life. Tragic after another. In what way, our money could help us ?. Money does not always bring happiness.

First we, out to ask for God's, blessings. He will look into that. Even if we, don't get rich with a wealth. We could have many other blessings, Into our lifetimes.

There are, a lot of rich people. Who only act, or pretending happy. The truth is they are not, all the time. In major they don't have enough happiness. Or much peace in their life.

At the meantime, there's, a lot of people, who are very poor, but humble, and down to earth. Very grateful most of the time. They are, happier than, many rich people.

The way, I see in life. There are, two types of rich number people.

First rich person, who make, his, or her money, at the honest way With faith, never takes advantage, of anyone. 100% fair, considered, thoughtful, generous. Never, cheat, deceived or steal from anyone. Always, charitable, and merciful. Living a simple life, and always appreciative and grateful to God. For all, the blessings. Always share, and trying her or his best, helping others Especially, the less fortunate. This type of rich are already working on gaining, treasure of next world In heaven with God. This one is Also very lucky, to be able to enjoy,what God has given them here on earth, and more likely, will have a chance, of treasure of here, and after.

Second type, of a rich person, is the one who, gather his, or her money. By cheating stealing committing frauds using people. Especially, the poor, of the poorest. Takes advantage, of every one, very ungrateful very greedy selfish, and in considers, they are, only good. For the ones who are making lots of money from, or having big business with. They deceive people, very cruel, and heartless. This type of rich person. They are, very critical, and are facing their own consequences they will lose their treasurer. They could lose in next. The treasurer, they gathered in this world when they die. They leave it, behind. Those people, never found time to enjoy. What they were gathering, in their lives. They don't only lose that. Chances are losing what they could have in next world, with God.

When people work, at honest way, and gather, to make a living,at the honest, pure way. Even if they don't get rich with money. They get rich, with a lot more blessings. Than others throughout their life.

Money alone does not make. What person is. Without mercy of God, and his blessings peace. Happiness comes along with it. We are nothing.

Being, too much, in desire for money. That would lead us, to lust greed, and living sinful life. Also makes people, blind from doing enough for themselves, and others.

Many with faith, and holy who becomes rich, and very wealthy. They feel, very fortuned they give credit to God, and Glorify him. Because, they expect, their wealth, and treasurer to be not from this earth, and life. But from next with God. They become, very grateful to God knowing that he fortune them just. The way, he gave, to our fathers Abraham, Isaac, Jacob, and Joseph. They are, example of God blessings. Here, and forever, in next life(See The Old testament).

God recruited, many Kings, and leaders, so they can serve him, and make his name great For generations, to come. Until the end.

My father told me a story, no base or prove to how accurate. It could be, used as an example. For a rich, who's great full to God for all the blessing of this earth.

My father put it, this way, and he said. Once upon a time, there was this one honorable and noble king used to send his workers, to the town to invite, all the homeless and the poor to dine with him. After they finished eating. Every one of them, got to take, their plate. Made of silver, or maybe gold. Each individual can sell it, and to make a living out of it.

My father, told me another story, and he said. Once upon a time. In this one region. There was this rich, and famous person,but humble. He wished to contribute, and to show appreciation to God for what he was, awarded with. He didn't want to have a pride of himself.

Instead He want to help, and feed his people. He went around his town, finding people. Who were suffering So he can bring joy, and happiness into their hearts. He did not want to be, noticeable by anyone. He didn't want to look, so great in people's eyes. He didn't want to look like a hero in people's eyes. His intention was to look great, in God's eyes, and to please God.

Getting rich, and wealthy. It could be, test of our faith. For God to see, how much we can do, for the less fortunate. Many times, God chooses who gives to.

Jesus fed,five thousand, Jesus fed, four thousand. John 6:1-14,Luke 8:1-9.

So Many Christian, go around. The world feeding, the hungry, and the less fortunate because of Jesus. Their wishes are, to do what Jesus did. When, he fed thousands of people, in couple, of occasions times. Jesus, new testament. When God saw, all those hungry people. He had mercy on them. His heart wished not, to let them go hungry.

Jesus said, what favor you have toward God. If you do, for the ones who are able to do for you. Luke 14:12-24.

If we do, for the ones, who are able to do for us. Is like favor, for favor, no one gain anything. I mean return the same favor. We break even.

Jesus said, do for the ones. Who can, never repay you back. That's how, we, receive our reward, from God directly. Earthly rewards, are temporarily. Gods rewards they last forever.

Lord Jesus Christ, came into this world. When he knew. The world desperately, need God. For God to speak touch, heal.

Jesus, he is, God with us. In the time of trouble, and misery. To free us from evil, power Because, of Jesus Christ. We discovered. Love of God, for the world. God also knew how much our world, in need of love. Mercy, and compassion.

In poor guests. Jesus said, when you give dinner, or a supper do not invite, anyone friends, or brothers, or relatives, or rich neighbors, Because, they are able, to invite you. Also can return. a favor. Luke 14:12-24.

Jesus said, when you give a feast, invite, the poor the crippled the lame, the blind These kinds, of people they can never return the favor, to you. Your reward will come directly from God.

Jesus, and Zacchaeus. The tax collector. When Zacchaeus, saw Jesus. He did not think of his wealth, he was willing to give half of it, to the poor. In exchange for peace and happiness he, found in God. Luke 19:1-10.

Zacchaeus, yes he was rich, powerful, famous. All that did not bring him, any joy, or happiness. Something was missing. What comes, from the heart. He discovered God, in the person of Jesus Christ. He received spirit, of God. He did not know, what he was missing. Until he saw our Lord Jesus. Jesus reach our hearts, and mind, and soul.

Jesus is the son the living God. When we, seek him he will take us, directly, one way to the father. Jesus never judged anyone. But he touches our hearts.

So much, people judge others.

Once upon a time, this friend of mine, he came to me telling me. So many people are talking about, this one individual. Who used to, gamble drink alcoholic, he is divorced. He continued saying. Now he should be a shame of himself. He now comes to church, and he also became a decanis. I Immediately, smiled at my friend, and told him. Do you know, you are judging this person ? When at the mean time you, supposed to, be proud of him. Because he took, a wrong path. Now he is trying, to please God. He is repenting. My friend immediate response was I did not think like that. Sometime we need to change the way people think.

We all make mistakes. Fortunately, decent people usually, correct their mistakes, and they make up

In our world today, people don't get too many chances anymore.

Money is the root of all evil. Timothy 6:9

Because, love of the money. People could easily get tempt it. To do bad things. Like greed, and many other,sinful desires.

The ones who want, to make their money, at honest way. Because they want, to be in success, and wanting to have everything. It is blessing.

People, who want to become rich, in wrong ways. They are critical, and the price they pay, is huge. Greed, and desire lots of money. We could, go stray from faith. Eventually we get tempt it. Follows by so much pain. Sometimes people become slaves to the money, and it became, their God.

Some people suffer, and die trying, to get rich. But never happen.

Love of the money, and greed. Drive people to do so many stupid things. So many got hurt, or killed over money. Innocent become victims.

Because of money, people, don't realize, everything is in right time, right place. If anything mean it to happen, will happen. Nothing can stop it.

All the bad things it is absent of God. It would be, in our best interest. Our intention through, our life to remain grateful, and faithful to God. So we don't, get into too many temptation.

Righteousness, devotion to God, and patient. It is, the key to the success.

Humanity, can never repay God. For, what he did for us. God humbled himself for us He came down, on earth for us. In the person, of Jesus Christ. Reveal his, heart to us to save us. To see, God face, to face to feel, and to touch him, to love him.

It is very critical, and important, to God, to build our relationship. With him spiritually The reason God want us, to continue focusing on him only. So we don't go astray.

Jesus Christ said, before we judge others look, at ourselves everyone have some kind of faults, no one perfect Matthew 7:1-5.

Beside the point, if we treat people good, with respect. They will do the same for us People usually, judge others the way, they act. Normally we get treated, the way we treat others If we put anyone down, they will do, same thing to us.

We need, to understand. People, will always stand against each other. They have every right to protect, themselves.

It is not fair, to judge anyone. Because nothing in the world, can make anyone better than anybody else. Because we all sin. We all make mistakes. The same, we all die. First we need to look, at our wrong doings, and correct ourselves. Before we look at others wrong doings.

May be help them. We often passed bad judgment, against someone else. Sometime intentionally. Just looking, at people we judge. To see, what wrong with them first. We are not supposed to judge anyone. Because of their look.

Another common thing. Sometime we see, the way people acts, and we don't like. They are, but truly insight are different. The way I see it, and feel it. There is goodness in every human being.

The golden rule to do others, whatever you would have them, do to you. Treat people just, the way you expect them to treat you. Matthew 7:12

We can't go, around treating everybody bad, and terrible way, and expect them, to treat us very good.

When God create us. I mean human being, he create us with his the mercy. Was insert it in our heart. We teach, and trying to help people. Not only feel,but to learn. How compassionate they are. When we show them mercy, kindness, goodness. They will find, mercy of God, into their heart. Just like everyone else

Once upon a time, I was working, in a convenience store behind the counter. One day Waiting, on customers. I always helped, my customers. Whenever, they were short of change. The line, grew longer one day. I was waiting on one of the customers in line. Once I was done ranging up her purchases. While trying paying me counting her money, she happened to be short, little bit of change. She immediately began, to ask me, if I could let her go. Before, I open my mouth, to say, it is OK. I did not have the chance to. A customer, who was supposed to be next in line after her in. Immediately said. I got her cover, he asked.

How much she needed ?. He was, generous enough to help. From his heart, he yelled out with excitement saying I will help her, and with. How much, she was short ?. Respond it quickly. He wanted to be the first, to help someone in need.

Everyone is born, with God's mercy, in their heart. Some don't know it. The point is, this person was not, a good person hardly. I was surprise, and felt humble. The goodness came out of that man. From that day, and on I try not to judge any one, how could I.

I learned in, bigger ways not, to judge anyone. That man, he was not a good guy at all. He created too many problems into, the neighborhood. Still did something, good came out to him. That is mercy, and compassion. He helped someone, who was completely, and totally stranger, to him. *This is why, we only let God judge. Because he is the only one, who read* hearts.

Obedience to God. He is the, highest authority. No power higher then God. Romans 13:1-2.

Those who have, the power to judge, and living on earth. They have been appointed by God, and they have to go by his laws

If we don't, obey commandments of God, and laws. We will be tempted by the evil, and lost, in Sin. We could face severe, judgment. Besides, that no one is allowed, to judge except God, himself.

There is not, no power on earth, or sky. Above the power of God. Therefore, all the good, the just. The fair judges, are descended from God. All lawmakers, and the ones who practice the law, on all face of earth. They are appointed by God. To protect, and bring justice to the less fortunate, victims, innocent, and innocence. To gain freedom, and peace, for the ones who are seeking it. Usually the bad, and the ones, who abuse the justice system. They are usually revealed 100% of the time, and castaway from their positions. The ones, who betrayed the law they become published. Everywhere. Also the, ones who take power over others For evil purpose. They are, revealed eventually.

Jesus said, to his followers, false witness, and swearing is work of the evil. Instead be, truthful with everything you do, and say everything. Only to please God. Matthew 5:33-5

God is he light, of the world, that shine. God laws are his love for us. If we help everyone, go by the laws. God will gives us comfort, peace of mind. His mercy, and goodness.

People who, miss use the law. In bad ways, and wrong ways. They face, their own consequences. Also the ones who neglect the law. They face their own consequences. They are sinning against God.

Gossiping, behind someone else back. Putting out rumors, about someone else falsely That's evil. It is judging. Especially, if we're not sure about things. If we, hear anything about anybody else. Would be fair, before we pass judgment, to that person, to make sure. If it is true. What we heard, because everyone have, the right, and freedom,To defend themselves.

So many people, make up false stories, about others. Only so, they can have something to talk, and gossip about.

They are, selfish, inconsiderate. They don't care if they are ruining someone else's life by hurt, their reputation. Myself if I hear a story, or anything about anybody else. Before I believe, that person, or even wondering, if it is true, or not. I would go, and ask that person who was absent at that time. I would go, and ask that person, if that was truth, or not. Of course, I never tell him, or her, who told me. Because, I don't want to create problems. As a courtesy giving, the right, to the one person, or individual, to defend her or himself. Everyone has a right.

It happen to me, my cousin once told me, he heard things, about me from someone. He did not mention their names. He sounded like he believed. I reply is not true, and I added, I would appreciate it. If you did not instantly believe next time ask me, how true, and accurate these people are. The ones, who talks about me. I also said, when the judge preceded with any case in court. It would not be fair, to have the plaintive present in court, and not the defendant. It would, the right thing to, is to have plaintive, and defended. So he can hear both site of stories. To decide which is right, and which one is wrong. So the judge can do justice. My cousin answered. I always knew, but never look at it this way.

Abraham became, the father of all nations, because of his faith, he obey God. He was righteous man. Therefore through his faith. Promise, was made to him. Romans 5:33-35.

Without, the faith, will be no Justice, or fairness. Without faith, it will be to be abuse greed, deceiving, and suffering. Faith makes us holy, and determined, to obey God, and his commandments.

Faith, is the reason, we have wisdom, grace, mercy love. True faith, bring justice for everyone. God choose Abraham, to be father of the all nation. Because he, trusted in God he had, the most profound, faith in God. He depended, on God. Abraham put, his entire life into God's hands.

Many people, act like they have faith in God. But they don't like others, and refuse to be. Their brother keeper. One thing, they usually figure out for themselves. Which is they think by only loving God. They are, practicing their true faith, not knowing concept of faith.

The most profound, faith is love, goodness, mercy compassion we show others. Love our neighbor, and the people around us. Even if they were strangers. It is impossible to love God. If we don't love each other unconditionally first, and the most. Love, and goodness, from all our hearts, and mind. That's when, In our hearts spirit of God will reside.

No one can ever deceive God with their lips, heart, and mind. Because God create. Our hearts, minds, and souls. He doesn't have to read it. He knows what we are thinking to 24/7.

The LORD bless the righteous. Psalms 5:12.

God favored, the ones who bring hope, mercy, peace, relieve. For the poor less fortunate, and the ones will bring justice for all the people. Especially, who are less fortunate, and who desperately, need of help. So they don't feel, they are abounded. b y God. What truly please God. If we continuously rescuing, the ones who are lost.

God commanded us, to be our brother's keeper. We are, obligated toward each other.

Especially, to help each other to become good people. God put, all that into our hands. We are, responsible.

Jesus said, as the father has loved me, so I have loved you. Now remain in my love John 15:9-17.

Jesus, commandment, is to love each other, as he loved us. Can anyone imagine, or think how great God's love for humanity. Jesus lay down himself, for us. He suffered, and died on the cross. All that he did, so we can be saved from evil sin. If we don't forgive unconditionally Or if we don't show any. Compassion for others. Our faith will be in vain.

Once upon a time, I seen this person. I happen to know his brother from the past His brother, lived most of his life in the streets, homeless. Hardly, found a place to stay. Day after day. Sleeping, out site. can anyone imagine. How much, suffering that person endured ? Anyway, he indicated to me, his homeless brother, had passed away. He continued, by putting his deceased brother down, with no pity. Because, the way his brother lived, he sounded like It was in his brother's control, to have the life he had. I interrupt him by telling him. First, It is not right, to talk about your brother. He is in God's hands. There's, nothing we can do except pray for his soul. Secondly, I told him. Did you ever tried, to reach him to see. What he needs, or you were, too busy with your life. Not worrying, about your brother. Or maybe it was, his destiny the, way he was. I continue it, telling him. Don't you, think your brother ? Many times, he wished, if he could have life like yours. Un fortunately some do, some don't That's life. Life is destiny. God is, the only one who can change it. By miracles. I gave the living brother something, to think about. Or to feel guilty. Because he, wasn't there, for his brother

Jewish, and Christian, takes their our moral values, from the bible. Being guided, by the holy spirit of God. In the, most profound way. By teaching word of God. For all the, generations to be civil. God want us, to unite together, and to be the team.

My father had, too many Jewish friends. He told me, they never let, any of their people go without. This is, why they succeeds. Besides being, the minority in the world.

Christian also, feed the world. Because of Jesus, Christian go around the world feeding the, hungry clothing, taking care, of the sick, the needy, and the less fortunate.

One of the main commandment, in the old testament, is to love our neighbor. In the new testament, Jesus remind us again, to love our neighbor, as ourselves. Mark 12:31 Matthew 22:35.

Many, who don't understand concept of love your neighbor. I mean is not only by word. We can say, to our neighbor. I love you all we want. It very nice, but will not help her, or him any. If our neighbor, have problems. May be we can reach to them, to see. If we can help. To make their life better. That what will, please God. Our neighbor is not only the person, who live next door, to us. God he is talking, about anyone. Even if is stranger

All Christian, in the beginning, where one community, and believers all one heart, and mind they, shared everything that belong to everyone, of them. Therefore, was no needy person among them. Acts 4:32.

But now these days, Christians, they are, not only few. But they are, in billions, around the world. There's, no way. They can be all there, for each other. But a lot of these people gather together, as group, that's the church. This is why, you see so many churches.

Jesus want us, to practice heaven here on earth. So we can feel, and touch the heaven. God like us to conquer evil with a good.

This is why, it is very important, to God. We take care of the poor, the needy, the neglected, the persecuted the orphans, and the hungry. Around the globe. If we do, all that where the evil would fit. Evil cannot be, will not be, were good is. Evil, cannot stand goodness.

About the woman, who got caught, in the adultery People were trying to test Jesus. To see what he would do about that. Their Laws was to stone, the adulterers. John 8:3-11

Jesus was able, stop them, from hurting her, by remind them. They sin also. They left her alone. Jesus, did not condemn her, but he advised her, not to sin no more. God has, no intention, of condemn anyone. Because he is good, and full of goodness.

Jesus is, the good news. He is preparing room for us with him, in heaven. Jesus did not only revealed to us heart of God. He is heart spirit, and divinity of God. Which was delivered to us by, the person of, our Lord Jesus Christ. So we can be saved from evil.

God sentence, his own self to death, on the cross. So we can be saved. Can you imagine or think how awesome God is. Absolute, and perfect love. Unconditional, love for us.

Whenever we sin, God don't, make it his choice, not to forgive us. Because, he often say, to himself. They are, only human being. What do, I expect. God knowing, we all going sin anyway. He loves us, and want us for himself. God told us over, and over. He forgave us before we sin. Because he knows, we will eventually go back to him anyway.

In old testament, many prediction of his coming, in the person of Jesus Christ. He talked about the future events went, on before they happen it. God is, the present, future, and the past. Everything is, done by him.

God he is the good shepherd. John10:1-18.

When we are, lost, and gone astray. He, do not rest, until he find us. once he, do so he rejoice.

Who are we, or do we think we are, we point, our finger, at anyone, and judging them What give us, the right. How could we. When we, all somehow sin, and make mistakes.

Everyone, make mistake. Everybody, is guilty of something. We all make mistakes. People who always judge others. They are, often sad, and miserable.

Anyway. My father often, use to teach a lot. He told me, a story I don't have the proof to it, but it means something.

My father said once upon a time, there was this person. He had a brother was always quiet. Never smiled. He always, acted like he was mad, at the world. He hardly said anything This person, was very concerned, about his brother. Therefore, he hired someone. May be, can gets his brother, to smile, and laugh. Or some kind of help. The professional, did a lot of work with that person brother. Took a while to come up, with this great idea. The professional, came up with this idea. Because of many meetings, had with the brother. He found out, the brother was too judgmental, he complained a lot about people, he thought, he was perfect, Therefore the professional took, the brother, to the market area. Where they would be, gathering of people usually, and more likely. Once they were. At the market. The brother seeing, all different people with different habits, different attitudes many goals. He begin, to faced real world. He found out, he was not perfect after all. He began to laugh, at himself. Because he, was doing nothing but fooling himself. After all he discovered, he was not right all the time. The professional, fix him The professional, took witness with him, to the person he was hired by, and he got paid.

For the love, of money is, the root of all evils 1 Timothy 6:10.

Some people,when they desire the money. So much they, stray from their faith in God. and loved ones. Many who lose their moral obligations.

People don't think, in how much pain they are. So many get hurt abuse, neglect prosecuted many got, killed because of, the money.

God don't mind, for us to become wealthy, and very rich. Because God made this earth, for a human being to keep, and use it forever. That is, all into our hand, anyway.

God, main plan for us to be, wealthy with happiness, and that comes. When we become spiritual, and to have a pure heart.

God also want us, to understand, and know that, true wealth comes from our hearts Bible specifies, the love of money is evil.

Because, people love, and lust for the money.

When it is only material. Instead we should put, our hope in God, for their joy.

The money itself is, not evil, and Sin. Only if we don't put the money, before God himself Love of material, and treasurer of this world does, not please God. pure wealth it is gift from God.

Put to death, then the part of you. That are earthly Immorality impurity, passion evil desire, and the greed that is idolatry. Colossians 3:5.

God said, let go things of this earth. Focus, on him What, he had given to us We will leave it behind. He said none of that,will make us pure, and spiritual. God wants us to be, his descended.

There for, we out to be virtual, ethical, righteousness to honor the law, and the commandments, of God. Because, the laws keeps, morality in check.

Immorality, impurity, passion, greed, lying, deceiving. Anger, and idolatry. Idolize, all that is. What the evil desire from us. Evil hopes, we live this way. So we don't belong to God, any more.

That is all, who have not, believed in the truth. But have approved, wrong doing may be condemned 2 Thessalonians 2:1-8.

Not knowing the truth. But they, don't acknowledge wrongdoing. Defines, as lust, and unrighteous. These, who don't, acknowledge Sin. They judge for themselves, and they make it right. Even if they know. They are wrong. They could be, condemned by God They are, displeasing God.

So many people, don't read the bible: Because, they don't want to see they are, doing wrong. So they can continue to do wrong, and not feeling guilty. Or a shame. These are the ones. Who don't want to face, the truth.

Evil is, deceiving power, to get us apart, and far away from God. 2 Thessalonians 2:12. For I am, not ashamed of gospel. It is the power of God, for the salvation of everyone who believe. Romans 1:16.

So many, are a shamed to read the gospels. Bible is the truth, and for the conversion of hearts, to almighty God. The holy bible, revealed to us righteousness, and grace of God. Feed the poor the hungry, and who is asking for food. Romans 14:3-4,17.

God does not allows, withhold from the poor.

For the kingdom of God is not a matter of food, and drink, but of righteous, peace, and joy in the holy spirit. We worship God in spirit,and the truth. John 4:24.

All good we do, mercy, charity, comes from the spirit. This is, how we get rich spiritually Those who, trust in their wealth, and boast of their abundant riches.

One cannot redeem one self, and pay ransom, to God Psalms 49:7.

Even if we own, all the money, in this whole world. With all that, we will never be able, to have enough to, please God. Or bale our self, with him.

Un conditional love, and goodness, toward each other. That what please God. If we have all the money of the world will not be enough. Even for the sake, of our salvation. Only by our actions. Which is, how much good is goodness. We had done, while living on earth.

We Love, and glorify God always. If we, always belonged to God ?. Evil will not recognize those,who's always, do what is right. The evil, will shy away. From good, and vanish.

The riches of this world, will stay behind. Heaven is spiritual, and is richness of hearts. Conversion of hearts toward each other. That will be enough, ransom to bail us out, to enter kingdom of God. Because, that's what surely please God.

Jesus said. So do not worry about what are we to eat, or what are, we to drink. Or are we, to wear, all these things that, the pagans seek. But for you, your heavenly father knows that, you need them all. But seek first kingdom of God, and his righteousness, and all these things, will be given to you beside. Matthew 6:31-33.

God saying, to us only, the people who don't know him. Should worry about. Making, a living. How, to eat, or drink. Every one face, their own consequences.

But because, we know God. We believe, he will take care of us. God telling us don't worry, focus on him. To humble, our self. When asking for his kingdom. God wants what it is best for us.

About judging others. Stop judging, and you will not, be judged. Stop condemning and you will not be condemned. Forgive, and will be forgiven Luke 6:37.

If we don't forgive someone, who sin against us. That person more likely makes peace with God. Therefore, if we don't, make peace with that person. We remain guilty with God. If we don't forgive. We live with sin. Also not to condemn, anyone. For the wrong, or mistakes they have. Because, we all make mistakes.

Jesus will judge, the nation, and rule over people and the lord shall be the king forever. This is, one of the prediction of coming, of Jesus Christ.

Power of God, to judge the living, and dead at the end of time. God will establish his kingdom over, and all humanity. Wisdom 3:8.

The holy ones, of the most high, shall receive the king ship to possess it forever; holly are the people who go by the law of God, walk with God their entire lives. They serve and obey God always. Daniel 7:18.

The holy ones, will judge the world. Hopefully, we'll have someone, was fair salute the justice.

The holy, the just are, descended from God. The unjust they don't, fear God 1 Corinthians 6:1-4.

Person should, examine, him, or herself first. It will be in our best interest. First to judge ourselves. So we know we are doing wrong. To have, the chance to stop. Before we face God's judgment. Judging ourselves, give us a chance, to correct our self.1 Corinthians 11:28.

At the end, everyone. Will be judged, according to their deeds. By what was written, in the scroll. Revelation 20:12.

At the final judgment all the rich, poor, humble, loyal the faithful, the meek, the holy and the sinners. They, will all stand before God. They will all be judged, according. All the people we did good, or bad to them. There will be standing there, to remind us. Each face to face, to be a witness.

Let your life, be free from love, of the money. But be, content with what you have Hebrews 13:15.

Be grateful, to what you have. There's so many who don't have nothing. Be grateful there is, always someone worse than you.

Be happy with, what you have. Nothing can guarantee in this life. The only thing we can do, is count our blessings every day. Proverbs12:1-7.

That people who work for you. Especially, poor workers make sure do not hold, their wages. Their cry, and complains reach God, God always hear cries of the less fortunate. James 5:4. We need to make sure. We pay the workers enough to live. They need to live. God said, and pay them enough. So they can live.

False witness, will not go unpunished, and a liar will be destroyed. Proverb 19:9. There are, so many, who makes up stories. About others wrongfully, and false witnessing against, the innocent. They don't go unpunished. When we sin, against anyone We pay for it. Sometime in the big way, or in the small way. There's no way out.

But at the end, the truth come out, and the innocent win. Then the false witness. Will be put to shame, and get in trouble with law. Lying is deceiving someone.

Even white lies, are worse, because all they are empty, and false promise. Something will never happen, or come, true.

Through time, there's some time people exaggerate about something. When they, are not sure. Then, they come back, and correct them self. Almost everyone in the world lie.

Allot we say, when we are not sure. Once we, find out we go back, and correct it. Lying, to get, or gain anything, it is evil. Sometime we, overstate, about something. Therefore we go back, and correct ourselves. After we find out we were wrong. Also some time, we say things were not sure, of what to say. Anyway we find out, what we said is wrong. We go back, and apologize.

People who, make lying a way of living. People begin to see it. They lose a lots friends In process hardly anyone want or like to associate with them. Allot who assume things. Before making sure.

Judas Iscariot, betray Jesus for money. Judas said to himself. I have sinned in betraying Innocent blood. Matthew 26:50. 27:3-4.

When Jesus, was condemned. Judas repent it, and felt guilty but that the 30 pieces of silver he gave it back to the chief priest, and Elders. But they did not take it. Because they said it was blood money. Judas threw it in temple, and went hung himself. Because he felt guilty

Passing judgment, to someone else that means. The person, who is passing judgment he, or she think. They never make, any mistakes. The ones who, past judgment, on someone else. Especially, when they see mistakes of others. They go in shock acting like, they never made any mistakes before.

Chapter 7

Marriage, Marital-Solutions, And Relation Ships

About marriage, and relationship hope fully life time until death do us apart. During marriage. Arguments. That's not, the point. Stress. That's not the point. Financial hardship That's not the point. God forbid sickness, and disease that's not the point. Argument that's, not the point. Harsh relationship, that's not the point. Sex that's not the point. Feeling lost, in life. That's not the, point. Having bad luck that is not the point.

Unfortunately. Majority, of people in the world have some, or all these problems. It is unfortunate thing. There is, some people in the world who have all the above,and even more.

If you truly think, things will be perfect. Once you get married? I got news for you Therefore, our main focusing, on life. Should be, on each other happiness. Because, whether we like it or not ? We will always have problems.

You need to make your mind, and look around you. To see what you are getting into Chances, and possibilities you might have some of these issues. Are you ready to live through? What will be outcome of it ?

Not only, marriage relationship. But all kind of relations. They are identical the way they work, and what is the outcome of it.

Everyone, guarantee will have problems, issues. Critical moments anger every one, of us will have. What we need to do is. To focus on each other's life happiness, and being together always. All the things comes ahead of us. To be ready willing, and able to fix. For each other sake. Because, something is bound to happen always.

Before getting married, you need to analyze, all these futuristic, events. They, could come your way in marriage.

If you are, not willing to get married?

First - you lose, the beauty of marriage, and the rewards, you get, in marriage relationship

Second - you will miss, the opportunity, to wake up. With someone next to you every morning, and to get, to bed every night. Someone to share with you. Life, and the challenges Only to know, you're not alone.

Third- you'll miss, the opportunity of having someone. Who is, part of you who understand you, more than anyone else in the world. The one who is willing to share. Your happiness, your sadness. Because he, or she understands. How you feel more than anyone else.

Fourth- if anyone tell you. They are, having a perfect marriage. They are exaggerating nothing is perfect, in any relationship, everyone somehow suffer

Fifth- getting merit, it is the final step, to kingdom of heaven. When we are young, and single almost everyone do everything a lot of younger people do. It is harder to become 100% holy, and faithful. That is, why life to so many is different. When we are single. Society demanded. It is also hard to have 100% faith. I mean follow up faith. Because, we become too busy doing. What every single person do.

Fortunately, once we get merit. It is our opportunity to say. First to God I do,before we say to our spouse. During the holy matrimony. We also have a chance, to increase our faith So we can overcome temptations.

During marriage truly nothing, should go wrong. We don't have, to sin no more. Besides the natural. I called normal things people go through. What truly makes a perfect relationship Is unconditionally love in any relationship.

Mainly in marriage is not about laughing, or crying alone. Everything, should together 100% Life in marriage, supposed to be crying together and laughing together. Selfishness, greed and inconsiderate holding grudges, does not work in marriage or any relationship.

Once upon time someone. I knew came to me trying to get my advice about a friend, she had. He always cry, and complain about problems. He had, not even once he wanted to listen to her. Always all about himself. Not once. He was ever happy. He was being very selfish. All he thought of himself only. By him being very stressed. She was depressed.

Unfortunately he never came to her with, any good news. He never want, to share her feelings. He just don't know when to stop. He cried, and complain all the time. He was very inconsiderate, not respecting her feelings. Thinking to himself only to gain her attention. She always wished and hoped, if he can have, any happy moments. So she can be happy with him. It was hopeless She tried to get my opinion. I told her, You know something ? You need to have someone to laugh together, and cry together with you.

I did not suggest to her. to stop being his friend. I left it up to her to decide. What she wants to do.

Life went on, for her. Someone else found her. He fell in love, with her she asked me in my opinion. I knew the person. He was someone, I can trust. It was fine with me. Quickly he got engaged to her.

She was very open with me, about her relationship with him. Myself I always open for advice. For her, or anyone. Especially the people, I love, and care about.

One day, he was about to have minor surgery done, for his arm. He was going through a lot of stress. Worrying about it.

A day before surgery. He was acting very weird, and strange with her. He acted like. he don't even want her to be there, She came to me. Being concern, to what's happening or why this happening. At the meantime, she plant to be at the hospital next to him. To make sure he's OK. But he kept telling her, you don't need to. She did not know what to do. I told her. He does not want you to see him, in this situation, and critical. It might hurt too much to see him in this condition. Secondly, he is crying for attention. I remind her, how they were out a week before out together. Celebrating their relationship. Laughing together and happy together. Now it is time, you are crying together.

That's what, makes a perfect relationship. Always to be there, for each other. In good times, or bad time. When he, cried for attention. You did not, stay away. I told her.

We should, be willing, to do it together, and being there for each other. The same way we must be,willing carry each other during. Bad times, and good times. With no pressure for either one, or side.

That would make us, as one. We think like one. We are, not two persons, anymore. In marriage. We grow up together. Like from the time. When we were, just babies.

The couple together, their focus should be always on happiness. But not forgetting Things always, will come their ways. Need to fix, and taking care of it immediately. Knowing always, will be daily issues. Need to face that, and deal with it. The reason is, that eventually tragic things happening around us, daily anyway. Also things can happen, in our own home Among our friends, or relatives. Have you seen anybody with no problems ?

There is, already too much hate, and problems in the world. This is, why we need to start in our own house - hold to make things better, and to fix our own.

Over all, If we are good people. ? We should, know how to make things better. If we don't have it good, at home first. Will be harder to help any-one else.

I believe there's, many psychologists, and therapists. Some who work with very sick people. But they have, their own problems at home. It would be easier, for them to work with patience If they have happier home. How can they help someone else ? If they cannot help themselves first.

What you should do, is say to yourself. There's, already enough hate, out there in the world today. Why should, I add more to it.

Basically what you ought to do. Is to be grateful to. What you have, and to focus, on your own households. Happiness first. If you have extra time. Will be, a blessing to share it with someone else. Who are less fortunate, than you. To help someone else, with their life's.

Many saints, they came from broken, and troubled family. Many of them, had severe disease, and under severe pressure. They were willing, to endure anything, and everything. They still loved God. To the fullest from all, of their heart. From all, their mind from, all of their spirits, and their soul. They knew their life, did not belong to them. But it belongs to God only They knew that, God loves them. He is, willing to take all their problems, and get it fixed They also knew, they are going, to die one day. Like everyone else. They will, face

God. Saint only become. When they get to heaven. They were, very patient, and understanding. Saints, were compassionate, humble Lived in virtue, grace, and charity. That's how they became saints. Saints can do miracles. They become saints, when they die. Because they, became favored by God.

When God created, Adam, and eve. His plan humanity. To live with him, in paradise that a perfectly happy life. (Creation Genesis).

Because of the strong faith, saints had. They felt free of suffering, free of problems Perfectly, pure spiritually.

Gods goal was for us, to live with him forever, and multiply. Until our first parents Adam and eve sinned. Before they sinned, that is, when they were spoiled. They had everything. Genesis.

By disobeying God, evil found a way, how to tempt human. To sin, and suffer, because of it. Before Adam, and eve committed, the sin. Evil was more, miserable than ever. Because he had no one to tempt, and make their life miserable, like he was.

Once we are merit. Our life does not belong, to us anymore it belong to God. To Christian our, salvation is through our lord Jesus Christ. He laid down himself for us, so we can be saved. He was innocent. But yet, he suffered. He was tortured nailed, on the cross. He went through all that. Because, he loved us.

Jesus like us, to carry our own cross,and follow, in his footsteps. In order for us, to have our, own salvation through him. Jesus heels, our heart mind, and soul.

God give us, the sacraments to go by. In order for us to grow, and to work our way to become saints. Eventually, to be with him one day. God he is a spirit, and we are human being flesh, and blood. We live on earth. Therefore, he depended on us human being To glorify his name, and always to be great in his eyes mind, and spirit. We put evil, to shame by doing good. Goodness, cowards the evil.

My favorite figure, of speech is. Why do we, do any evil what? There isn't, enough evil in the world. Of course will be always more evil, in the world. Evil love, to tear apart. What God put together.

God gave us instruction. How to live a moral life, so we can be happy. God created a man He did not want him to be alone. Out of the man. God created a woman. out of Adams flesh (Genesis). God said everyman need a woman, and it is not good for a man to be alone (Genesis).

God is, very unique the way he thinks. That is, when a man loves. Himself he is loving. His wife also. Because, she is him. Part of him. She is himself. She is his body. His mind. His heart and soul. She is 100% him. Can you ever hate yourself. Your wife is yourself. Also because, she came out of your flesh. I believe during holy matrimony. God he is at, it again I mean at creation When he create Adam and eve. We become new Adam, and eve at marriage.

My wife of 32 years. I never even, think of getting disappointed with her ever. That is unconditionally. Because just to, think about it. I laugh at myself because, if I do. Actually I will be, disappointed at myself. Because she's me. We try not to live with things. That help running our relationship. We always figure, we're more valuable, and important than, all the material of the world, hold together. Even when, we were poor we're happy. As long, as we are together We grow up together. We go up, and down together. It is what everyone else go through ? Our goal is to serve each other. We focus, on each other 24/7. We both humble, ourselves, we don't care if we live on bread, and water alone. As long,as we are happy and together.

Believe me, we don't have a perfect life. We have our own issues, like everyone else We don't shove things, out the way. Or void anything. We take care of it. One out of the time. If we can't fix it. We figure at least we try. From the time, day begin until day end. Our love for each other never depart from us. No matter, how much things we have: going on in our life. We don't let anything. Touch our happiness. The reason that we know. Will always be many, bad things happening like everyone else.

When my son was very young. When ever heard us arguing. He used to think, we're about to get divorce. My innocence child. Can you think, or imagine ?. What our children are going through, out there. Into society today. Normally that. what, they hear, or sometimes see every day. Maybe somehow, he heard it all the time. People are divorced. Nothing can hardly be positive. Negativity, almost every corner. Or else you, don't think children speaks to each other about their life ? And you don't think children get hurt. Even though, they are innocence ? Still they feel, everything in their heart. One of my nieces, lost her father that is my brother. He died, when she was only seven years old. Once upon a time, in school. All the children were asked. What their dad do for living ?. My niece, did not know, what to say She came home crying to her mom. Well dying is, something everyone got to go one day Something we could not prevent it. No matter what. But divorce, we are able to prevent. Many children with single parent.

Later on growing up. My son began to learn. What relationship, should be about. It is not about any problems, any kind of problems. Life is should about us, with each other first. How much we are willing, to please each other?. How much we are willing to serve each other ?. That what pleases God the most.

Almost everyone, love dollars store, my wife love dollars store. One day I took her to one To do some shopping After she picked, a few items we came to check out. My wife jokingly telling the cashier. Oh I love dollar -store -my husband don't bring me, here very often. Immediately, the cashier responded saying, oh controlling. I also responded and said no. I don't control my wife. I serve my wife, and my wife serve me. I did not hold anything against the cashier. But it is, a shame that's, how people think these days controlling, controlling. They always want to make sure. Who is in control, who comes first.

If we're out, to be a leader. If I ever thought of myself as a leader. What leaders do ? Is serve, take care of their household. Leaders make sure, their people live, to be free happy, and peaceful. and to have peace of mind. Presidents governments, officials. They are, leaders and their job is to take care of their people. That is, their number one goal. To make sure they're OK. To become a leader, is very powerful, and they can be very aggressive. But they don't become arrogant instate a humble themselves. Because they know one thing they, have to do. Is to serve. People becomes their extended family. Try to do what they promised.

Christian when they, get married. It is the promise, to obey God, by serving each other always When it, comes to God, there's no excuses. It is against God to take apart. What he has put together, and that is man, and woman. God wish us to be one. Just the way he made. Us in the beginning(Genesis).

The point is if we live, as one. Evil will not have, any room to squeeze himself between us. To put us apart.

God made man, and woman to be, one flesh. Therefore, a man leave father and mother, and take his wife they shall be to one flesh. Genesis 2:2,21.

When a man find, a woman of his dreams. He actually and spiritually found, his missing rips and the missing part of his flesh.

We become one, as God intended to. I mean as to grow with, God's love, and each other. The moment you go through, the holy matrimony You bound together, and become one. By the holy spirit of God.

God takes marriage, very personal to himself. From that moment your wife, and self. It don't belong, to you anymore. Belong to God.

One thing, to remember every single day. Life is full of challenges. It is common sense Everyone know it. Even children figure that out from early age.

People who thinks. They are, getting married, to have free sex. They are, very critical. That is the way. Of lust. Many of these marriages, they end up committing adultery.

Sex in marriage, is allowed. In marriage, sex should be spiritual. Spiritually is, when sex is not, an issue, it is spiritual. When the two hearts United's, and become one together. Otherwise if sex become big issue, between the partners.

That is when it, became lust. Spiritual is, not about,who want more sex, or less. Spiritual is, and whenever your hearts, come together. As one, As we are one in marriage. Some are selfish, and inconsiderate, when it comes to sex. Complain, how their partner, do not want to have sex all the time. They are, very critical. They are, only pleasing the evil one. If you love your partner, you must. Also respect,her or his feelings, and desires. Then turn around, and look at your partner. You don't always, see yourself. You also see, the one who belong to you. and you belong to each other. You have, each other 24/7. Why worry about anything?

It's been said good sex during marriage. Is contribution, to the good, and healthy marriage. I say it is true. As long, as we do make, an issue out of it.

In marriage, there's no such thing. This thing belong to this spouse, or the other spouse Everything, you have to belong to both of you 100% It does not make a different. Who make more or who makes, less.

Fussing, or complaining about. Whose last, or first You are opening the door. Making evil to, be able tempting you easier. Evil always want, to destroy what God put together. God plan for humanity, to multiply to be good. So we can represent. God here, on earth. We put evil to shame with our goodness.

God said, if a man seduced a virgin, who is not to engaged to any one, and sleep with her, he must pay the customary dowry, and take her for his wife. Exodus 22:16.

God honoring woman. God trying to protect, every woman dignity, and to have pride in herself. So no one, can put her, to Shame. God do not permit for women, to be used, or even touched, or have a sex before marriage. Sex before marriage is forbid. God said if you have got, any serious contact with a woman. Must be only for her, to be your future partner that his marriage. Because God, knew he create us to be pure. No premarital sex Adultery is forbid. Because if you commit adultery, with anybody ? Someone is stealing. The love you have for your spouse Also your spouse committing adultery with you. Because, you are one.

Jesus teaching, about adultery. Jesus saying about committing adultery, even if anyone look at woman with lust,in his eyes has already committed adultery, with her in his heart. Anyone who marries, a divorced woman commit adultery. Matthew 5:27-32

Step one, in relationship will be a proper, to begin with, one thing on your mind. There might be a chance, to be the one. Might spent, the rest of your life with.

Growing up, you will have all your friends. Suddenly one day you find one, whom you are very attached to. Then you look, and think of a way to approach that person, and once you do so. There's a chance, that person having the same feeling for you. It could be one of your friends,or someone you run into occasionally. Then you grow together. Building your relationship based on love and understanding.

Love is, very powerful. Some people complain, about the one, they love. But they still stick around. Because, I say if you love the person. Especially, your spouse. You don't have to do exactly like, his, or her way. But if you, love that person? You need, to get used his, or her habits as long, as it is not. Offending you, or offending anybody else. It is to like, you can't live with, or without.

A lot of people dates, to find a long lasting relationship. Unfortunately there's no guarantees There's a time, where they fell. It is the destiny. If is distant happen, it will happen. We all need to date, to find our partner. Of course now these days. People have to date, in order for them to find our partner. It is essential. But as long as, they have one thing, on their mind from the first, second. We meet, that someone hoping, to be a potential lifetime partner

It is unfortunate thing now these days, so many dates for convenient for sex, or sometime They go from, one person to another. When people date, more than one person, out of the time. Going from, one person to another. Insecure jealousy. Having a corrupt, relationship living in fear. Too many heartbroken. No self-respect, people don't feel shame, to be touched, and felt they don't, value themselves. When their body is involve, they are being used. Also giving up their purity for lust. They don't understand, God created them, with dignity.

So many don't know. The meaning of dignity, and pride in their shelves. So many who have, many relationships before marriage. They are very critical and have more problems Than others during marriage. Some who have good marriage they feel guilty thinking about their pass. In fact a lady once told me. How guilty, her husband felt. Because, he dated someone else, beside her Because, she was given him such good life. Therefore, it will be great. If you have one memory when it comes to finding life time relationship. The first, and the last. Who you are, about to spent the rest of your life with.

The faithful, and others now these days, are giving kids sex education, and how to have a safe sex. It is really great thing, they are doing. So kids don't get, any diseases. But are they teaching, our kids to have self-respect to protect their dignity. Or are they telling, any of the children,will be shame If they miss used their body, and how much. They should be concern Are they teaching their children. How to, save themselves for their future partner. Or else are they telling their children, dating is not about sex. It is about the future finding, the right person, to spent the rest of, her, or his life together. So many, who don't know, how to be a shame, or even care for them self. When kids grow up, and get married. They should preserve, their body for their future spouse. They will be honored, and respected Beside they could have a very healthy a prospect relationship. Parents should explain to their kids. To understand. What dates is about. We have to insert one thing, in our children mind. Which is do not let anybody, use them. But only to find someone, hopping to be their future partner. There is no sure thing, about anything. Sometime things can go wrong. May not be the one hopefully, one more try. They can find the one.

Parents, uncles, aunts, and friends can be great example for kids. Especially, whole life began, when the two, together man, and woman. Get married, and have children. Having girlfriend, or boyfriend is not only. For sex, and pleasure. Or for their own enjoyment. So many kids because for adults miss guidance. They look at it So awesome, and cute when children have a girl friend or boyfriend. Instead of the explain to them that just a friend. So they don't think, otherwise. By not doing that, it open children's eyes.

We called, to teach our children. The meaning of life at the early age. Now these days majority of teenagers. If you ask them why ? and for what reason you're dating. They won't even have, an answer, or their answer might be for sex, without feeling any shame more likely. So many teenagers, are out of control. We need, to teach our kids how to live life of virtue, and to have a moral values to instruct children, to have self-respect, and to protect, their dignity, and good reputation. Now these days. We need to search, for a solution, for children, So they don't make, any mistakes or bad decisions, When it comes to relationship. Dating someone, with commitment. Is safer, and you're not taking, a big chances. You are taking, good chance.

Some kids, and teenagers, they don't understand or realize. How tournament it is for themselves. The anguish, the suffering, stress, and how miserable, they can be, if they date different people all the time. What make them think. The same people. They are dating Are not doing same thing, with others. They could very well be dating others, as well. We need to help, our children. To set for themselves guidelines. To have, a rewarding future

We are obligated to help our children, to make sure once, and when they grow up to have a great memory. So they can live, a happy human being. With no clouds on their mind. To help, our children grow up having good memory, to feel free with themselves.

The olden days people. Put everything comes from bible, into perspective. Also in olden days parents raise, their own children. Their uncles played, big rolls Their aunts were also, felt responsible to help guide, and monitor children. After all this is part of family value. Values are, how much you, express yourself among people. How people look at you, about your reputation among people.

We can find, our partner, in many different ways. Some who grew up together from the childhood, and some love, at first site, and many other ways.

Meeting someone, to grow together, Loving each other. Is a miracle. Because can you imagine. Someone who was stranger, destiny bring them together, don't know nothing about each other, finally they meet they fall in love with each other. Together they become one.

First the golden step. Is getting engage, after the commitment. That is, first celebration, among people. May have little, get together relatives, and close friends to celebrate their first step. From then, on be aware of troublemaker. People who gossip. Some people have nothing else to do. But stick, their nose here don't belong. There are, also jealous people, be aware that. Be private, and don't let anyone know your business.

From then on, practice to be, as one. Do everything together as one. Planning for wedding party is not easy. Be extra careful some people, act like they want, to live your life for you. Almost everyone around you. Want to have their point, in the wedding party you're about prepare, to have. No one want to be left out. Your relatives from both sides friends. Seems like everyone, wants to have a piece of you.

Sometime there's, corruption among all these people they'll act like. Who want be,first or last These things really happen to some people.

There, will always be someone. Who will drive everyone crazy sometime disappointment and hard feelings. All these things come from people, who truly love you,and they want to be involved.

All for stupid reason, because no one wants given in, people are very persistent When they, want their way, and these are the people. Who want, to run the couple's life. Without knowing. Or rather not knowing better. When at the meantime, should be only up to a couple to do for themselves.

One of the best thing. You can do. Is to try to bring everyone together. Two out of the time, or four, or one On one. Get all these people, to know each other, to become good friends. If you ever, run into the situation's Will be in your best interest, first to start with, future mother in laws. Take them, out altogether get them involved, together in your wedding. Before you know They will become close friends. You can do the same thing For the future, father in laws. You can, do same thing For your, friends from both side. Get them all to know each other. To become tight friends,and all the people who don't know each other. From bride, and groom get them together. So know each other. You'll never have any problems. By that time everyone, gets to your wedding party. You don't, have to worry. About having, any problems. Will be wonderful to have, many people around you. Growing with love, and peace, and mercy.

Everyone will remember, your happy day for a long time. Especially, you will never have, any problems with mother laws. Because they're, both mothers too and they both love to get attention. But they are friends. No need to be disappointed, or jealous. They are already friends, and for a sure they spent, lots of time together. If you have, children someday No one will feel, left out maybe, there will want to watch the kids together sometime.

Because, they both love them the same. When there is love. love is not jealous.

If everyone know each other, love each other. They will become humble, about everything. Especially, when it comes to the one, they love. Also love comes with natural respect, and unconditionally. It is not a difficult thing, to have lifetime commitments relationships.

The gift God give us in marriage

Many rewards children, and grandchildren, we can be proud of. Hopefully, they become our joy. Good grandparents. They become parents all over again.

I often make it, sound like a joke, to my son. I say hurry up, and make me a son I truly want him to take his time. Because he is, young. But one day, if he do get married and have a child's. Will bring joy, and happiness into my heart. Just looking, at his baby will be like looking, at my son, when he was a baby.

Marriage is, the final step to heaven. We have a chance of living life of virtue, love mercy, grace, and charity. This is your final chance. Marriage it is the most profound way God ever give us. Because he did not want us to be alone and lonely.

The lord God said, it is not good for the man to be alone, I will make a companion who will help him. lord God made a woman. From, his rib, and brought her to Adam. Genesis 2:18,22.

Evil despise God, and all what good, and always want to destroy. What God put together.

Evil knows how weak, and imperfect human being are. When it comes to temptation and falling into sin. Also how easily we can become deceived. We were made as temple God.

We are all born, with mercy of God, in our heart. We are all, made like God's image in spirit. In marriage. We obey God in every way. Trust in God, and give him all the challenges, we are about to face. God know how, to fix everything, because, he made everything The things we see, and the things we don't see, God able to, fix everything

In marriage, nothing of this world Should stand, in the middle of love, for each other We should fix everything, on the spot. Issues, and problems. When they begin are very small. If we don't fix it immediately. They could get bigger. During marriage we are as one body, also as one spiritually. Because of small issues, or problems we have, if don't fix it will become like, a little gap between, the couple pulling them a part. One gap small enough, to give room, for evil squeezed through, to make the gap, bigger wider Until the couple, are so far apart, where it becomes so hard to close gap. Evil is, leading one thing to another.

Therefore, these problems, are temptations Given in, to the devil I mean, when the problems get bigger, it is hard to fix. That is, when it's too late. This is about, any relationship, not only the marriage relationship.

We fall in love, we get married. But that's not whole thing. That's just, the beginning I mean begin to work, on your love relationship. Takes a long time. It could take, life time

You also have, to remember. You were strangers, to each other, when you met Suddenly destiny brought you together, to be, as one that is the hardest thing to do. But the love, you have for each other, that makes it easy. To be one act like one, takes a life time. When I met, my wife she told me, about the places, she went to like shopping places Parks, fewer shopping, or park's. Same places, I went to. More likely we ran into each other before we met.

Marriage, should be built. On Mutual Trust, and understanding. Should never, be about material. We should treasure. Every moment. We have together. You know. How everyone. Get separate, by dyeing. Because you just, don't know, how long, you're about,to live to be, with each other.

My father, lost my mother, after 57 years of marriage she passed away. I believe her, spirit never departed from him. I know because, she often came, in his dreams The reason, that happened because. In spirit they were as one,also. He was always in contact, with her spirit in his dream, and that is his spirit, at work. My parents, with them was never, who was, first or last always run for each other. All chores all homework, or taking care of children work, or anything. Should never, be your job, or her job, your job, or his job, or neither one you. Who's duty is it. Or who is turn to do, particular thing.

We should always think, like one. Because, we become one should not make any different, who would run, first to take care of things. We should do, everything As one mind heart, and soul.

Truth in marriage, builds on Mutual Trust. It is not about. You should, or don't trust Your spouse, or each other. To be ethical to understand. It is being understanding person. Being positive. It is the best thing you can do, for your relationship If you take your vows seriously ? Yes you can, keep your marriage together. But will not build a happy home If you want your home to be secured, and happy. It must be built, on real understanding and constant communication. That what makes, marriage successful.

In marriage relationship, if you look at things, and you say this belong to me and this belong to you, that is separation, does not work. You are not acting, as one God intends it For you both. To be one, to have Hundred percent, of everything Each one expected to give in 100%. To be, completely happy marriage need to be stable to achieve all the goals and dreams, you will have together. We must understand and accept God's given rules, and work on it to fulfill it. Jesus said, we're not supposed to leave, each other's in the divorce. When they are joined together by God. New testament.

People don't understand. The great gift. God give us, in marriage. God made it holy, grant us eternal love. It is God's higher power, to make us as one. The same love made the couple,as one.

Like God's, the father the son, and the holy spirit as one God. With three, persons each one. God give them duty. God is one spirit, one holy temple. Therefore he, want us to be one. To resides in us. So we can become his temple.

The holy spirit of God makes, two persons as one. Because we were, made, of image of God'. Therefore, he is one image. He chooses husband, and wife, to be one image, to live as one, God in us.

Marriage should, be taken into consideration. Honesty, is the only way to the happiness. Life time commitment.

Marriage is not a game. When you, obey God in marriage. living with God's love In marriage, God created, the new garden of Eden. Everything supposed to be perfectly happily ever after. With Gods directions and instruction.

For all Christian around,the world. Jesus told us in the new testament. He explains why we aren't supposed to leave each other in divorce. Once we joined together in marriage.

The society, does not understand, the great gifts God give us. When, he made it holy, and bring to us his eternal love. How great, and powerful it is. The word of God makes man and woman just the way, it was from the beginning. Genesis.

Once we joined together, to love, and become one. We supposed to spend the rest of our life, as one. Also is the promise made. Reaching the highest point to please God.

Our main goal, is the opportunity, it was given to us to have a happy, and prospect life, to be faithful, to each other, and to make our love stronger thru our entire life. Pray to God. So he help us, to live life of purity, chastity, and virtue. Nothing will survive, or last without God help. Especially, marriage.

Christian honoring, Jesus Christ, by submitting themselves to each other. It said wives submit, to your husband, in the same way you submit, to the lord. Ephesians 5:22

Also husbands show, the same kind of love, to their wives, as Christ showed us the church, became his body. When he died for her.

If anyone wants to be a leader among you. You're supposed to be, the server that's what leaders do, is to serve. Controlling, does not work.

I believe when, we meet, and fall in love, it is destiny. God has it planned. Especially when two hearts join together.

Relationship should be, equal. To grow with respect, wisdom, and faith equality, and to respect each other's feelings. Strong love foundation, it will become example for our children, and grandchildren.

Having children, is not only carry our family name. It is gift of love between men and women from God. Children, are future generation. One day they will take over and continue. What we started.

When the two meet together, for the first time, and begin to date. There are many reasons, why people date each other.

There are, two tape in particular.

First - dating for convenient of having self-enjoyment, free sex, and lust might be some feelings toward each other. Usually those couple, don't have much respect, for each other. There's also a chance. They might have multiple, relationship. Behind each other back. Both always feel insecure, and jealous. Corrupted relationship, and more obstacles Many hearts breaking. No self - esteem, or self- control. They don't care about their reputation, or dignity. Their relationship only fulfill each other, temptations, and desires. In many cases.

People, who have multiple relationship. Before marriage More likely, you run into more problems than. others. Something, or someone always, remind them of their past Or if they have. Good marriage, relationship often. They feel guilty, and wish, If they had only, one memory. That is, with their spouse. With my,own ears I heard some people feels bad, or guilty, their spouse was not the only they dated. Because, have they beautiful marriage. Often wished, if they do not have other memories.

Second - When the two meet. Full in love with one goal to have long lasting relationship, with potentials. Hoping to grow together, to be great couple, in the marriage and fresh memories. The two, they started together.

We are, always willing to give kids, a sex education or safe sex. It is great, besides we should, be testimonial, to teach our children. How, God created them, with dignity and self - respect. Teach children to respect, their body. Because, they deserve all honor, and respect, God made them this way.

We need to teach, our children to look up for their parents. Their goal to be first, to be couple like them. To get married like them. To be parents like them. This is what children in general. Should learn, an example.

We should, teach our children. Their main, goal to be finding their made. Even if they don't date at, all until then. It is cute at first stage. Many put, in very small children, head that's boyfriend, grill friend. It is ugly cute. Children are, innocence They need only to have friend's, to grow out of their innocence, on their own with our guidance.

Many children. Especially teenagers. They are, so much in the dark. Much of, it is our fault. We don't teach them, or spent much time with them. Lots of them are gone astray. When at, the meantime. They are our, future generation.

Number one problem. If we ask many teenagers. Why they are dating someone ? Most of them, one thing they, have on their mind. That is sex. Especially when, they are at the age, of preadolescent. Their juvenility goes out of the control.

At home, we need to help our children. To grow in virtue to be moral, and proper Instruct them to respect themselves, and others.

In olden days. Especially, in some part of the world. Might be still going on today That is, arranged marriage. But now all that has changed, in many parts of the world big different. Which is great. So we know, what that person is like, before deciding. It great to know each other for a long time. It is better, because is about life. We are, about the one to spend the rest of our life with. There is, nothing easy about it.

A priest my friend. I ask him once only to get his opinion ? About dating my wife before my marriage to her. Telling him. I am dating her. Because, I love her, and will for sure. Marry her. He answered, your spirit is safe. He also said, were love is That is. Were God is because. God is love.

Unfortunately, these days we are very critical. Putting marriage, and relationship in question. Evil trying to redefined, marriage. Taking away our dignity.

It is not only, parent's responsibility, to teach children. How to behave, helping. Them to establish, a relationship with others. It is churches, uncles, aunts relatives, good neighbors friends. They all, have kids also.

Our goals, and dreams. Should be, creating great future generation. Out of our children. Anyone who's able, to give advice. Should put, to practice always check. On children trying to direct them, to the right path. Always to see, what kids are up to Before we give our children birth control, or condoms. Should also let them know, the consequences. Helping kids, making the right design it the key.

Marriage, at holy matrimony. When the two bond together they become one. By the power of holy spirit. That is when. God takes our relationship personally to himself God always wanted us to be, as one with him. From then, and on is not about who makes more,or less money. Which do more, or less around the house. It is not any more. Who is first, or last. Everything is 100%, together.

It said good sex, is contribution to good, and healthy marriage. Some think, they get free sex. in marriage. Obsession with sex, next will become abuse and lust. God allowed to have sex during marriage. It should never be. Who want it more, or less. Or like to have it now, or later. Should be spiritual. Which comes from, the heart mind, and soul out of, this world. Sex should never, be selfish. Is not about, one person. When the merit couple. When their hearts meet, at the same time. We could have better marriages.

If we teach our kids. Should dates having, one thing, on their minds hoping, to find their made.

I understand people find. Their partners in many different ways. We need to remember, nothing guarantee. We can still make it happen. The first thing, we should do is to focus on better life to come ahead of us.

The first golden step. When you, get engaged. Small party with some of the closest friends, and family. The ones who truly love you, will help you. Accomplish your dream, and happiness.

There are also some, who want to put, their two cent, in your business. Some because of their jealousy, like to cost problems. Usually people gossip. Everyone, try to make their point, and opinion counts. People do that. They go, out of their way. When at the meantime. They know, it is only about the couple. Who got engaged, to be married.

Everyone goes for, a different type of experience. The wise couple, should take it to prospect.

The future bride, and groom. Booth have friends parents siblings, and relatives. They both have, their own life with their people. But soon, the couple. They are, about to become one. Therefore, they should introduce, friends relatives, siblings. Future in laws, to each other. So they can become, one big family big circle of love, and great relationship. The reason is, many think just because you're getting married. You let go, all the people you had before. It is good to let, all these people around to get involve in your love happiness. Once you are engaged. You become center, of the attention. Everyone want to walk with you. Every step of the way, until you reach your goal. Especially the ones who truly love you. Those are, the ones who, truly want. What best for you. Now in this time, and age. People are not,taking marriage very seriously.

God don't want us to be alone, and to obey him alone, to bring good, and holy children. So we can have better world.

Many things, in the marriage.

1- It is great gift, God grand it, for us. The final step to eternity. That is, having a chance, to live holy life. Pleasing, God in every way.

2- Evil despises, God, and all the good. Always try to destroy. What God put together. Evil knows, how weak, and imperfect human being are. When it comes to temptation. Eventually sinning against God. How we can, easily be deceived.

3 - We are temple, of the holy spirit of God (Genesis) We were made like his image in the spirit. We need always to invite him. Into our hearts mind, and soul.

4- In the marriage obeying God, should be number one goal, and he will be our protector and shield, from all the dangers of evil.

5- Evil hate love it is the point. Where, he vanishes

6- During marriage. Not about, any material, or anything, made of this world. Should come before, our love for each other. No matter what, you should always find, a solution for whatever,comes ahead. Never let anything stand. Between the love. You will have for each other. You do nothing to please evil. Fix everything on the spot.

Not fixing the must smallest problem. It is like leaving a gap between the couple. So the evil squeeze through, to make it, bigger, and wider to pull. The couple apart until they are not together anymore.

7- In marriage. We need to have, a spiritual life, and to live life of virtue, mercy charity, faith, and true holiness.

8 - In marriage love. Is like being, a child all over again, to grow with love. One step out of the time. The experiences, and challenges. Should make love relationship very strong, unconditionally.

9- In the marriage, should be continuously,every moment focusing. Doing on acts of love toward each other

10 - In marriage, the couple helps. Raising supporting, each other. To be each other's guidance.

11 – Marriage. Is life time relationship. The wealth, we have for each other in marriage. Should be with, our respect. To the quality of our feeling emotions. To share that,with your spouse.

12-As one, until death do us apart.

Family values

The image of my father's. The image, of my mother's

Introduction

Throughout the world. Especially, in our country America. Family values, has being the main issue among everyone.

People are, very concerned about the subject. We are, always thinking about. What to do. Salvation is right in front of us. We just don't pay attention.

That has been done in the world. There are, so many children. Who don't, even know their relatives. They don't, even know anything about their grandparents. Much less the generations before them.

Many of us came, from different countries. To make this country our, home, sweet home.

Made America, so unique to have many nationalities. With many, different cultures Came along with their values. The values soon, are forgotten.

Here in America, and around the world. We are, becoming a material society and not spiritual. We are, losing our moral values.

Marriage, relationship. They want to make it, thing of the past. Children are being confused. They don't know which direction to take. A lot living with a single parent or no parents. Some are, in the middle of big fight. Many divorced parents becoming very inconsiderate. They do not think, about their children. But only think of them –selves No one respect, children feelings.

As the parents, they brought the child, into this world. They promised to give him, or her, good, stable, and happy life. The older, that child become. The more critical parents, feels. When they, were at the beginning. Were very excited they have a baby.

So many, problems within marriage. Mainly because of financial, suffering Declining in jobs, makes our economy very bad.

Greed,and jealousy. Makes society lose touch. Foundation, and stability of families is shaking. So many are, running scared, and confused.

Poor decisions, greed, sex, alcohol, drug abuse gambling. Becoming, things of today We are, becoming blind, to see how our society is in decline.

It is all about, money of this world. It is also about. Who will, get there first Being a team among, any family,or any one. It is essential In order to succeed.

I don't recognize, or have proven, or base. How true, it is. The story of. Seven wood. It is wisdom, we learn from it. Story of seven woods. I did heard of the story When, I was young.

The story goes as following. Once upon a time. Older man he knew,he was getting old,and his last days are very near,the end of his life. He had seven adults kids. He called them, to his house. He want, to have meeting with them. When they were in his house He brought, seven sticks of wood. He had it, waiting for them. He put all, the seven sticks of wood together in bundle, and typed to hold it together. Then he handed, to each of his kids asking each one of them to break it in half. It was very hard to break it Then the father took that bundle. Separated, into single stick, and handed each stick to one of his kids. Asking each of them, to break the stick. This time they were, all able to break the signal stick. During all that time, they did not know. What their father trying to do. They were, trying to figure out. What their father was trying to do, and wondering. But he was quick, to explain to them. First he asked them all, to sit down and to listen. He said this the sticks together means. When you are, a team working together, backing each other. You go up, and down together. Happy, and sad together With love, understanding each other. You have bigger chance, to succeed in life, and bigger chance to be in success. If you are together. Their father also, told them. If you are alone, you'll be weak. If you are, together you will be strong. He also told them If you're together. You will be each other's strengths. None you will go without. He told them. He add it, you will become one mind heart, and soul for each other. When you are together, as a team you share ideas, and you all have one goal, and dream.

Secondly the one stick means if you are alone. It is a lot easier for others, to take your advantage, you will be weaker less strings. When people, have no one lean on. They become sad, and measurable.

Family values, are giving an example, to others. The way you express yourself I mean the, way you treat people. The way you act, toward others. That is how people will know, the way you were brought up. If you are bad person. Will give your family Bad reputation. If you are good person. Will give your family, good reputation. Actually it is not fair, the way people look at it. But that is how people are. They past judgment to entire family. Just because one of them, do one wrong thing.

More likely. People think that's, how the entire family is. Therefore, we should raise great children, to go into society. With good, and moral values. We only try our best

Nothing work without, faith, and religion. Faith is 100% charity, and that is unconditionally love, mercy compassion, peace.

Being faithful. It is not deceiving, or lying to anyone. Faith is, always being forwarded, and speaking, the truth no matter. How much it hurts ?

Religion it is rules, regulations, Laws. We put rolls, over our self's. Come from the Bible. Gods laws to walk through, the right path. Also to learn what is right, or wrong. Disciplining our self. All the above, comes from the bible.

Jesus Christ church, put all teachings, into prospect for millions. So they don't go astray. This is why ? We need to, attend church more often. Because, a lot of us Hardly make, any time to read the bible.

We need to, teach our kid the values. How to be morals. Letting them know all that comes from God. Bible teach us to forgive. We learn forgiveness. It is not our choice We are obligated. We must. We learn that, is the only way, we will be forgiven by God If we forgive others.

Good values are being responsible, toward each other. Helpful, considered Generosity. Kind. Relationship to be built up on Mutual Trust. Honesty, is the key to success always.

From Old, and new testament. We learn if we earn our living. At the honest way Even if we don't get rich with money. We will always have more blessing, in our life than others. We also learn if we work, and earn our living, at the dishonest way ? We will suffer and struggle more than others. We could. have less blessings

People who cheat and steal to make their money. Even if they are making millions They have, one tragic after another. They are, always critical. Because, of the greed and love of the money, make them blind. From knowing, how much they are suffering

Many people. Who are, very innocent suffer. Because of others. greed. Greedy people will do anything, for money.

Values is not only, the family. Also Includes, your friends, and the people around you. Especially, your neighbors. You should always check, on your neighbors.

Faith is a gain given, by God. So we can reach the heaven.

What makes family, as one. The love, they have for each other. Love is not only by saying the word, but also, by action. Of course everyone, has their ups, and downs. As long, as you are still together,at the end of the day.

One thing family should have, on their mind. Knowing that. They need each other. Could not live without one, and another. We should, teach each other. How we can get along.

I lived small town, majority of people, try to live according, to the commandment and God rules. We figured, if we feed, the poor. We will, give them relieve. If help thief's Would they have, any reason to steal? If we forgive. They will not have, any other choice but to forgive. If we love them, the only choice, they would have. Only to love.

I often reminded myself. If was not for my grandparents, my parents hadn't exists. If was not, for my parents I would not exist.

Therefore, family values began. With our grandparents. Many of them, knew how to keep us, as a family. They had learned. The only way. Is to have a business hoping to past, to their children. Not only to have everything. But to make sure. Their children stay together, and to make a habit out of it.

Last it 100 years after, my grandparents passed away. My father, and his brother My uncle, took over family business. They were, very successful, business men. They did not get rich. But they lived very well, and gave allot to the needy. But that, was not the only point behind it. It was giving a lesson, to their children, and their friends to teach them. Family, stay together always.

For over 100 years, until his day. Many of us, we have business together, or somehow. We are, associate. From my, grandparents, to my parents, my brothers. and sisters, my uncles children, and grandchildren my nephews, and nieces, and their kids We all associate with each other. Somehow. Of course we have Ups, and down. Only one thing we, always have, on our mind. We need each other. We extended this love to our friends.

We know, life with our children. Does not, end at age of 18 years old Actually that's when restart. My father always told me, to take care of my brothers, and sisters. When he's gone. I mean when passed away. My mother used to say the same thing. They meant to, love them always. Every and each of my brothers and sisters. They were told, the same thing. Mostly my brother's. We father, each other, just the way our own father would do for us. My sister's, they did not only mother each other. But mostly, took care of us brothers. Just the way our own mother, would do for us. We are truly the image of our mother, and father.

Chapter 8
Why We Suffer

Natural Suffering

Fundamental, of natural suffering. We inherited from our first parents Adam, and Eve. In the book of Genesis. We read, when God created Adam, and Eve. Before evil tricked them, to eat from the forbid fruit tree. They were pure, and immaculate Genesis 3:1, 16.

They were able, to see God face, to face. They did not, feel any pain. they did not have, to work either. They did have a spiritual body, also. They were able live To the eternity. Forever with God and his angels, of course. Along, with their children and entire humanity. I mean their children, and great grandchildren until now, and beyond. They were, innocence and lived with Grace.

When Adam, and Eve sinned. They disobeyed God. It was a very hard, and unhappy experience of losing their innocence purity, and grace. Because they disobeyed God. He said to Eve You will suffer at conceptions. Genesis.

That being past, to every woman. But always good comes, out of bad things I mean joy, and happiness mother has. When, she have the baby. Especially becoming mother for the first time.

God said to Adam. Just because, he listened to his wife, and broke God's commandment, when he told him, not to eat from that tree. Genesis 3:17-20.

Adam will labor, to eat all the days, of his life. The herb of the earth. God told Adam, in the sweat of they face should eat bread. By the sweat of your brow you will eat your food, until you turn into the ground. Also God told Adam, cursed is, the ground, because of you.

Jesus said, to his disciple. If anyone, wishes to come after me let him deny himself, and take his cross and follow me. For he who, would save his life will lose it. But he who losses his life for my sake, will find it. Matthew 16:24-25.

Jesus is trying to say to us. I have done nothing wrong, and did no harm to anyone. I am innocent yet. I will put, my life down for you. So I can save you from evil sin. I will die for you. I will suffer for you.

Jesus also said we have, to be patient in life, and keep good faith. We were all born with free will.

From the time of Adam, and Eve. When they disobeyed God. They were cast out, of the garden of Eden. Genesis 3:23.

Because of, their free will. They chose to bring the suffering, upon them self- allowing, themselves to face the consequence. Of accepting the offer evil gave them They listened to the evil. They created their own suffering, and entire human being,as well.

A child is, born blind, deformed, or mentally affected. Life can also be racked by pain, because of a hopeless disease, that can only, end up in death. That what many suffer with.

God put the, sentence upon woman after, the disobedience. God loved human being. He for gave them. Therefore, he promised, he multiply them human being But because of the disobedience. God said to a woman I will greatly, multiply you, and your conception, with sorrow. You shall bring forth children. Genesis 3:16

To the man, God said. In the sweat of thy face shall eat bread till. You return, unto ground. For dust thou art, and unto dust shall thou return. (Genesis)

So death is, common to all human. It is natural everyone will die.

Jesus wants us, to be patient, and calm. To believe, keep up the faith, to carry on the burden of this life.

Jesus is, talking about the natural suffering. Which is, personal suffering Commonly everyone go, through in life. Cross is, the sign of the suffering Jesus endured on. See. New testament.

When we are, going through, whatever comes ahead of us in our lifetime. We out to follow Jesus. Showing him our loyalty, and love to him. Jesus also said, I will come to take you, to my father.

God himself involved,in suffering of men.

Because, he loved the world, out of his love, he gave us his only son to die for us John 3:16..

God allowed himself, to suffer too. Jesus was wholesomely innocent, untainted by sin of, any kind. Yet he voluntarily, laid down his life for entire humanity.

Jesus suffering, was injustice. But, he did it for our salvation. God gave his beloved son to suffer, on the cross. For the redemption, of all humanity New -testament.

So who are we to even wonder. Why we should suffer ? Jesus carried our suffering. He takes it, gladly. Because, he loves us.

We suffer, and mourn, when we watch, our loved ones die.

When Adam, and Eve disobey God. Genesis 3:1-6

God changed, everything. Every human person to be born with sin, and die Earth, and universe cause, effect, and the consequences of certain cause s are inescapable. Even, the earth is cerise. Because of Adam, and Eve. (Genesis).

We will have, all the disease, and germs, that destroy. Because, we were made from earth. We have the same D. N. A. Will always be, facts of our lives. What we go, through our lifetime.

We suffer, with our children work, and home or whatever. We suffer. In this life. These facts have, a moral implications. Responsible, beings with free will. To choose how we will act.

Because of Adam, and Eve first sin. They neglect, and misuse their life they end up corrupting the stream, of human life itself and left evil to fall. On succeeding generation, after generation.

God enforced, on human being, natural laws. Because of our free will, we face the consequences. It is not only facts of life. What human go through but so much personal suffering. That is, natural suffering.

Besides earth, was not perfect anymore. Because Adam, and Eve sinned God made the earth, go through climate change, earth quakes, and floods. We call this act of God. We have, no other explanation, for their occurrence. That's how God made Earth system. After first sin. Natural disaster Earth, will always have. Earth goes through changes throughout time.

More likely. When the evil got Adam, and Eve, to disobey God.

Because man made, out of Earth. Therefore, the Earth, and man are alike. Same D. N. A Is not only the evil had, the control of men. Also from then, on Evil took control the earth, as well.

Therefore, evil cost it, for all of us to suffer. Evil is not only against, earth but also, and against human being.

Suffering is, problem in life. Comes home, to everyone. Pain sometime hopeless disease. Can only end up in death.

Jesus said, whom loses his life, for my sake will find it Matthew 10:38

The way of the cross. Is sign of suffering. Jesus want us to follow. In his footsteps. In order for us to gain power. Over evil, and put him to shame.

God did not cause our suffering. But when we do suffer, we use it for purpose of salvation. Through Jesus.

When he endured, the suffering. See. Crucifixion. Mark 15: Mark 16;

When we discover God. We find, comfort in him. Jesus want every - one, of us to find faith, through suffering. So we can learn, how to be patience.

When we suffer, we are able to have self - discipline, trust. When we suffer. That is, when we experience, the love compassion. When we, receive all that love compassion With help from the ones around us. That's when we know, God he is with us.

When we, help someone. Who is, suffering we find significance amount of love in our own lives.

Suffering, is deep evil. Suffering is, the consequence. Through history, we faced God want us to be strong. With continuing prayer.

Job had strong faith in God. Very devout. Yet the evil want to test his faith. By bringing disaster to him When he lost everything even,his children, his wealth,all at the same time. Job 2:1-13

Even when evil striking him, with disease. Job still kept the faith. Because he knew. There is, no power above God and he is nothing without God. His wife tried, to make him feel bad, and weaken his faith. Job told her, don't be a fool. God always want. What is, best for us. Job did not sin, with all his ups, and down. Job was simple, and upright, and fearing God and avoiding evil. Job knew God is all powerful. He could not, do anything without God. Job kept, his faith.

God rewarded him,for having such strong faith.

God gave us assurance. He will eliminate our suffering, and give us comfort when we die. He fulfilled his promise with our savior. His only son, Jesus Christ.

Job said we cannot only, be happy, when we get the good thing from God But avoid worrying, about, the bad things. We only please, evil. When we, lose side of goodness.

When things go wrong, and begin to struggle. We begin to blame God. That is not fair More likely most, of the time something good. Comes out of bad. Look back into your life. You will find out, for yourself.

From the beginning, we allowed evil to take, control over us and entire earth Our first parents Adam and Eve, when God created them. He did not only gave them life but he gave them, everything they ever wanted. They were, able to have anything. They want, and needed, as long, as they followed, God will. God warned them to stay, away from the tree of knowledge of the good, and evil. But we read. They listened to evil and ate from, the forbidden tree (Genesis).

Evil tricked them, by making them believe. Their lives will be better without God.

Because, of their free will. They were able to disobeyed God.

Were cast out of Garden, of Eden. Genesis3:19-23

They themselves caused, their own suffering. It was their own choice.

We too, because of our own, free will, we cause some of our suffering.

The choices we make,and the situations, we run into Sometime harm come to us.

The evil one is, very powerful,and the evil forces attack us, and cause suffering In an attempt to attempt us. So we full apart from God, when we sin.

Evil test It job, in book of job. So he would hate God, and blame God. For his suffering.

When God create Adam, and Eve(Genesis) God intended for them, and us to have perfect bodies perfect health, and free from pain, and suffering.

The world God created, would being perfect just as. It was, before Adam and Eve, sinned. Evil took over from the time of, first sin.

God whenever he find it, good necessary and essential, to he give us the relief by miracles. God is able to change, and intervene, to change our destiny. By miracles.

God intervene. Whenever, something is not meant, to happen, to any of us (God). He come on emergency. Whenever there is crisis, like a tragic thing. If is not our time to die. God intervene. Always to stop it. And stop the evil one from making it happen. Many who being saved. From dangers. Because, God was there for rescue Just because was not the time, or end of someone's life.

Whenever someone survive a sickness, accident, or death. That is, God stopping it. When at, the mean time the evil trying to make, feels like. That's, the end of our lives. So we would lose, our hope in God. Just the way evil got Adam, and Eve to suffer. Evil one does so for the entire mankind.

In the bible old testament, in the book of job He trusted in God. With all his suffering. Job knew that God has control, and power over all, anyway. Job was a very good man; he was blessed in many things. He lost everything, he endured very terrible suffering.

We often question, ourselves why ?

Such faithful person, has to suffer. God has a mysterious power. Goes beyond human, understanding. Whenever, we are suffering. God is with us, to give us the strength to go on.

In Job's case, his suffering. Was not because, of the sin. It was the test, of any ones faith.

Evil put us, through test. Just like Job. Even when,he was angry with God, he did not lose his faith either abandon it, his faith in God.

Job was convinced. Even in his terrible suffering. God was there with him. That's what gave Job a reason.

To thank God. Jesus said simple. Word, believe! Mark 9:23

Whenever, we are in middle of suffering, or feeing confused. We need to put our trust in God. knowing, God is in control. He is, the light that shine God he has, unlimited power. He can, accomplish anything that we want.

Suffering is, the consequence of human sin. Is not caused by God. We have moral responsibility. God so loved the world. There for, God has not abandoned the world, eternally to suffer, the consequences, of sin.

God gives us assurance. He will, eliminate our sin, and give us comfort.

When he gave us his son Jesus to endure, the suffering, on the Cross - for our suffering in sin. Mark 16:

Complete avoid once, suffering is not an option, for any of us. Our option is to waste our experience of realizing. God's purposes in the middle of suffering Through suffering, we can learn patience self-discipline trust, and many other virtue.

When we, suffer we can experience, the love compassion, and self - denial of those who help us. When helping someone, who is suffering. We find significance amount of love in our own lives, as well.

So much more, natural suffering. Suffering can also be direct. Just consequence of our own actions.

Natural suffering, in losses some loved one to the death loneliness, as human being. We all have a moral conscience.

Even corrupted, by sin, and often ignored our conscience should not rejoice in sin, suffering, and death. We all face. Hebrews 12:2

For the creation waits, with eager longing, for the revealing of the son of God expectation are not worth, comparing with the glory that will be revealed in us. Romans 8:19.

God revealed to us, suffering, in this sinful life is not without remedy. The only reasonable, response we have in suffering. That God's promise, us eternity

Jesus said, Blessed are those who mourn, for they will be comforted Blessed are, the merciful for they will be shown mercy. Blessed are those, who are persecuted because of righteousness, for there is the kingdom of heaven. Matthew 5:3-10.

So much suffering in our lives, we face. Because of our free will, and choices. We often put ourselves in situations. We might get hurt, or cause harm to others. It's not, fair of us to say. God caused that. It is our own free will. We chose, to place ourselves in these type of harems ways. They are the result of our own actions.

We must take the responsibility.

Miracles are emergency. God loves us, and wants the best for us. God is with us in the most troubling, and painful times. He never, leaves us alone.

If we continue, calling out for his help. He will come, for our rescue, and aid. Throughout history. So many miraculous, events attributed to God. He gave us signs of his love. Whenever we, are in the most difficult time. If we have, bad situations in our own lives. God give us love, and assistance.

God give us knowledge, how to handle. The worse, and difficult situations That come ahead of us.

As long as, there is evil will cause us to sin, and the reason we sin.

Nothing will be ever, so normal We are always going to struggle.

All books, of bibles warn us. To be aware of evil one. Also being revealed us How much God loves us, and wants only what's best for us.

God's alternative, goal for human being. One day is to be with him in heaven Just the way it was at the time of Adam, and Eve. Before they sin.

Sometime pain and suffering cause, to us with no fault, of our own, like car accident. When God created us, and gave us free will. We are, blameless. That we. bear the consequences, of the gift of free will. God give it, to all people.

God did not restrict. Free will of others, and only gave it to some. But to all of us.

Natural suffering is all the personal human tragedy. These are, more likely everyone get sick physically, and internally. These are, problems we dread. Disease and much more is bound to happen. Sometime, in our life time.

After all God never leaves us alone. We have the knowledge, God give, us to make medicine. It ease our pain, and heal us in many cases.

Still some things will come,through until the end of time.

Suffering from flood, natural fire there a lot facts of life earth quakes, disasters and natural calamities. Famines, and floods are called act of God.

Usually there, is no explanation. For their occurrence. They are, natural acts. This is, the way God made Earth.

Germs that, gives us diseases, and destroy,many by death. Germs are part of earth.

Therefore, they are part of our body. Actually we have all, the diseases in our body. Some they react in our lifetime. Or some time don't. Some may be hereditary Weakness of body.

God said to Adam that. Earth will, be cursed Just the same way that Adam and Eve were cursed by God. Genesis 3:17.

Both the Earth, and Adam, and Eve, were not perfect no more. After, the sin. I can imagine. How perfect the earth, would being. If our first parents did not sin.

Everything surrounding us, would being perfect; The heaven, Itself would being the earth. Moon, sun,and all the stars. It would being, paradise.

Human being, would being able, to live to the eternity with God, and his angels Only if they had not sin.

The earth was not going to have, no floods, no earthquakes, no disasters or change of climates.

People would, still multiply. Because that's what God said. When he created Adam and Eve. Genesis.

They also, would not become sick ever. If Adam, and Eve did not sin. We could see them today and all humanity. Would have being alive today living life, like angels.

All humans, could of produce, and multiply, forever or as much as God allowed us to.

God is love. 1 John 4:8.

He will not cause any of our suffering. Evil is to blame, not God. Evil one is responsible for the pain and problems.

To God the, most important, for him is our souls to gain one day. Healing, our spirit is God's main goal. Because, our spirit is God's main goal. Our spirit will live in heaven. With him to the eternity.

When we see, others suffering, God transform, our suffering into grace.

Beatitudes in sermon, on the mount Jesus said Blessed, are you suffer persecution for justice sake for their is, the kingdom of Heaven. Also who suffer through their life. Matthew 5:9

God will reward us at the end.

Most of people who suffer. First they, seek Gods help. Because,they know. God made everything.

God created Adam, and Eve perfect, and the Earth for them to enjoy as paradise

God literally gave, them everything, under the sun, the moon, and the stars.

Because, of their sin they lost it all. But God still, gave them a chance, and the entire humanity.

Especially, Christians around the world. If any of us complain. We will be very un great full, and selfish, because God so loved, the world he gave his only son John 3:16

Jesus was innocent yet. He laid, his life down for the entire humanity. So we can conquer overcome evil. Jesus suffer, injustice, cruelty, for the sake of humanity

God did not need, to do that. But he chose, to come down on earth, to live among us. To reveal himself. Through our lord Jesus. So we can feel him.

He brought the heaven, with him, to draw the entire world to himself. God shared, into our suffering, he made himself visible.

Natural suffering, it is for greater good of all humanity. If we look once, at the cross. That Jesus suffered, and he was crucified.

So many, who claimed that. When if you are good. You suffer more. They do say the magic word. If they just, can analyze. For themselves.

That they are only suffering, in the way that Jesus suffer, to concord, the evil By walking, with Jesus to the cross. Only Jesus did it, without sin. But our sin Is great.

In the passion, until death of Jesus. Jesus endured all that suffering. He shed blood. Jesus did all that for us. He is all about us. He want us, to be like him.100%

Jesus did not, even think, of himself. But thought of all human race, to be saved from evil through, his passion until his death he thought only of us. John 11:1-18.

Being in agony, in the garden. Jesus prayed with, all the sorrowful passion. He ask his disciples to pray. So they do not enter into temptation. Luke 22:44

That same thing,goes for us. We need, to keep praying. Especially, in our, most difficult times.

Jesus never gave up for us. He was arrested after he was betrayed, by Judas. Jesus was denied by Peter his disciples. Jesus just like a criminal, he was taken. Mark 14:43-52

Just like they say, everyone has, a certain calling from God, we are all for a reason. God went us all, this is our calling. To choose him.

Sometime, people say. Why the good suffer more, than others. Because the good, are walking with Jesus, and his passion, he endured.

The good suffer more. Because. the closer you get, to God the more the evil will try, to interfere with our life and try to make us fall into temptation.

Our life, is all kinds of trials, will eventually, bring us Into heaven. Our God is the one, whom comfort us. When we are in, the most depths of our sorrow.

Are you afraid of dying ? So many, especially Christians, are afraid of dying Some who had nightmares. But the ones who truly believe in Christ, Jesus Christ said, if we do,what he commands to do according. We will be saved.

If we live life of Grace. will be transferred from this life to the next in.

But as Christ raise from the dead the first, of those who have fallen asleep will take us to his father.1 Corinthians 15:19-20.

Therefore, death is like a bridge. We cross from this material life, to the spiritual life. With his life only in view. We have hope in Christ.

Job predicting saying. I know that my redeemer is alive, and in the last day. I shall rise out of the Earth spirit, and flesh will joined together. And I shall be clothed again with my skin, and in my flesh, I shall see my God. Job 19:20.25

And it came to pass while, they were, wondering what to make, of this that behold. Two men stood by them in dazzling raiment, and when the woman we struck with fur, and bowed their faces to the ground. They said, to them why do you seek, the living one among dead ? Lukc 24:4

Jesus was not, in the tomb. Because, he was risen. We will rise, with Jesus one day. Also, it was written that son of man must be betrayed into hand of sinful men, and be crucified, and on the third day, he rose. Luke 24:7

Jesus came here, on earth also, for people conversion of hearts, to win over those who, do evil things.

But when, this mortal body puts, on immortality, then shall come to pass the word that is written. Death is, swallowed up in victory. 1Corinthians 15:16-17,54

Paul said, Christ suffer, die for our sin, and rise again, for our salvation Because Jesus Christ, was risen. Therefore, all the dead will rise, by the power of the holy spirit.

If Jesus Christ, did not die, for our sins. We could not, have the chance. Christ took our sins. On himself, by dying on the cross.

God bless, who mourn for sake of the truth. He said they shall be comforted Matthew 5:5.

Suffering with faith. It is glorifying God, here on earth. It said come to me all that, who mourn, you find comfort.

Wide Gate, if we have easy life. Especially if we spend our life enjoying this world without Faith. Living sinful life. Matthew 7:13.

It is like getting into, a wide gate. That will lead us into darkness That is, when We live fast, and sinful life. But the narrow gate is life itself. All the suffering we endure in this life, struggling of all kind. We expect it lots of faith. Narrow gate is all the hard time. We face here on earth. We will, get into real life with God.

He will welcome us, with open, arms at the end. God will take all our suffering struggling, sorrow. What we endure in this life.

God will turn all the bad things happening to us,in this life. Into everlasting joy and happiness. Only if we take, and endure all that happening, in this life to us.

With Faith, and patience. Always have pride In God.

Moral person, being morally. Should unconditionally, be considered, thoughtful. Out of this world, goodness.

Chapter 9

Un Natural Suffering

Natural suffering. It mean things that happen. Naturally. To everyone. For instant, personal suffering everyone have Sickness, diseases, and things majority, and most of the people have in common.

Un-natural suffering is. What some people, cost it to happen to others, like abuse murdering. Especially someone, who's innocent. Stealing, from someone else. All kind of greed taking someone else belongings. Taking advantage of someone else an- awful ways.

People get hurt, because of others fault. All the above, and much more. It is un- natural suffering. People don't need, to suffer off someone else hand. Everyone, has enough natural suffering.

First crime, of the history.

When, Cain killed, his brother Abel, When God ask him where, his brother is?. Genesis 4:8-9

He said, he did not know, and he was not, his brother keeper. God cursed Cain, upon earth. God had, compassion toward Cain. God put mark on Cain. Anyone to see him, not to kill him. That was first murder, and crime of history. Abel did not ask, to be Murdered He became a victim. He had all of his life, ahead of him. It was taken away, in seconds How is it, any fair ? Cain tried to lie. Not knowing, God see everything.

If killers were in right mind, they would know. They will, get caught any way, or get murdered too.

Same old story, we hear people saying. What am I my brother keeper ? It is so rewarding many have faith in God, they pray. and go church. They say, they love God Often talks highly brag. How faithful, they are. At the meantime. Not understanding, concept of their faith very much, or often. Many, who refuse to do, for others, or don't make enough time. To look around, them self. To see what needs, to be done. For the less fortunate. Even if, they were strangers. Knowing others are, Gods children, as well.

Many, who believe in God. But they are, not too sure. Because, they are good colt and good colt. Only having mercy on each other. Within, their circle and no one else. God he is a spirit. No one, can see God. But If we begin to have mercy, on everyone no matter who they are what they are, or were they come from. We will truly feel God present. Try it.

God demand of us. To take care, all of his children. What will, please God is. If we are charitable, merciful, and show compassion. Mercy gives relief, for many. Beside unlimited, and unconditionally, goodness. Will glorify God. If we do good, where evil can, or could fit.

Many of people, who think, they have strong faith in God. They are, doing very well pleasing him. They really think, in their mind. They are, doing so well for their spiritual being. At the meantime. Many who add, one magic word saying, in selfish way. If am doing, so well for myself Others, is their problems.

There are, so many among us, capable of doing something. To help. But they choose, not to. There are, so many as long, as they make a living. They just don't care what, might happen to everybody else. Many, of those people. They are, willing help someone. Who, is rich like them. Who is, capable of paying them back. At the meantime. They think. They're, doing great deed toward God.

God made us, our brother's keeper. God command us, to take, anyone who need help Even, if we have to take by hand. If we have to take them to the end. In order to do what take to help.

In fact Jesus did not even thought of himself hardly. He thought, of us always. Jesus never stop loving us. Even If we sin. He take it, on himself. He died, so he could wipe sins of the world. Jesus Christ, himself, for gave. The ones who crucified him. Luke 23:34

Do not be deceived, God cannot be mocked. Galatians 6:7.

Pure at heart, people. They are, the ones who always do. What is right, for them self and others. They never deceive any one, ever. Always speaks the truth. Strong, in faith always Honest, and forward. He or she treat everyone fair, and equal. Faith is never to cheat, or deceive anyone.

Jesus said, about rich man. Lazarus, and Abraham. The rich man lived fast, and sin full life, and the poor man Lazarus who lay at his gate. Luke 16:23.

When poor man, Lazarus died. Angels, put him in Abraham bosom. When the rich, died he was tormented, in the flame of hell. rich man looked up, and saw Lazarus. The rich man asked Abraham. If he can send Lazarus, to his family, to warn them what will, become of them, if do not change their life. But Abraham told the rich man. They have Moses, and the prophets. They need to listen, to the living, for sure they would, not believe the dead, come back Rich man, was never great full to God. He did not humble himself. Instead, he lived life of fun, lust, and temptations. He done a lot, for his earthly body. But nothing, to in rich his spirit.

The poor man, he was homeless. Yet he was humble, and kept the faith along. With the suffering, he endured. He was rewarded. When the rich man, knew how much he was suffering After life. He knew, it was too late for himself. He want to see if he can try to save, his family So they do not end up like him.

If everyone, in the world read, sacred scripture. Will learn, and understand in the, most profound way. People who come to the knowledge. They are. inspired by word of God. His spirit will never depart them. The holy spirit, will become their 100% guidance.

We learn how to live, and know right from wrong. From holy sacred scriptures. We get deeper knowledge, of the truth. Bible give us insurance, and hope in God. Because, of the Bible we are able to put our full trust in God. We also learn, we are truly his children.

God is, very concern,about all of us. Through old testament. God predicted, and prepared his coming for our salvation. In the New testament.

Jesus Christ, he is our savior. Our salvation, it is only through. He is truly heart, of God He is, the God who heal us, feed us, forgive us. He took our sins, up on self.

He was crucified, to pay for our sins. Mark 16:

Jesus Christ, will also lift us up. With him, to heaven Jesus forgave all the ones, who crucified him, and tortured him. Christ he never think of, himself first. He'd always think of us first He wants us, to have like his, mind, heart, and soul. So his spirit to live among us, into all of us hearts, and mind.

It is very bad. Many people are, a shame to read the bible because they don't want to know, if they are, doing wrong. So they can continue doing wrong, without feeling, any guilt Those are, the ones who don't acknowledge sin.

In the new testament. We see Glory of God.

Jesus forgiveness, it is unconditional. Therefore, he would want us to do. Same thing for each other. That is, unconditionally, forgiving each other. It is impossible to know God. Without knowing Jesus 'first.

We all sin, and make mistake. Repenting, means promising God. We will not do that again. But, we can only try our best. God knows that.

Therefore, God did not give himself, other choice but to forgive us. Because he often say to himself. They are, human being. What do I expect.

If we all acknowledge God, and become devoted, to him in every way, we will succeed

I mean like trying, to live life of virtue, love, peace, grace mercy, and goodness. To do all that toward God. Because, he is good. Therefore, all the goodness go to him.

Without charity, and forgiving others unconditionally. We could, never please God.

Jesus through his teaching he expressed, and pointed Gods passion, for the oppressed hungry, widows, orphans, and the poor. If we don't care for them. Will be like, turning our back to, Jesus himself. Jesus Christ, take it personally.

At the judgment, of all nation. Jesus Christ, the king will says to the righteous, answering I say to you, whatever you did for one, of these least of my brothers of mine, you did for me Matthew 24:40.

At the end. When, we die. There is, a chance, we might suffer, the consequences. I can imagine. Before entering the gate of heaven. We will be reminded. How, we did not do enough or nothing, at all charity, unconditionally forgiving, take care of sick, the poor, the lonely, the depressed. Did not matter. If they were our relatives, neighbors, or strangers. We did not reach, to each other for the glory of God. We are human being, and are all short of something.

If you, and I think. We are, better persons. Than others, I mean thoughtful, considered compassioned, helpful, and honest. We are not suppose, to judge anyone. But we are, able to help, and teach others, to be like us.

The main, reason is God give us guarantee, to be able to help anyone. Because we were all born, with mercy of, God into our hearts. As much, as we give mercy. The more mercy we received, from others. The more, mercy comes, out of our hearts.

Many, who always do bad things. They, feel locked. With then, themselves. They just don't know, how to quit stop, or get out. The only things they how to do is bad. I believe they do feel, the agony, they endure. Or guilt because, they just don't know how to get out Often they wish, If they can learn how to stop. We need, to reach to them, to teach them To encourage them,and giving them a chance. To become better citizens, giving them hope Will be rewarding.

Without faith in one God, people began, to believe in many Gods. Especially, material of around this world becomes their God. Not thinking about paying. More attention to society, all around them. May be they try to do something about it to fix what is being broken.

To make it better, safer, peaceful merci full, compassionate society. For themselves, and their children.

If everyone have a job, to make a good living. Why would, anyone steal, or cheat anyone? There is, so many poor people. Have moral values humble, pure, honest, with a strong faith. They only want to make a living. To provide, for their families.

We are so connect it, to each other. If someone. Do one good thing can benefit many If someone do one, bad thing, could hurt many. Also if someone, declined financially so many could get effected. So many get off work. When company slow down or go out of business.

Because love, of the money, and greed. Makes people, blind from doing enough for them self, and others. They hurt them self, and others around them. They, feel it when it is too late.

Many companies. When they were, making millions. When they saw Changing, or decline in neighborhood. They could easy stay. Remain making their millions, they were making The way, they could done it. When they knew. Their neighborhood declination. If they were to invest, into the neighborhood, to keep it strong, and going. How much good, anyone could do ?. Without, having too many people around. If anyone go in some major cities will see so many closed down, abandoned, and vacant buildings. Many, of those buildings were successful, doing good company. They were, wholesales, manufacture, and stores. Some of those companies, were relocate somewhere else. Or may be out of the country regardless.

We end up, importing more goods, then exporting. We can make everything here in U S A The more company closed down. The less opportunity, people going to have. We lost many jobs were did not,require. Much education, to do the job, or work.

Most of, these company, was very convenient for workers. Especially, when it was in walking distant.

So many people. Who lost those jobs are too old to go to school, or have the chance Like younger generations have. 100% chance. Many people cannot make time to go to school. What need is a job so they can live. Many, has children.

It is very bad those companies did not invest, in neighborhood. Would being, the keys to success.

People need, to unite together. In order to succeed. Because, hardly anyone can do it alone. Without, help of others.

We need to set, all our differences a site, and help each other. To make a decent living There is, so much we can, get from earth. Should be enough, for every single person living. On face of our planet earth.

Things always go up, and down. America, will always remain, land of the opportunity It is, up to the people to make that possible. We can go, to church all we want. Thinking that is, one best way, we please God. Even if we help others become full of faith. We will only please God, in some ways. But God want us to look, at bigger picture. Which is, the people around us. God wants us to be our brother' s keeper. The way, we reveal God to others. The way, we treat them.

Jesus speaking of faith, explaining the way we increase it. By putting it to work. Not keep it, for ourselves. But to share it with everyone.

Faith it is not privet,Jesus parable, of three servants. Their master, gave five talents, to first. To second one gave two. The third gave one. He want it them, to put it, to work to see, how well each of them, can do. Matthew 25:14-25.

God give faith to everyone, according, to our ability. We increase our faith. By reaching, to everyone, Unconditionally. Our faith will multiply. When we, reach others, in need, and give hope to the less fortunate. Charity, mercy. If we have faith, knowledge, and wisdom. We must teach others Also to reach the misfortune in order for us, to please God.

Compassion, mercy. Will bring relief, and will enrich our Spirit. God called us, to be spiritual Not materialistic. God he is not, about money.

We need to pay attention, and focus, on all the terrible, things are happening around us. We need to stop hunger, starvation, abuse, killing wars. There's, so much need be done About, hate, lust, anger, abuse, greed.

If we truly, believe in God. We need show our loyalty. That is, doing something. About all the above. That what will,please God.

When we sin we are, asking for evils rewards. What kind of the rewards evil gives ? Very terrible, and a lot of suffering. When we, do good things. We're asking, for Gods rewards They will be great, and out of this world.

Spiritual= spirit that what God is. A lot these days believe, in many Gods, and not the one God. Who create them. Their number one God, is the money. If they only know material of this world, would stay behind.

Many who use Gods words, for their own evil purposes.

When Simon Saw that. The holy spirit was given. When the apostles placed their hands up on people heads. Acts 8:18.

He offered money, to buy this power. So the apostles, can let him have the power, of the holy spirit. Simon exclaim. So that when, I lay my hands on people. They, will receive the holy spirit. But Peter replied, may your money perish with you, for thinking, God's gift, can be bought. Peter told Simon, can have no part in this, for your heart is not, right. Before God Peter knew Simon was wicked. Peter told him, pray to the lord, perhaps. He will forgives your evil thoughts. Pray for me, Simon exclaimed. That these, terrible things won't happen to me There's, no mention, in the book of acts. If Simon ever received the holy spirit.

This Simon he was a magician practice magic. He made money, doing that. He figured he could make more. If he has, the power. The apostles had.

God is light of the world, that shine on everyone. For free of charge. Holy spirit comes upon, the ones who seeking him. With all their heart, and soul. Especially the pure, meek.

Christians are called, to have mind, of Jesus Christ. Believing in God, and having a strong faith, without action. Does not reach God. We are, being called into special way. To become children of the holy spirit.

There is so much, natural suffering, like disease illness growing old, and dying. There's a lot, more unnatural suffering. Others faults, or our own faults.

Once upon time, I had out of state automobile insurance. Every year I had to renew the policy. One of the year's the price doubled. Before, I paid for the coverage I immediately called my agent, to find out why. I told the agent, I did not have had, any violations accidents I figured that will be, the reason why, my insurance doubled. But the agent, said to me, the reason your insurance went up. Because, they were many claims in Michigan. Anyway later. I found different insurance, and switched to, and paid less.

At the meantime, I was the victim, and many more people who were victims. Because of other people's fault, like accidents, and other violations. Many like me, were affected.

Stores, and company close down, because of theft. Sometime their own workers, or public. In the event. One of the stores close down. Al l the workers, lose their jobs. Those workers were making a living, out of that job. They supported their families, pay their bills

Some lose their homes, cars belongings. Many times financial hardship, they face. Some people, end up in divorce. Things always full apart.

The Key to success in any business. For the workers, to treat it. Like their own Unfortunately, some are deceived, by not thinking. Their work could be, their future, and bright one.

When people become greedy, and Steal from their work. They are, hurting themselves and others.

People who steal. They are, facing the consequences. Many don't care, as long, as they are making the extra money for time being. They don't think, they might be hurting themselves and others. In the long run.

I can only imagine. When prices go up. It could very well happen. Some stores, would very well add, extra percent. Because of the theft. The profit,they lose. In process they want to gain that back.

There is, a local car dealer ship, next door to, the family business. One morning I happened to be, at family business. First customer came in give us, the sad news. About next door. Dealer was broken in, the night before. Most of the cars were vandalized. I immediately told the customer. It is crying shame, what people do. I added, they will more likely want, to gain more profit to make up for Lose. Maybe by raising prices, of the cars. Therefore, people who done that evil act. May be their friend, relative, neighbor, may be buying car, from that dealer. They may, end up paying higher prices. The dealer have to make up somehow for their lost. That customer agreed with me. Maybe I taught him something.

There are, so many. Take good care, of each other feed, clothes they give each other They can afford, to do that all the time. Only because, they care about each other. They think they are doing something amazing, toward God. Yes it is good, because God is love. Where is love. That were God is. But what will please God more. To do, for the ones. Who is, not able to do for us in return. That is, doing good favor to God. Our rewards will be bigger.

Rules of charity. Jesus spoke of charity. He said if we love those who love us. We only please each other, and if we lend to those, from whom you hope to receive, can return. What favor we're doing for God. Luke 6:27:27-35

Jesus said. Even sinners lend to Sinners. They may, get back, as much in return Jesus said do for the ones who can never do for you. let God reward you. Jesus said love your enemies. Luke 6:27-36.

Jesus said. Don't hope for a return, and your rewards will be big,and you shall be great in heaven.

Jesus said you shall be, children of the most high. God is kind to the wicked, and un great full.

He wants us, to be like him. To show his mercy to others. Whenever, we repent God takes, and except us. Like champions, and heroes. Especially when we over com temptations.

God weep for us. Jesus wept, for the sinners. John 11:35.

Hoping to return to him. Because with him, we don't suffer, no more. God know, how much harm, evil can do to us. When, we live in sin. We are, being controlled by evil.

Just as our earthly father love us, and give us everything. So do God. And always take us back always.

The prodigal, son Jesus spoke of. Man who had two sons. Luke 15:11-32.

The younger said to his father. He want his share. He went away spend his money on pleasure, until he run out at the end. He could not have anything to eat. He want it to go back. But he were not sure if his father would take him back. But returning home his father. Notice his son was coming back. He was full of happiness. When his father saw him, was moved with compassion ran, and fell upon his neck, and kissed him, and welcome him home. His older son, did not like that. His father, explained saying your brother was, lost and found. But you are always by me.

When we live in sin, and repent our heavenly father. Except us with open arms, every time, we go back to him. The faithful, he always has next to him. Therefore, he often call sinners.

Un natural suffering. We cause to our self. Or others who give us the pain, agony, and suffering. It is not our fault. Just, can't blame God. For whatever we do we are facing the consequences.

We also sin because, freedom of will. God give us, to choice. Which road to take. Freedom of will, might be restrict from some. But likewise, God gave it to entire men kind. It is our choice.

We need to, bring God, into our hearts mind, and souls. God he is, pure spirit, he in every, and each of us. It depend on us, the way we love, care, and forgive. Evil always enjoy watching us. Hurting each other Also he celebrate our suffering. He has control over so many. Evil always try to stop. What God had accomplish into us human being.

All the horrible crimes, murdering the unborn. When we, know from the moment, of conception, the fetus has heart, and soul. That is, life God given to become image of God Every baby, in the beginning, in mother's womb. In the heart that is where spirit of God reside. Soul gives life to every unborn child. After the brain, get develop. The blood that flow, in the vain goes to the heart.

God makes his temple. God takes spirit of parents spirit, and give them children, to their image, and likeness they all become image of God in spirit. Genesis 1:27.

From the moment of conception, God he is, at the creation once again. Our first priority, should be, to do everything in our power. To save, and stop murdering the unborn Those babies, they will never have a chance to live. They could have been some Important people. The ones who are pro- choice, may be, or can be. Because, everyone have the freedom. But are we going, to give choice to the unborn. When at the meantime, they are, innocent victims, and innocence. Can the unborn choose whether they want to be born or not. We have, to make this choice for them. (unborn).

Mothers who, aboard their babies. They end up suffering the consequences. Most of the time they live with guilt, shame, and pain. Having, hard time forgiving themselves even If they only know, God did forgive them.

Evil forces attack, humanity. Causing all kind of suffering. People continue hating, and blaming God.

Evil loves divorce. So he can, take the happiness away, from people. Evil love to see children. Becoming victims, with heartbroken. Beside, people around them, and close to them get hurt too. Especially, the ones who shared, their love.

Evil love to put us, into temptation. Lust drive, people to commit adultery. Evil hate what good, and hate stable families. We need to work, to put, and to keep our families together. We also need to, bring social justice to the family's. Our dignity, pride. Should be our family's. We need to learn the meaning, of the family values. We need, to build our homes on the rock, and not on the sand.

My main purpose of writing the book. Especially, this chapter. Because so, many people don't, have the one to lean on.

If you, or I think, we are good person's. People around us, sense that. Whenever good people go down. Helps always is on the way. Just need to find it. Whenever they struggle they get the help they need it.

God favored poor people. Because, lots of them, are simple, and pure. All they do make honest living.

It is very bad, and crying shame, the rich always helps the rich get richer. Some rich use the poor, and makes sure. The poor remain poor. So they continued to use, the poor. For the rich, help the rich get richer. This kind of natural. Because, the rich has the power to do so. Unfortunately, if the majority of people becomes poor, and minority are rich. The rich will not have many, or hardly any people, to trade with them. Eventually, will shut down maybe a chance, they also lose everything they own also.

Sometime we can be fools, and deceived. Thinking, only of our selves. When, at the mean time. We are, hurting our self's.

Love of the money, and greed. Makes people blind. From doing enough for themselves and people around them.

Many people, are starving for attention hoping, for a miracle. Mercy, and peace into our world today. Peace bring comfort, to our minds. But mercy give us relieve.

Our world today is, so much in need of mercy. All the bad, and horrible things, are getting close, to our doors steps. There is, so much needed, to be done. So much, hate, wars abuse killing greed starvation = hunger.

We are, becoming so busy. We don't, even make time to think of our self, and others Especially, our loved ones. It is not fair. There are, so many people in all world today. Especially the faithful, who claim, they have faith in God. They can, and have enough money to build company manufacturers. So they can create jobs, for the poor. So they can live. The rich will get richer. Making more money, and benefit themselves too. Having, everyone the job, will lead to healthy environment.

There are, unfortunate ones, become homeless. Also some being tortured by suffering They need, all the help. They can get.

Many, who want to have power. Over power less. Just like death being imposed, on the helpless. But millions, by mistakes. The distraction of un necessarily. Modern wars, losing Countless, innocent lives. Also the biggest acts of evil Is terrorism.

Brutality, and hijacking trying, to crash airplanes. So many innocent, become victims of these crimes.

Also human ears, that lead to destruction. Because, of the greed cost oil rig to blow Unsafe work, can become very dangerous. Drinking, and driving cost so much death. That does not have, to happen. People can stop drinking, and driving easily. Also accidents, brings casualties Always people should, only die naturally.

We need to, show the devil, we are not made, to listen to him.

We also need to take, everything back to ourselves. It is possible to do away with evil Believe me, God does not will not punish anyone. Who please him.

Jesus said "Let not your hearts be troubled, believe in God, believe also in me. John 14:1-2 God goal is to reward us, with good things. God always welcome us with open arms.

Jesus Christ wishes are to unfold evil off, face of earth, and replace it, with good.

Jesus Christ brought the good news, from heaven. He taught us how to concord, and over com evil with good.

Jesus Christ said, he want to bring us, to the father and said there are, too many rooms in his father's house John 14:23

Faith is always speaking, the truth, acting in good manners. We should never tolerate suffering. Especially, the people around us. Because, it could easily, get to us.

It is very actively done to many people. When they take advantage of one person Then move, to another person so on, and on. Like there's, no end to it. Needed to, be stopped Many continue to endure. So much suffering. Because of others, trying to control their life's.

It will be ethical, morale, and humane to protect anyone. Who is being hurt in any way, or for any reason.

A typical human being, with the faith. Should do something. Also if we believe, we have strong faith. We must, put it to practice.

Christian around the world. They should, have mind of Christ. Because he is the truth. Through, Jesus Christ. We have, our salvation.

So many who sin, and don't know, they are doing that. We learn what is wrong, or right from the 10 commandments. (Exodus).

We ask Jesus Christ, to give us the grace. So we can understand, and overcome the temptation.

If we all give our hearts, to Jesus Christ will not please him, as much. But, what will please, Jesus Christ 100%. If we become, like him. Throughout, our life. He want us, to be him. So he can dwell. Into our hearts, to live with his spirit and to do. What, he command us. Which is, to love each other unconditionally.

Our Lord Jesus Christ, did not even owned a home. He wanted to always focus on us, help us to enrich our spirits. He said, God always know what we need. Be more concern what will be. In to the next world.

Jesus said, son of man has nowhere, to lay his head. Matthew 8:19-22.

Christ said, he didn't even own something, to lay his head on. And here we are, only worried about, this material of this world. Even if we suffer,and get hurt because of it. If we have lots money, we don't take it with us. When we die. Even If we, leave it for our kids. We don't even know. If they can keep it, Or will.

Jesus spoke of forgiving, and how rewarding it is. He was asked. How often we should forgive our brother ?. Or whoever, might be sinning against us.

He did not give us, any choice. He said, unconditionally Matthew 18:22

That is, if we want to be, Gods children. Children always belong to their fathers Our Lord Jesus Christ. Know. If someone, sin against us, or hurt us, in any way. More likely, they make peace with God. If we remain angry at them. We remain, without peace with God.

If we ever, go to church, we received spirit of Jesus Christ into our hearts. Also flesh blood divinity of our savior. We try very, hard to keep it this way.

Christ always, spoke the truth. Even when he knew was going get in trouble. I mean before the crucifixion. Mark 14:43-52 He was, thinking of us.

People don't understand. Concept of family value. Families, are falling apart. If you truly want, to be happy. Nothing in this world should come. Before, your relatives friends Your neighbors, or even. Stranger. Whenever, we feel related, to anyone, we meet instantly feel secure, and free. Family, should be one big circle, to include friends. Every, so often someone comes out, of the circle. To extend to bring more people into circle, to spread love, and charity.

My sister, told me once. If you need something ? You should only, go to a family Because, if you go to a stranger, or anyone. Who is, not the family. They, will be putting your family to shame. Thinking, your family don't care about you.

How often, we ask our self. Why people have, to steal, to make a living ? Or why people hurt others ? Just to gain something don't belong to them. Why people have to starve ? When there's, so much food, be thrown away every day. There is, some people, who wish if they can have that food.

If we truly believe in God, and love him? is to prove it. We make sure, no one go hungry and without job. There is many, who have relatives brothers, sisters, and friends. Still they have to depend on charity foundation. When at the meantime, charity foundation. Should be for emergency We need, to let them have more time to provide, for the needy.

People who can afford, to build company, factories, office buildings manufacture. They can help others working. They, will eventually make more profit also. Help everyone else becoming successful.

They are, around the world, talking millions, billions and trillions. If they can invest some into neighborhood, and cities. Building jobs for people. They can, double their money eventually. We are, importing so much from other countries. Can you imagine. If we can make most of it here, in our country. How many more jobs, we can create ?. We let other countries import from us.

True faith is, whenever, we hear cries, or see suffering of others. To be moral enough. Is to become outrage, and run to rescue the sufferer.

God create it us, to enjoy a perfect, good, loving happy fellowship with him forever God he is glorified,over and over again. Because of, the goodness. We have, for others. When people are, humbled. Because of us. That is, when they see, and feel God. We are made of his image. (Genesis). God want us to live with him forever.

God want us to live happy here on earth. Overcome, evil with good Hoping evil will vanish someday.

When it comes to God, and evil.

There is, no competition. No comparison. What is, good goes always to God. What is bad goes to evil.

It is our choice, which road to take, or how much we gain. Or how much we lose. Is it worth it ?. Evil admire suffering, because. He is suffering in hell.

We heard of seven deadly sins, are you frighten ?. How much ?. When we sin, we give evil the authority, over our lives. Evil putting, sentence on us When, we sin.

When we, become greedy all we do hurt our self, and the people around us. The more people, lose their jobs. The more things goes up, in price. Because, everyone business go down, of course less profit. How else, they will make up for the profit. If they don't raise the price.

Many people, are losing their homes they needed places, to rent. Therefore, owners of the rental are taking advantages. By raising, the rent. Even, the faithful among them do that Thinking it is only business, and part of life. Not feeling, compassion toward people.

Feeling guilty, something we cause it to our self. Anyone, whoever claim to have the faith should have good conscience as well. Good, and faithful person. If he, or she makes a mistake or offended anyone. Should go, and apologize, and make up.

Sometime, we get confused. When, we know everything is with possible God. Pleasing everyone. It is the door to success.

Trusting in God, will lead us, to the right path.

One of the reasons we must care, about each other. Just look at people's life. You will see yourself. If we only take a look. Figure of speech, we are all, in same boat.

We all somehow suffer, and struggle. We all go, through good times and bad times. People don't realize that. Because, they are so busy. Thinking, of themselves only.

Now more than ever,many people are very selfish All they are doing, is hurting themselves Self- centers, and selfish they. Act like they're, saying all for me, all about me. Only me. This is a selfish person for you.

God he gives, unconditionally love. He is good, loving and merciful. Therefore, he want us, to try, to be good 24/7 not 23 hours 59 seconds.

Becoming spiritual, takes a lot of work. Reaching people. Especially, the misfortune Living life, of virtue, grace, mercy. Purity, humbleness, and goodness.

Evil always waiting, to squeeze himself, into our life. Also evil always try, to pull apart What God put together.

To avoid having, any problems, in your life. Give everyone, their place. Give everyone the honor,and respect. Just the way you want, to be done to you.

What would possibly, go wrong. If put your love in right places. Always, were it belong There's always people in your life's. You have no choice, but to get attached to. Because they become part, of your daily life, as well, as your relatives. Therefore, for instant. If you love all these people. What could possible go wrong ?

Or what kind of problem you will have ? If you love, and honor friends of your father like You would love, and honor your father ?. Any friends of your mother. You love them like, you love and honor your mother. Even friends become, part of each other spiritually. My father when all his friends passed away, before him, he missed them, and always cry for them. Besides his past away Relatives. Any friends of our children. They should be like our children, to honor and love like our own.

Any friends of our brothers. We should, love them like brothers. Any friends of our nieces and nephews. We should, love them like nephews, and nieces.

Once upon a time, a friend of my deceased brother. He was looking for my brother lost contact with my brother for long time. Hoping to see him. He was my brothers, childhood friend. When he finally got hold of me hoping to see my brother. I told him, my brother passed away long time ago. He began to cry. He cried so hard. Like he would for his own brother. He also had picture, of my brother When they, were young.

Anyway friends, of our sisters. We should, love them like our own sisters. Cousins they are, like our brothers, and sisters.

We are all, part of each other. Flesh, and blood. All the good we do, and the love we have, and show for each other for each. Rumor will spread fast in heaven. Nothing above, or below can broke chain of love. Pure love, will not suffer the consequences.

I do have the most, profound experience, in this field. When you love, there's no chance Can never be defeated by evil. When it comes to love. Evil become helpless.

Many governments, of third world. Especially, the rich among them. Their people, are poor. Many of them live in condition like 2000 years ago. While the high officials lives in luxury lavish life, great life style. Living in castles, and mansions. Why have, to be like this. Always the strong control the weak. And take advantage of the poor. why ?

The seven deadly sins. Are you frighten ? Are you aware, every time we sin. We face the consequences. Also many suffer along with us. We have good reason, to have fear of these deadly sins.

Sins is giving evil, full authority, over our life, and increasing, his hope of gaining, and getting our souls at last judgment.

Suffering, is from evil himself. Devil put sentence, on human being. Evil justice is to punish the sinners. Who always lives in sin. Because, he is continually being tormented. In burning fire. He wanted to, include every -one of us. In hell with him.

We pray one day, hell to be empty without. Not one spirit. That is, when God himself comes down to put his justice, and peace on earth.

Jesus Christ, talks about last judgment. Matthew 25:31-46.

Saying how will happen. He said that everyone, will be Judge according. We will be reminded, of all the things. We did, and throughout our entire life. Let us hope, we did more good than bad. Our true home is with God in heaven.

God gives the freedom, to the poor, and less fortunate. God doesn't like it when someone takes advantage of the poor, and the week.

People who refuse, to know God. So they continue to do wrong without feeling, any shame. People with faith, whenever they make any mistakes, their faith never shaken. Instead they fix correct. What they did wrong. They are, wise enough to depend on God.

We pray to God for guidance. God never punishes anyone. He Is, fully and 100% good His rewards are, always great. Extremely, merciful.

If we try to please him. We will automatically belong to him. Rooms in heaven, will be prepared for the good.

God gave us free will, and taught us. What's right,and what is wrong. Hoping we take the right path, to be with him one day.

Every one sins. We all sin. We have for longtime being critical. Might not be easy. With us But with God. Everything, is possible.

We could be forgiven, by God, over com temptations. Before they turn to sins. Romans 5:12.

The seven deadly sins. People talk about. They are, frightened. Hoping trying to prevent our self from committing, any of those. Hell is not a joke. Committing, all those sins, is working Some one's way to go hell.

1-Lust- Beauty is, also a gift from God. Decent people will look, at you, and praise you Sometime could be critical, and danger. Be aware, of the mentally sick people. Who lust for you. Wearing obscene clothes. tops, or shorts. It is becoming normal. What people, are wearing Everyone, is free. Some they may, want to look sexy. They are, facing, the consequences. Some go with, the style of today. Some they just don't know, any better. Also ordinary, people they may have, the desires just by looking at you.

When men, or women have desires, over someone else there's a chance. They might commit adultery, and destroy life.

More likely many end up in divorce, heartbroken, and hard feeling. Because, of divorce Everyone becomes victims. Especially, children. Also affects loved ones around.

We need, to always pray to God. So we don't have, any desire one, except our spouses Believe me, is being working for me. If this working for me. It will work for anyone else.

Unfortunately, there are lots of sick people, out there. So many got kidnapped, and raped Was that worth it. Innocent people hurt often. We need, to do something about that. We need to stop, any one from getting hurt.

Once upon a time, a friend invite me, to the club. I did not want, to put him down without asking, any questions I went along. Soon as I walked in the club. It was a strip dancing woman, exposing, their bodies dancing naked. From head, to toe. That was, my first, and last time. I ever went. I was in shock, any woman would, do such thing, to herself. Over money I felt sorry for her. Because, God created everyone of us with the dignity. She did not feel, any shame, for exposing her body.

2-Pride. Taking too, much pride, in our selves falsely and foolishly. Showing off, can get us, in big trouble. If we brag about, things don't own. We are, only living in denial. We are deceiving our self. Trying to get everyone's attention. Brag about things we don't have, or own That is, living fake life.

It is good to be proud, of our accomplishment. Expressing that to people. May be they will learn something. That is, being serious about life.

Taking too much pride, in our self. Only to seek, someone's attention. We become critical What we need to do. Whatever might be, accomplished. We can, proud of our accomplishment. By speaking the truth always, we will be respected. By most of the people, around us.

Taking pride, in our selves, it is very serious sin. It is showing people, we are better than them, more important, attractive than others. Putting people down. By failing to acknowledge others.

Taking pride of our self. It is for selfish. Selfishness is like, you are saying to yourself All for me all about me, and only for me. That is, how selfish people do, and say, feel. Even think

Jesus Christ heard, his disciple, arguing, discussing Who was, the greatest. Jesus sitting down he called all the twelve disciples, and said to them, any man wishes to be first he shall last of all, and servant of all. Who- ever put himself down, he will be rise. Mark 9:35

3 - Greed it is lusting, for the material of this world. Greed is, the desire for wealth, power, and control. Greedy people are, always very selfish. Often tried to get, what doesn't belong to them, and still keep theirs. No matter how much they have, is not enough Their personal gain, it is unlimited. The money, and material of this world. Becomes t heir God Some want to get quick rich. Especially, if they get involve, in theft, and robbery, violence trickery, or manipulation.

Greedy person, do not care. If everyone starve, as long, as they make their money Greedy people only help the people. They are, making money from. Or they only help anyone They are, doing big business. Otherwise they never help. Who is less fortunate. In fact they use and take advantage of the poor.

4-Envy. It is like what, it said in ten commandment. You shall not desire. What your neighbor own. Exodus20:1-17. Deuteronomy 5:2-21

People who lives, watching what others have. Wishing to have, what other people own They do live, with stress Live in agony. Also people like that,they are always angry. About what others have. And they could not have.

I say instead of getting jealous, at someone. We could, gain more than losing. If we join them. Because, if someone has everything.

If we are always, loyal to them. We would always have the chance, to get the help. If we needed.

5-Wrath - anger, rage, and temper is feeling, hatred inside. Therefore, hate sometime lead to murder. Anger can be tragic could leads, to suicide That is rejecting, God gift. Which is, our life God gave us.

When people are in state anger, they are, not mentally thinking, of consequence. Angry people are quick to past judgment. Anger can be control, with allot of patient.

6- Gluttony eating allot, over stuff our self. To hurt our self-eating. It is sin. Because we become, inconsiderate. Not thinking, of others around us. Especially, when we hold food from the hungry It is sin wasting food.

7- Sloth- is laziness. God call us, to keep trying, and never to give up Laziness ruin anyone's life. Lazy people It is hard for them, to make decent living. They do not want to work. Always depend, on others, to do things for them. All they want to do eat drink, and go to sleep. The hardly, have or own anything. They also struggle, more than others. Lazy people they hardly have any success in life. When we, give up we please Evil. And displease God.

If anyone commit, any of these sins. It destroys life of grace, charity, love, peace, and mercy. God call us, to be virtual, spiritual.

Fathers, shall not be, put to death for their children. Nor the children for their fathers,but everyone shall die for his own sin. Deuteronomy24:16

Everyone responsible, for their own action. In this life people who ignore God, and his mercy. They are, critical.

The ones, who don't believe in God. They call, themselves atheist. Atheism, It is denial of existence, of God. Along with that, could bring catastrophe, into the world. Believing in God along with that, comes moral value.

The ones who don't know God, or believe. They are, empty shall. They are, more liable to sin. It will would be easier to be tested by evil. If the ones who don't believe in God ? If they have any, moral values. They would not try to stop others, from practicing their religion Or else they are jealous of others. Who want to, have faith in God. Also they don't have any idea, how to **know God.**

Here in America, supposed to have, freedom of religion, freedom of speech. There is some, who's trying to take, the American pride, and the joy we experience. The way I look at it. People who try, to take my freedom. They are, doing act of terror against me. Terror It is hate. Showing hate toward, the faithful

Especially wars, against Christian, and against Christmas trees. Decoration, lights, nativity scenes, and displays. When Christmas season. Bring people together. It is time of love, peace joy, and sharing. During this season. Any moral people. They should be move, by their spirit Even they if do not believe. It is the holiest times of the year.

Only evil could not stand, grace, love, charity, peace, mercy, and giving. Do you honestly think, Evil want us to be happy ?

Christmas time is, not only spiritual. It is also time of renewing our self. During this season sales go skyrocketed. Throughout the country. Great economic growth. More jobs.

People who has tried, to stop good things. They need to know Jesus Christ, he reshape the world, and made it what it is today. His teaching, his wisdom. Hospitals, good Samaritans feeding the hungry, taken care of sick. Charity foundations love, peace, mercy, and much more goodness. Came about because of Jesus Christ.

The same way, he reach it to of all our hearts. Jesus Christ give, *us* the freedom. was delivered from God through. Our Jesus Christ. We owe our existing to him. Read. New testament.

It is not fair to take someone freedom. Especially, their beliefs, and if they are not hurting anyone.

It is wrong,to convert anyone to what you beliefs. Or try to make anyone changing their religion. Only if they, choose to do that themselves.

Because, of persist, constant, and steady guilt it. Become, very difficult for some, to continue to believe in God. They stop believing. So they, can do what they want, without feeling guilty.

We have, the gift of the holy spirit, to receive. Grace wisdom, knowledge, of the truth and much more.

Our world today, and for the entire, and through our existence. We will, need God always We all belong to God. Because, we all have, the time. When we die, we go to him.

Many are, waiting for an answer. God is, the answer.

The planet earth, was created by him. People who don't believe in God, are attacking the faithful.

Existence is our only hope. Avoiding the imminent destruction of our homes. Our kids are going astray.

The first murder, and crime of history. Abel did not ask to be murdered, he became a victim. (Genesis).

He had, all of his life, ahead of him. It was taken away, in seconds. How is it any fair? Cain try to lie to God. No one, is able to hide from God. If killers were, in right mind They would know, they get caught, anyway, or get murdered too.

Same old story we hear people saying. What am, I my brother keeper. Also so many this common saying. Especially who are doing, so good in life, and it is so rewarding for them.

They do have, the faith in God they pray, and go to church. Not, or doing very little charity, they often talk highly how good. They are doing, for them self's. Which is, great, But a many, who add one magic word, saying. I am doing so good for myself. Why should, I be my brother keeper?. Or some who often say that is, their problems. About others.

Well God made us our brothers- keeper. In fact Jesus, did not even taught of himself hardly. He thought, of us always, and never stop loving us. Even If we sin. He take it on himself.

Jesus died, so he could wipe sins of the world. Luke 23:21,34.

Pure at, heart people. Always do, what is right, for them self, and others. They never deceive, any one, ever. True, strong faith always, to be honest, forward treat everyone fair, and equal.

God said we must take care, anyone who need, any help of all kind. Also to see, what need to be done for that person.

Where ever is, one hundred percent goodness. There, will be none evil. Faith is never, to cheat or deceive anyone.

But Abraham told the rich man. They have Moses, and the prophets. They need to listen to the living. For sure they will not believe the dead. Can come back. Luke 16:23.

If everyone in the world, read sacred scripture. Will learn know, and understand. In the most profound way.

People who, come to the knowledge. They are, inspired by word of God. His spirit will never, depart them. The holy spirit of will become, their guidance.

We learn how to live our lives, according to the holy bible. We also learn, how to be moral. We also learn if we are doing right, or wrong.

From Holy sacred scriptures. We get deeper knowledge of the truth. It give us insurance, and hope in God, and puts our full trust in him. We also learn. We are, truly children of God. He is, very concern about all of us.

Through old testament. God predicted, and prepared his coming for our salvation. In the new testament. He was here to stay.

We all sin, and make mistakes. Repenting, means promising God. Will not do that again But we only try our best. God knows that. Therefore, God give himself no choice but to forgive. He often say to himself. They are, only human being what. I expect?

If we all acknowledge God, and highly devoted, to him In every way, and live life of virtue, love, peace, grace, mercy, and goodness. Doing to all that toward. Without charity, and forgiving others unconditionally. Will not please God much.

Jesus through, his teaching. He expressed, and pointed Gods passion, for the oppressed hungry, widows, orphans, and the poor. If we don't care for them. Will be, like turning our back on Jesus himself. See last judgment. New testament

Jesus Christ, take it personally. At judgment of all nation, Jesus Christ the king will say to the righteous. On his right side, while wondering. What they did so good for Jesus Saying to him. Lord when we did all this goodness ? He answered. I say to you. Whatever you did for one, of these least of my brothers, of mine. You did for me. Matthew 25:40

At the end. When we die There is, a chance, we might suffer the consequences. Before entering gate of heaven. We will, be reminded how we did not do, enough, or nothing at all charity, un conditionally forgiving. Take care of sick, the poor, the lonely, depressed. Should not matter. If they are, our relatives, neighbors, or strangers. If we did not reach each other for the Glory of God.

If you, and I think. We are better, thoughtful, considered, compassionate, helpful, and honest. We are, not supposed to judge, anyone. But we are able to help, and teach others to be like us. The main reason that. God give us a guarantee, to be able to help anyone. Because we were all born with mercy of God, into our hearts. For more mercy received from others The more mercy. Comes out of our hearts.

Many who always do, bad things, they feel locked, with then themselves. They just don't know how to quit, or stop. I believe they do feel the agony, or guilt. They just don't know how to get out. Often these, people don't have no one, to encourage them to show them. How to, become better people.

Without faith in one God, People began to believe in many Gods. Especially, material of this world. Become their God. They are, deceived, by not thinking, may be pay more attention To our society, all around them. May they can do something about it. Hope fully To make it better, safer peace full, merci full, and compassionate society. For themselves, and their children to live.

If everyone, have a job to make a living. Why would anyone steal, or cheat anyone There are so many people are humble, pure, honest, with strong faith. They only want to make a living. and provide for their family.

We are so connect, it to each other. If someone, do one good thing can benefit many. If someone, do one bad thing Could hurt many, also Or, if someone declined financially? So many could get effect.

Many get laid off, when company slow down, or go out of business.

Love of the money, and greed. Makes people blind from doing enough for them self and others. They hurt them self, and others. They feel it. When it is too late.

The more company, closed down, the less opportunity, people going to have. Things always, go up, and down. America will remain land of the opportunity. It is up the people to make the possible.

We can go to church all we want. Thinking, that this one best way we please God Even if we help others becoming a saint. When they go to heaven, will not please God much. God want us, to look at bigger picture. Which is, the people around us. God wants, us to be, our brothers- keeper. The way we, reveal God to others. The way, we treat them.

Jesus speaking of faith, explaining the way we increase it. By putting it to work,and not keep it for ourselves but to share it with others. Jesus. parable of the talents. Matthew 25:18,27

To increase our faith, is by reaching, to everyone unconditionally. Our faith will multiply. When we reach, and give hope to the less fortunate. Charity mercy, being compassioned toward others, will bring relief. And will enrich our Spirit.

God, called us to be spiritual, and not materialistic. God he is not about, how much money. He is about. How much we love each other ?

So much needed, to be done. For our world to make it safer, peace full for ourselves and generation to come. We need to pay attention, and focus. We need to, stop hunger starvation abuse, killing wars. There's so much hate, lust, anger, abuse, and greed. If all of us believe in God, and we don't do something. Will not help God in any way. Because, that is how it works.

When we sin, we are asking for evils rewards. What kind of the rewards evil gives? Very terrible plus so much, suffering. When, we do good things, we're asking for Gods rewards. They are great, out of this world. Spiritual = spirit, that what God is. Many their number one God is the money. The material of this world, would stay behind. Also many, who use Gods words For their own evil purposes,and gain.

This Simon. He was a magician practicing magic. He made money doing that. He figured,he could make more, if he has the power the apostles had. Acts 8:18-20.

God is light of the world that shine, on everyone for free of charge. The holy spirit comes upon the ones. Who seeking him. From all their heart, and soul. Especially, the pure and the meek.

Yes there are so many take care, feed, and clothes, give for each other. Because, they can afford to do that all the time. Because, they can afford it. They think they are, doing something, amazing toward God. Yes it is good because. God is love. Where is love that were God is.

But what will please God more, to do for the ones. Who is, not to do for us in return That is, doing good favor to God. This is, how we glorify God. Our rewards, will be bigger \

Unnatural suffering, we cause to our self. Or folds of others. Who give us the pain agony, and suffering. That is not our faults. Just can't blame God. For whatever we do. We are, facing the consequences.

It is our choice, whether we want, to bring, God into our hearts, mind, and souls. God he is pure spirit. He in every and each of us. He depend, on us. The way we love, care, and forgive

The evil one, always enjoy, watching us hurting each other. He celebrated, our suffering He has control over so many. Evil always, try to stop. What God had accomplish Into us human being. Luke 15:11-32

All the horrible crimes, murdering the unborn. When we, know from the moment of conception, the fetus has heart and soul, and that is life. God given to become image of God

Every baby, in the beginning. In mother's womb, the heart. That is, where spirit of God reside, and is soul, which gives life to every unborn child. After the brain get develop. The blood that flow, in the vain to go to the heart. God makes his temple.

God takes spirit of parents spirit, and give them children to their image, and likeness They all become, image of God in spirit.

Our first priority to do everything in our power to save, and stop murdering the unborn Those babies, they will never had a chance to live. They could have been some important people.

All the ones, who are prochoice. May be, or can be. Because, everyone should have the freedom. But are, we going to give choice to the unborn. Whether, they wanted, to be born or not. Or whether they wanted to live, or not. We need to choose for the unborn. At the meantime, they are innocent victims, and innocence.

Mothers who aboard their babies, they end up suffering, the consequences. Most of them live with guilt, Shame, and pain. Also has hard time. For giving, themselves even when they know. God did forgave them already.

Murdered babies, they go back to God. The parents whom lose a baby for abortion That child Could have being someone. Who was to care, for them. At their old age. If they were, to get sick, and many other things.

Evil forces, attacks humanity. Causing, all kind of suffering. So people to continue hating and blaming God.

Evil loves divorce, to take the happiness, away from people. The children become victims with heart broken. All the people around them, as well. The ones who shared their love.

Evil love to put us. Into temptation. Lust drive, people to commit adultery. Evil hate what is good,and hate stable families.

We need to work on keeping, our families together. We also need, to bring social justice for the family's. Our dignity, pride should be our family's. We need, to learn the meaning,of family values. Practiced. As well Protecting our family's. Should be, our number one goal.

We need, to build our homes, on the rock, and not on the sand.

My main purpose of writing this book. Especially, this chapter. Because so, many people don't have, any one to lean on.

God favored poor people. Because,many of them are simple, pure, and they make, an honest living. They do not ask for much.

It is very bad, and crying shame. The rich always, helps the rich get richer. The rich use the poor, and makes sure, the poor, remain poor. For the rich, help the rich, get richer. It is kind of natural. Because, the rich has the power to do so.

Unfortunately, If the majority of people, becomes poor, and minority are rich. They will not have, any one hardly to trade with them than. Eventually will shut down. And maybe a chance They may, lose everything they own.

Sometime we become fools, and deceived. Thinking only, of our selves. All we do is hurting are self's.

Love the money, and greed makes people blind, from doing enough, for themselves, and people around them. Many people are starving, for attention hoping, for a miracle, mercy, and peace into our world today.

Peace bring comfort to our minds. But mercy, give us relieve. Our world today, so much in need of mercy.

All the bad, and horrible things, are getting close to our doors steps. There is, so much needed to be done.

So much hate, wars, abuse, killing greed, starvation = hunger. We are, becoming so busy We don't, even makes time to think of our self, and others. Especially, our loved ones. It is not fair.

There are, so many people in all world today. With faith. They can build companies manufacturers jobs For the poor. So they can live. The rich, can make more for themselves Having everyone the job. Will lead us, to healthy environment.

It is unfortunate. For the ones. Who become homeless. Also some being tortured. By life of suffering. They need, all the help. They can get.

Many who want, to have power, over power less. Just like death, being imposed on the helpless. But millions by fault of others. they suffer.

Destructiveness of, un necessarily modern wars. Losing Countless, innocent lives. Also the biggest acts, of evil is terrorism. Also brutality, and hijacking trying to crash air planes.

So many innocent, become victims of these crimes. Also human ears, that lead to the destruction.

Because of, the greed cost, oil rig to blow. Unsafe work, can become very dangerous Drinking, and driving cost. So much death. That does, not have to happen. People can stop drinking,and driving easily. Accidents brings, casualties always. People should only die naturally.

We need, to show the devil. We are not made,to listen to him.

We also need to take, everything back, to a ourselves. It Is possible, to do away with evil. God job, is to reward us with good things. God always, welcome us. With open arms.

Jesus Christ wishes are, to unfold evil, off face of earth, and replace it with good.

He brought, the good news, from heaven. He taught us, how to concord evil. We ask Jesus Christ to give us the grace. So we can understand, and overcome the temptation Because he was tempted too. Plus he took all our sins of on himself.

If we all give, our hearts to Jesus Christ, will not please him much. But what, will please Jesus Christ 100%. If we become, like him throughout our life. He want us to be him. So he can dwell into our hearts. To live with his spirit. He command us, to love each other, unconditionally.

Our Lord Jesus Christ. He did not, even owned a home. He wanted to always focus on helping us, enriching our spirits. He said God always know. What you need. Be more concern What will be, in to the next world. Jesus Christ said, he didn't even own something, to lay his head on, and here we are only worried about this. Material of this world.

Even if we have, all the money we need. We don't take with us, when we die. Even if we, leave it for our kids, we don't even know they can keep it.

Jesus spoke of wealth. But it is, more important forgiving, and how rewarding it is Jesus Christ, was asked. How often, we should forgive our brother, or whoever might be sin against us. He did not give us, any choice. He said unconditionally. That is, if we want, to be God children. Children always belong to their father.

Our Lord Jesus Christ know. If someone sin against us or hurt us, in any way. More likely they, make peace with God. If we remain angry at them. We remain, without peace with God

Whenever, we go to church. We received, spirit of Jesus Christ into our hearts. Also flesh blood divinity of our savior. We try, very hard to keep it that way.

Christ always spoke the truth. Even when, he knew was going get in trouble. I mean before the crucifixion, he was thinking of us. Matthew 18:21-22

People don't, understand concept, of family values. Families, are falling apart. If you truly want to be happy. Nothing in this world. Should come. Before, your relatives friends, your neighbors, even strangers. Whenever, we feel related to anyone we meet. We Instantly feel secure, and free.

Family should be one, big circle. Include friends, and every so often someone comes out, of the circle to extend to bring more people, into circle. To spread love, and charity.

Relative told me once. If you need something?. You should only go to a family. Because if you go to a stranger, or anyone else. Who is, not your family. They will, put down your family. Thinking your family, don't care about you.

How often, we ask our self. Why people, have to steal to make a living ?. Or why people hurt others ? Just to gain something don't belong them. Why people, have to starve? When there's, so much food. Being thrown, away every day. There is, some people who wish. If they can, have that food.

If we truly believe in God. Then we have, to prove it. We make sure, no one go hungry and without job. There is, many who have relatives, brothers, sisters, friends. And still they depend on charity foundation. When at the meantime, charity foundation. Should be only for emergency. We need, to let them have more time to provide for the needy.

People, who can afford to build companies, factories. Office buildings, manufacture. They can start, businesses to help others have job. So they can work. Owners will, eventually make more profit also, and help everyone else. Becoming successful.

Here, and around, the world people. Who are talking millions, billions. If they can, invest some into, neighborhood, and cities. Building jobs for people. They can double their money eventually.

We are importing, so much from other countries. Can you imagine. If we can make, most of it here. In our country. Many more jobs, we can create. We let other countries, import from us.

Faith is whenever, we hear, or see suffering of others To be moral, is to become outrage and run to rescue the sufferer.

God create it us, to enjoy a perfect, good, loving happy fellowship, with him forever God he is, glorified over, and over again. Because of, the goodness, we have for others.

When people, are humbled by us. That is, when they see God. We are made, of his image. He want us to, live with him forever.

God want us to live happy. Here on earth. Over com, evil with good. Hoping evil, will vanish someday.

When it comes to God, and evil. There is, no competition, no comparison. What is good always goes to God. What is, bad goes to evil.

It is our choice. Which road to take. How much do, we gain, or lose ?. And to see If is worth it ?.

Evil admire, our suffering. Because he is, suffering in hell. We heard of, seven deadly sins, are you frighten ? and how much ?.

When we sin, we are giving evil. Authority over our lives. When we, become greedy. We hurt our self, and the people around us.

The more, people lose their jobs, the more things goes up, in price. Because, everyone business go down. Of course less profit. How else they, will make up for the profit. If they don't raise the price.

Many people are, losing their homes needed places to rent. Therefore, owners of the rental, are taking advantages By raising, the rent. Even the faithful among them, do that Thinking, it is only business, that's part of life. Not feeling, compassioned for the people.

Feeling guilty something, we cause it, to our self. Anyone Who claim to have the faith. Should have good conscience always, and come along with it.

Good, and faithful persons. If they makes a mistake. With anyone should go apologize, and make up.

Sometime we get confused. When we, know everything is possible with God. Pleasing everyone it is, the door to success.

Trusting in God, will lead us to the right path.

One of the reasons. We must, care about each other. If we only look at people's life. You will see, our self. If we only take glance, figure of speech. We are, all in the same boat.

We all somehow, suffer, struggle, and go through good times, and bad times. People don't realize that. Because, they are so busy. Thinking of, themselves only.

Now more than ever, people are very selfish. All they do is hurting themselves Self-centers, and selfish. They act like they're saying to them self's. All for me, all about me and only me. This is, a selfish person for you.

God he gives unconditionally. He is good, loving, and merciful. Therefore, he want us to try to be good 24/7 not 23 hours 59 seconds.

Becoming spiritual, takes a lot of work. Reaching people. Especially, the misfortune. Living life, of virtue, grace, mercy Purity, humbleness, and goodness.

Evil always, try to pull apart. What God, put together. To avoid having, any problems in your life. Give, everyone their place. Give everyone, the honor, and respect. Just the way you want to be done to you.

What problems, you will have. If you love friends of your father like you would, love your father, any friends of your mother, you love them like, you love your mother. Even with friends, become part, of each other spiritually. My father when, all his friends passed away before him, he missed them. Always cry, for them. Besides, his past away relatives. Any friends of our children, they should be like, our children to honor, and love like our own. Any friends of our brothers. We should, love them like brothers. Any friends of our nieces and nephews. We should love them, like nephews, and nieces. Once upon a time, a friend of my deceased brother was looking, for my brother. Hoping, to see him. He was my brothers childhood friend. When he finally got, hold of me hoping to see my brother. I told him, my brother passed away long time ago. He began to cry, he cried so hard. Like he would for his own brother. He also had picture, of my brother. When they were young. Anyway friends of our sisters, we should love them like, our own sisters. Cousins, they are like our brothers, and sisters. We are, all part of each other. Flesh, and blood.

All the good we do. And the love we have, for each other. Rumor, will spread fast in heaven.

Nothing above, or below, can brake chain of love pure love. Will not suffer the consequences I do have the most profound experience in this field. When, we love. There's no chance. Can never, be defeated by evil. When it comes to love, evil become helpless.

Many governments of third world. Especially, the rich among them. Their people are poor. Many of them live in condition like 2000 years ago. While the high officials, live in luxury lavish life, great lifestyle. Living in castles, and mansions. Why have, to be like this way. Always the strong control the weak, and take advantage of the poor. Why ?

The seven deadly sins, are you frighten ?. Are you aware every time we sin. We face the consequences. Also many suffer along with us. We have good reason, to have a fear, of these deadly sins.

Sins is giving evil, full authority, over our life. Also increases his hope of gaining, and getting our souls. At the last judgment. Suffering is from, evil himself.

Devil put sentence on human being. His justice is, to punish the sinners, and who lives in sin Because, evil he is continually, being tormented, in burning fire. He wanted to include, every one of us to live, in hell with him.

We pray one day, hell to be empty. Without one spirit.

That is when, God himself comes down to put, his justice, and peace on earth. Jesus Christ, talks about last judgment. New testament. Saying how will happen.

He said that everyone. Will be judge according, will be reminded of all the things we did. Throughout our, entire life. Let us hope we, do more good, than bad.

Our true home is with God in heaven. God gives the freedom to the poor, and less fortunate. God doesn't like it. When someone, takes advantage of the poor. And the week

People refuse, to know God. So they continue do wrong, without feeling any shame.

People who have the faith. Whenever they make,any mistakes. Their faith never shaken Instead they fix, and correct. What they did wrong. They are, wise enough to depend on God.

If we pray to God, for guidance ? We will be, able to overcome all the temptation God never, punishes anyone

He, is fully 100% good. New testament. His rewards are, always great extremely merciful If we, try to please him. We will automatically, belong to Him.

Many rooms in heaven, will be prepared for the good. John 14:2

God gave us free will and taught us. What's right, and what is wrong. Hoping we decide to take, the right path. To be with him one day.

Every one sins. We all sin. Feeling critical might not be easy, to over com. But with God everything possible. We have a chance, to pray for God to, give us enough grace, to over com temptations. Before, it turn to sins.

Seven deadly sins, people talk about, and they being frightened by. Hoping, trying to prevent it our self from committing, any of those sins.

Hell is not a joke. Lusting. Beauty is also a gift from God. Decent people will look at you,and praise you.

Sometime could be critical, and danger, be aware of the mentally sick people. Who lust for you. Wearing obscene clothes, tops, or shorts. Also ordinary people, they may have the desires. Just by looking at you.

When men, or women have desires, someone else. There's a chance they might commit adultery. And destroy lives. More likely, end up in divorce, heart, broken, hard feeling. Everyone becomes victims. Especially children. Also affects life of loved ones.

We need, always pray to God. We don't have, any desire, for the one except, our spouses. Believe me is being working for me. If this working, for me it will work for anyone It is becoming normal. What, people are wearing, some may want to look sexy. They are, facing the consequences. Some go with style of today. Some don't know better. Unfortunately there are lots, of sick people out there. It depends on, how much expose your body. So many got hurt. Pride, taking too much pride in our selves falsely, and foolishly. Showing off, can get us in big trouble. When we, brag about things. We don't have, or own. We are only living in denial Also we are, only deceiving our self, and trying to get everyone's attention.

When we, accomplish something. We can be, proud of our accomplishment. We speak the truth. Then we'll always. Be respected by most of the people. Taking pride in our selves it is very serious sin. It also mean, showing people. We are better, important. More attractive than them. Putting people down, by failing to acknowledge others. Taking pride of our self. It is being selfish. Selfishness. The way selfish people think, and act always like They are, saying to them self. Only for me. All about me. Only me. Very in considered selfish people are.

Whoever put himself down, he will be rise. Romans 5:12

Greed, it is lusting for the material, of this world. Greed is, the desire for wealth, and power. Greedy people are always selfish. Often try, to get what, doesn't belong to them and still keep, theirs. No matter, how much, they have, is not enough. Their personal gain it is unlimited.

The money, and material of this world becomes their God. Some want to get quick rich. They involve in theft, or robbery. Especially by means of violence, tricking others, or manipulation. Greedy persons, do not care if everyone starving, as long, as they make their money. They only help the people, they are making money from. Or they only help anyone They are, doing business. Otherwise they, never help anyone. They take a lot more than giving.

Envy it is like what is said in ten commandment. You shall not, desire what belong to your neighbor Exodus 20: 1- 20. People, who live watching. What others have Sometime makes them, angry. Especially watching what others have, and they could not have. I say instead of getting jealous at someone. You could gain more, than losing. If you join them. Because, if we have friend, who has it all. Chances are, we get the help. If we need it. Jealousy it is, when we hate someone. Because, they have it better than us. Wrath anger, rage, and temper. Is feeling, hatred inside in someone's heart. Therefore, hate sometime lead to murder.

Anger can be tragic. It could lead to suicide. That is, rejecting God gift, that is life When people are in state of anger. They are, not mentally thinking, of consequences. Angry people, are quick to past judgment. Anger can be controlled. With allot of patient. Learning to be patient is a decision. We should continuously make, and is to decide, to wait instead of becoming tense angry, and knowing everything can be fixed.

Gluttony, eating allot over stuff our self. To hurt our self-eating. it is sin. Because we become unconsidered not thinking of others around us. Especially, when we hold food from the hungry. It is sin wasting food.

Sloth is laziness. God call us to keep trying not to give up. Laziness, ruin anyone's life Lazy people, is hard for them to make a decent living. They do not want to work. Always depend on others, to do things for them. All they want is to eat drink, and go to sleep. They hardly have anything. They also struggle more than others.

If anyone commit, any of these sins ? It destroys life of grace, charity love peace, and mercy. God call us to be virtual spiritual.

Fathers shall not be, put to death for their children, nor the children for their fathers. But everyone, shall die for his own sin. Deuteronomy 14:16.

Everyone, responsible for their own action. In this one's life. People ignore God, and his mercy, they are critical. The ones who don't believe in God they call themselves

Atheist=atheism. It is denial of existence of God. The ones who don't know God, or believe. They are, empty shall, more liable to sin. They would be, easier to be tested. The ones who hate God, and don't know him, as well. They are, a lot more critical. Then the ones who don't know God at all. But they are good, and moral. Living, life of love mercy, and peace. I believe God, will claim them, at the end of their life. I mean when they die. Because where is always good. There is, no room for Evil. Where good, takes place.

Here in, America supposed to have freedom, of religion, freedom of speech. There is some, are trying to take the American pride. The joy we experience. The way I look at it People who try, to take our freedom, it is doing act of terror against us. Showing, hate toward the faithful. When, at the mean time they are not hurting anyone.

Especially, wars against Christianity, and being against Christmas trees. Decoration, lights nativity scenes, and displays. When Christmas season bring people together.

It is time of love, peace, love, and sharing, mostly brings hope into hearts; of many.

It is the holiest times of the year. Only evil could not stand grace, love, charity, peace.

Mercy giving Christmas time, is not only, and holly spiritual. It is time of renewing our self.

Sales go sky rocketed through - out the country. Great economic recovery, and growth Evil trying to destroy America. It is not fair to take someone freedom. Especially their beliefs It is wrong, to convert anyone to what you belief. People who are against, what is good, comes out of hate.

People who do not believe in God. Because, of persist a steady guilt, Become, very difficult for them, to continue believing in God. They stop. So they continue doing what they please without feeling, any guilt. Along that, they lose their moral values.

We have gift, the Holy Spirit to receive. Grace wisdom, knowledge, the truth, and much more. Our world today, for the sake of our existence. We, will need God always. Many are waiting, for an answer. God is the answer. The planet earth was created by him.

People, who don't believe in God, are attacking the faithful. Existence, it is our only hope In avoiding the imminent destruction, of our homes.

Losing traditional, and Godly values. Will lead us to the destruction, of our family's. Our children, are going astray.

Chapter 10

Problems, Bad Decisions

The very first verse in the Bible. Genesis 1:1. Identifies God, as the creator' in the beginning God created the Heaven, and the earth. We define God as creator also he is the light that shines in every corner, of the earth. He merciful father.

Believers, around the world. know God, from the holy scripture, and from the one who have spiritual calling to serve.

We, also know God from the miracles. He granted to us. I can define God love. Because of all great people. Who go, around the world, to serve the needy.

No one ever saw God. We bring him into our life,hearts.

We love God. We have the profits, and messengers. We believe in God he is spirit, even no one ever saw God.

But believers, bring him into their, life minds, hearts, homes. We live according to his teaching We honored him. We obey him,and follow his rules, and commandment.

My point is, If billions of people around, the world. Founded so easy, and not difficult, at all to worship, and to love God.

We don't see God. But, we find it easy to believe. How much easier everything else We should be, able to fix, and repair. Because, all the material of this world's is in front of us We can feel, and touch 24/7.

We can speak, communicate with each other on the spot. We should, be able to repair Anything that goes wrong, or comes ahead. In life It is in our control.

One of the things people are forgetting. Nothing, work without faith, Love, grace, mercy virtue, and charity.

Person of faith, supposed to be. Compassionate, decisive, and positive. Wisdom, and having common sense. Comes out of good faith. True faith.

Trusting in God except, his Glory, and mercy. God almighty he will give us. This insurance He will, never be abandon. Those, who trust in him.

True faith, teach us to have, moral values. Also to set for our self- standards, and principle Were given to us by God. God want us to take to him. All obstacles, problems, we might have So he can fix it for us. At the meantime. We give, it try to make, it work.

Our problem, we are facing today. Abortion. With respect, for Pro- choice. People, are free, and able to speak up. Defending woman right to choose. Whether, to aboard their baby or not. Prolife people, are being criticized. At the meantime. Everyone should be, entitled to have their personal freedom.

Unfortunately, they are not giving, the unborn. Their choice to be murdered, or not, to live their life, or not ?. Or is there, anyone defending, the unborn ? To have the freedom to choose. Or there's, no urgency for the unborn.

The way I look at it, we are taking advantage of the unborn. Because, women are here and adult enough, and able to fight, for their right. But the unborn they are not here yet, and they are innocence. What would you do for your children. If someone try to hurt them.

Beside, any good mother, should say. I will give my life, for my baby. When they, began to give choice to a woman. Will not be fair, not to give choice, for the unborn. Whether they want to be born, or not.

Writers of New testament like the old. Whether born, or unborn, baby is simply a baby many references. Baby are, gift God gives us. It is not their fault how they born, and was the reason.

The angel Gabriel, told Mary that she would be with child, and give birth to son. Luke 1:31

Unborn John Baptist. Luke1:41

Where ever there is, a genealogy distinct living human being there is a living soul and spirit 1 Thessalonians5:23

Behold, I was brought forth in iniquity, and in sin my mother conceive me. Each person has a sinful nature,from the point,of conception. Psalms 51:5.

Scripture condemn, the shedding, of innocent blood. Deuteronomy 19:10

Again, Balaam was not hallucinating,what was not there, but rather has his eyes Opened to what was there. Numbers 22:27-31

For the eyes of the Lord. Run throughout, the whole earth, to show himself strong, on behalf, of those. Whose heart Is loyal to him 2 Chronicles 16:9

Without faith, we face bad consequences. Without faith, we become immortal, and live sinful, corrupt, shameful life. Without faith, there's no love gain. We could, live life of misery anxiety, depression, and grieve. Without faith.

God, count on, us to be strong. True faith, accept all the consequences, occur in the life We pray, we will see God face to face, one day. To accept, his reward. That's when God, will tell us job well done. Beside, all of the suffering we indoor. But remained our self - focus on faith, in God. By living a happy, and prospecting life. That what, pleases God.

Myself whenever, I have an issue. Many people call it problems. I never ever worry about it instead. I began to think how, and find, a way to fix it. Usually, I'd try to find place, to be alone, and quiet. Alone but not, away from anyone. Trying to figure a way to fix it. Which way to go. At the meantime. I turned out to God. By prayer for him to intervene. Because, I could not do it without, God's help. Suddenly before, I know it, I get the answer I needed.

We should never, ever bring our problems home, or take it on someone else. Without worrying. We should begin to fix, our own problem. It is always good, to be open. Shared with someone else. We trust. So we can get, the help we needed.

Every individual, should hold their mistakes against their own self. If any one of makes any mistakes, they are responsible to fix it. Why bother anybody else ?. Because, if any of us make, a mistake, no one has, any chance, and knowing how, to fix it. Except us 'cause. We have, the detail. Others are in the dark. I mean knowing, about the mistake.

It is not fair, to let someone else carry, our burden, and heavy weight. The only thing we can do ask for a advise, or opinion on that issue.

Good man, out of his good treasure, bring forth good treasure, and the evil man, out of evil treasure, bring forth evil treasure. Matthew 12:35.

Good man, brings good things out. Evil man bring, evil things. Wicked persons bad things are stored in them. Good, and decent persons. When they make, a mistake with others. They try to fix it, and make up always.

All day of work. I just can't wait, to get home. So I can finally relax become happy, and comfortable. My home as always, my joy,and happiness. Our home it is the place, we get to do. Whatever, we please.

One of my friends once, told me. He made a lot of mistakes. I responded telling him Don't say, you made a mistake ? You only make bad, decisions. You need to fix. Many of them, is not too late to repair, and fix. Everyone, could creative. If one thing don't work. Try another.

In our lifetime, we always, do one thing, if it doesn't work. We try, another thing. It is one of the signs of success. Because, If we don't try, how we would know, if we make it or not Winners are, the ones. Who never give up. I often look at life, the following way. As long as We try everything until we find our calling.

Every morning, we ought to plan to have happy day, not forgetting things might come our way that day. We need to fix, and take care of. along the way. knowing that things may come ahead. Hopefully, we will fix. IF doesn't, get fix today. There's always tomorrow. Or it less try our best.

Problems issues, normally everyone have. Just face it. We will always be dilemmas, and difficulty. Why worry about it ?. Keep fixing it. Everyone has it all, or some of these problems.

Our life is more precious, and more importance, than all this stuff that occur in our life We have no choice, but to fix what is broken, all the time. Or we will not, be able to get ahead in this life.

Whose ever called, according to God purpose. 2 timothy 1:9.

God has reason, why each of us were born. God has, things work together for our good We are called according to his purpose. If we have Jesus, in our life? We could have, everything working always. For the moment things may seem to be, going against us. Then suddenly everything works.

If God is for us, who can be against us. Romans 8:28-31.

How anybody can catch up. If they have, piled up problems. As long, as we are healthy, and alive is never too late. God he, who created, and give us this life. He also want us to depend on him. God knows,we could not make it, without him. He want to remain in our lives. Otherwise, we go astray. If we distant our self's,from him. If we stop focusing on God. All terrible things comes head us. By praying, and being persistent. That is how God remain in us. We find out, when bad things begin to go our way.

We need to keep the faith. Without faith will be more abuse killing, divorce, hate Greed. Hunger, and thousands of horrible things occur daily.

Nothing, no one, with money, gold, or richness. Make them better than you, and I. Because, we all born, and die, the same way regardless. We all, turn to dust. Only one who's better is the one who will never die, and that's God. All the success, fame a priority will stay behind. When we die.

As an adult, we should know when, the dangerous is coming, and when we are critical. Even children, at young age, they act, and do whatever comes to their mind for time being. They are, innocence, and pure. They don't know better. They would touch fire without thinking of consequence. If we don't watch them.

My point is, they can tell when, they are critical. They also, know when the trouble coming. Especially, if someone makes, scary noise. They would run screaming. I saw that myself. Scary noise, makes them panicky alarmed. They know, the dangers coming. If children can sense that? How much, more us adults. We should know better, than children.

Once upon a time, my great nephew two years old, he was visiting with, his three years old sister, with their mother. They were playing, in one of the room happy together Few minutes later, the two years old he came running screening, and crying toward, the living room, and the reason was, he was scared. His sister, was making scary noise. She got his attention. He was alarmed. I was surprised. Because nothing scared, my little nephew But that noise, was big deal to him.

Once upon time, I took my son, by o'clock. I asked him you see what time is it ? He said 9:00 am. I waited until it was 9;01.am. I asked him again. What time is it now ?. He said 9;01. I told him, you see that 9:00 will never come again. He was wondering. What I, was trying to teach him. I Explained, to him that, he should make every moment of his life worthwhile. Because, for every minute, we miss will never come back. That is, why it make every moment valuable.

God is good, in spite our failing. He is ready to forgive. What we, all needed in our life to love. Unconditional love, conquers hardship, trial worries, and difficulty. So many of us often worry, and wonder what will be the next life. I say, just be good. What, can go wrong.

Unconditionally, good people don't have to wonder. Because, they always have the answer to. What will it be like, in life after death.

Therefore, goodness go to heaven to live forever Psalms 78:37-38. God will restore, to you the years which, the swarming locust has eaten, the hopper the destroyer, and the cutter, my great army,which I sent among you. Joel 2:25.

If we ever feel like our life is over. We need to go, to the one who can make us a winner. That's God. He is, the author of our existent. He author, of all time, and can make up for all what it was lost. Jesus, can turn thing around for us.

So many writers, wrote books about wisdom, and how much we learn from animals and creatures.

Once upon a time, my father told me a story, have no basis for it or prove. But it mean something. It is about not giving up, the only way, we make it. The story is about a creature, an ant this little creature is known, by storing their food. Throughout summer time, to be available for them throughout winners, season. They do so, before winter arrives. So they can have enough food to eat. Throughout, winter months. any way. Once upon a time, there was this army general. Who want, into the war hoping to win, and conquer another city. Sadly, he lost, the war. He was, defeated. He was about, to lose hope. Unfortunately, he the war. He was defeated. He lost many good, and brave men. He was very sad, and disappointed. Of course, he was hurt. It was very painful just thinking about it. Anyway, coming to his hometown with, what he had left form his army. On the way back, everyone was exhausted. Therefore, he decided to stop so he can rest, and in his entire army. The general, at the rest stop he leaned against this old wall, he was not able to sleep. But as his eyes were half way close. He seen an aunt, crawling up the wall. With piece of food in her mouth, trying to reach the hole up, and above, just before, that ant reached the hole, that piece of food fell off her mouth. Starting, all over. Went all the way to the ground, the aunt crawled down, to get that piece, of food. To climb the wall trying, once more to get it to the hole, to store it. Unfortunately, the tiny creature had to try few times until. Finally, made it to the whole. That was her home. The aunt could not afford to quit. She needed that food.

Anyway, during all the time, the general was watching, the little creature. How it was so persistent.

He was a amazed, by that. Just a point which is, that the creature did not quit, as he about to quit. He kept thinking about this Saying, that little creature was willing to take the risk. I could, do more. In such short time he trained his army. With more advance, fighting equipment. Then said to himself. How could I put my people down. Therefore, immediately in a very short time, he got his army together hoping to win.

He went back into the war. Only this time he won and concord the enemy He went back to his people as hero. Winner, not the failure. He learned, that no matter. How many times, we get defeated through our life. Never give up, as long, as we Are alive, and healthy. It is never too late.

Once upon time, my wife, and I were walking in the wood surprising. I hardly heard, any sound of animals. I told her. She answered, birds, and small animals live around people so they can survive. What will we gain, if we have all the treasure of the world but alone. Life will become very boring, and stressful.

Happiness is, everyone's choice. Should be the way, we want live.

My cousin, once he was talking to me, he sounded like. He was, having petty on me. I sense that. My answers, to him was. I would like, to tell you something. So you don't have, to worry about me no more. I said, as long as, I am not materialistic I am able to remain happy, and focus on my life, also life's of my loved ones. He agreed with me.

I say, if you really want to stay happy always ? Nothing should, come before your parents, spouses, brothers, sisters, kids, friends, relatives, and older people around us. That is when. We find, true happiness in this life.

All the people, who are around, should be. One wide circle of love to cover protect, to fix. Whatever occur in life. Always having, someone you can lean on. Once upon a time, one of my nephews and I, were driving, on the road. Looking, straight ahead, thinking about. There are, so many, who have no one. I told him. I think God, we have each other.

Especially, family they are, part of each other. Even all our friends, become part of us, spiritually. Once upon a time, my sister told me. Brother, if you need anything ? Don't ask anyone else, ask your relatives. I believe my sister, was thinking. If I go to anyone outside, of the family, for help. They will down, my family thinking, they don't want to help me, and they do not care.

After my mom, and dad passed away. All my brothers, father each other, and all my sisters, mother each other. I mean is that, we knew that mom, and dad were not there no more. We have, to be here for each other. All my sisters want, to be here for us, brothers because our mother was not here. We have our ups, and down. But love grow stronger. We were, raised to love, and care for each other, and others. That's what our parents taught us to be like. Always to be, a team.

How many disputes they have. At the end, they have compassion, for each other. Always makes up, and stay together, at end of the day.

God gave us, the laws, and the ten commandments, for our moral values, and happiness. For any, circumstances. God give us laws, and Ten commandments, for our moral values, and happiness. Exodus 20:1-17.

Also how to stay focused on life. When it, comes to forgiving ? God, give us no other choice, but to forgive. By doing God's well. Will guarantee, our salvation. We glorify God for every good we do. For any person. No matter, who they are. What they are. Or where they come from.

If we do good all the time ? Where would, evil fit. If Something distant, to happen would to happen. It will happen. Life is destiny.

God would only change things, by miracle. It is common thing every human being have something they worry about. If anyone, say otherwise. They are, exaggerating. It is so similar, what every human being go through this life. It is so similar. Figures speech" If is not, one thing, is the other.

No one, should be deceived, not knowing. God almighty created everything.

This is, why all the problems, we have. We hand it to him. Because, he has solution for it.

Worries: throughout entire world. Everyone, somehow struggle. Trying, to work making a living. We struggle raising family, and so much more through this life. When, we carry all that in our mind we get exhaust it. Also we make ourselves sick. All we do, is wasting time, could being working on it to fix things. Beside, all the struggle in our life.

There's a lot more, celebration in life, than anything else. life is good. We only have one life to live. Therefore, we should make every minute of our life worth living.

Once upon a time, a friend told after his greetings, I also asked how was he doing He said, as long, as I am healthy, I will be ok. I tell him, I totally agree with you. But would you be healthy, asking him ? If you, do not have your loved ones. Especially when you don't see them. He agreed with me. You will, become lonely, and depressed I told him. Also all the people, you care more about, and concern about. They feel it sense it, and appreciate. The connection, you have between you, and them, makes the different. The most, profound love comes. Directly, out of the heart.

Hezekiah received, the letter from, the hand of, the messenger, spread it, and read it, before the lord 2Kings19:14

We out to be wise enough with the burdens of life. Take them before, the Lord, and leave them there. Every day, we give our issues. In Gods hand.

Every morning, when I wake up. I plan to have happy, and prospective day But not forgetting, about things may come ahead that day. I need to fix, and take care of If I can't fix it today. There's, always tomorrow. Isn't it everyone's life ?

We should plan ahead, to fix things. Everything, is possible. Of course, we only try our best. I will, never get stress about anything, and making everyone around me miserable Because, people who love us.

When they see us hurt, they get hurt too. This is, why we should put everything in our control. To get it fixed as soon, as possible.

In our life time, we all do things, we take chances. Everything we do, should be prepared. If the worst comes. We already, have ideas, and goals how to fix it.

It is good, to have goals, dreams try, to accomplish. We should. continue trying to reach it. We should always try to think about. Whatever comes, into our mind, in order for us to make it.

Unfortunately, if we don't try, one thing, or another. We will not have a chance to know, if we are going, to make it, or not. Chances are, we might missing out. On big opportunities.

I believe everything, is destiny. If is meant to happen, it will happen. The way I see it, everything in life, is right time, right place. Only figure of speech. You either wake up poor, or rich. You just, don't know. Only God, change thing for us. Pray for anything. Try it will work.

The way I see things, I would take, two persons. They are, both intelligence, have the highest education. Healthy not lazy, very. Creative working very hard, and smart. One of them make it to success. The other may not. Or both make it. That is, part of life. Also there is some people. Who don't even have education. They made it, to the top. If it is meant to happen it will. happen, It is not only hard working. To some working smart. I believe it is a reality, any one, is able to live good, and have ever thing they want. As long as they are, not lazy, and they are healthy, and able, to work. If they don't let anyone take their advantage. People, can easily take, two jobs, or part time job. Or get higher education for higher paying job. Or maybe, you can team with maybe you're kids, friends, or relatives to start, some kind of business.

Financial problems, are very pain full. So many of us takes, big effect, into many life Sometime life can be, unfortunate thing. God forbid. If we have disease, or some kind of illness. We take, medication to get relieve from pain, and suffering. Or God forbid we die But financial problem. It is ongoing thing. We just, don't know when. it will end. Or if they'll ever be end to it.

I have this gift, no one can ever read, anyone mind. But myself just the way people say things to me. I know what, they're thinking for time being. Any way someone who cares about me, the way he was say things to me, I was able to tell. He was feeling sorry for me. I was able to feel it. He was, feeling sorry for me, also petty on me I respond to it to him, and told him not to worry, about me. I add it, as long I am not materialistic. I will always be happy.

It is always good to prospect, and try to make, lots of money, as longs, it don't become our life. Or if, we don't make issues out of It.

We should always, take our personal life more serious to focus, on our happiness, and our loved ones.

It not, good to be poor, at all But, I rather live on bread, and water, and happy. Money do not always bring happiness. A lot of poor people. They are, happy with what they have Because, they are simple, and humble. Especially, when you are humble yourself. You get your way all the time. I often say, I rather be poor living on bread, and water, and happy. Then being rich sad, and miserable. Money do not bring happiness all the time.

So many, who spent most, of their life. Making, lots of money. But they don't find time to enjoy. What, God has given them.

Some, act like they will live forever. I mean the people, who always complaint Some whom, waste their life complaining. People, who complain constantly being upset and disappointed. They are, acting like. They are, about to live forever, and they are working on making things perfect, for them self. Whenever, I see people like that. I remind them they will not, live forever here on earth. So why. worry so much. Some of these people if you ask them, what are they planning to do, with all the treasure, they own. Many times don't have an answer. Because, they don't even know. Why they are making, all the money, and for what use ? Many, who do not have answer. Sometimes, people get Confused.

We are afflicted in every way, but not crushed ; perplexed, but not driven to despair: Persecuted, but not forsaken: struck down, but not destroyed. 2 Corinthians 4:8-9.

We are not alone. God will never let us down. Even, when we are living in sin God walk along, our side. Until we can repent, and come back to him. He always take us back unconditionally. God will never, let the Evil give us, more then we can take. God put limit, on evil temptation against us. God never abandoned us.

Especially, in time when he know we need him, for the trouble we face. God give us mercy, and comfort, through others. Once we find someone to help us. God, putting into their heart, mercy toward us.

We acknowledge God. By speaking to him. Asking God to intervene in our daily life. The way God system work. We get the help we need. When we, find people. Who need the help too. We can team up. Together, we can fix everything.

When we pray, we humble ourselves, we receive the holy spirit of God. We pray for all people. We pray for God's, to grant peace, and mercy, throughout the world. World without faith, will crash, and collapse. This is why, we need, to trust in God, regardless Never give up even. If we are hunted down, by our problems. We needed to continue to work on it. Once we give up. We are pleasing, evil.

I grew up, in this small town, in Middle North of Iraq most of the people. They were down to earth people. They got, their values from the bible, and one help another, in time of need. They guarded their faith, and went according. Most them, tried to live by living word of God. That is, the Bible.

There was a lot of respect among people, In town. Younger people, were always honoring respecting the elder. Sometime people, have this one person, who do everything for everybody, help, charities Doing everything,to please everyone, even. Even If they were strangers. Always polite, plus truly good person. At the meantime. when people knew he had problems of his own personal life he don't care to fix, or make time. People in town used to come hard on him. Only because they love him. Used to say shame on you are such a great person, very Helpful, fixing other people problems. But you don't make time and afford to fix your own. Or even bother. There were, people who cared about him Because he brought, happiness to their hearts. Happiness, into heart of many but he didn't want to find time to make himself happy. When he fixes, his own problems.

It would please God when we find refuge in him. Psalm 131.

God old Abraham, fear not, I am your shield I will make your reward very great. Genesis 15:1.

Just because Abraham obey, and trust in God. He was not afraid of anything. He also knew, there was no power above God.

Every human being, is born with mercy of God in their heart. But, God chose Abraham so we can have salvation, through him. He was found favorites in God's eyes. God also told Abraham. God told him. Why are you, afraid if you know. I am with you.

Once we put our life, under God command. He becomes our strings. In our most difficult times. No matter,how deep we sink. God will pull us out. We need, to trust in God, and let him, run our life. It will be rewarding. We will have happier, brighter future Freedom according, to God grace love, mercy, and peace.

For sure guarantee, we'll have blessing life. Otherwise if we live sinful life. We struggle, and suffer more than others. It is our choice We have free will, to choose our life Which way to take ? Living hell or work our way to heaven. So we can live with God for ever. God don't wants us to be afraid. Because fear is, enemy of good. Faith is our hope in God. Because he is, the future, and the present. He's, the beginning of the end. Of our life here on earth.

Then this word of the lord came to Jeremiah, I am the lord the God. said I created all mankind everything, is possible to me ? Jeremiah 32:26-27.

Our God, he is spirit. He made our flesh. He made us like his image in the spirit. Genesis.

Therefore, our power, flesh, and spirit all belong to him.

We are temple of God. Corinthians 3:16.

Our entire life, belong to him. God spirit is sent out to us, to rescue us from all the dangers, if we only believe. Not even, one single evil force. Can come near us. Whenever we struggle. We call on God,and seek him. So he can, give us a strength.

Official said daughter, has died. Jesus said to him do not be afraid, just have faith Mark 5:35-36.

Our Lord Jesus Christ brought, that little girl to life. How much more, he will do for us. If we only invite, his spirit to live in us, so we can have like his heart. So he can hear every heart beat we have.

Our suffering. Jesus know, about suffering, more than anyone of us. He gave his life. For us, so we can be saved. He was innocent. Free of, any guilt. Jesus Christ takes, our crisis. That comes ahead of us, and turn it. Into happiness. Always there just in time.

There's no greater, than the power, of the holy spirit. God control, whole world.

Therefore, don't throw away, your confidence. Which has great reward, for you have need, of endurance. Hebrews 10:35-39.

So that, when we have done, the will of God. When we, please him in every way. He is, with us. What we have to worry about. If God with us, then we'll receive what he has promise.

It is not easy, to do will of God. When we have, evil power over us. Because, of so much wickedness on earth. Therefore, temptation become higher, and higher. Bigger and bigger When we give up. It became evil chance. To escape from hell, when we sin.

With prayers and fasting. We pleaded with God to make us holy.

Jesus said. Again, I say to you,if two of you agree on earth about, for which they are to pray. It shall granted to them, by my heavenly father. Matthew 18:19-20.

For where two or three pray, God will be there. Go to church more often,you will be praying with many.

God is love.1 John 4:8.

When we pray together, out of his love, and mercy. He answers.

Jesus said. I am going,there to prepare,a place for you John 14:2-4.

Jesus Christ said, I came to take you to the father, and the only way we see God. If we have, and become like Jesus. Jesus Christ he's qualified, by the holy spirit of God. Jesus Christ, he is the face of God.

One almighty God. Who loved us so much. He came down on earth to save us. Jesus revealed to us heart of God. Jesus Christ. He was, heaven on earth. Still live among us. Jesus.

He was to unfold, the bad off the earth, and replace it, with good.

The righteous deeds bring justice to all oppressed. God is all merciful gracious. Psalms 103:6,8,11

God love toward us is great. God takes over, all our problems, and turn it into good. He takes, our burdens, as well. Especially, when he knows, we're desperate. God bring us comfort, and carry our heavy loads, of this life. God he is, always with the faithful, and waiting for none faithful, to come back to him.

Lord Jesus Christ Said, so you also are now in anguish. But I will see you again, and your hearts will rejoice, and no one will take. Your joy away from you. John 16:23.

Gift of this earth, all we own. Well end when we die. But God gift, it is forever God will let us, share his Glory. He is our God. Who revealed. Himself, through our Lord Jesus Christ. Whom who, supply us with. what we needed, to get to the father, If we all get along, work together. What could possibly go wrong. God gave us the laws.

We know that, all things work for good those. Who loves God.

We trust in God. We prove our love, and loyalty to him. By following his commandments, and laws. Romans 8:28.

God gave us the laws, for our own good. God wants us, to be victorious 24/7 Not a failure.

Our goal should be, conquering the evil with good. What, could possibly go wrong.

That your trust may be in the lord and his word been known to you. Proverbs 22:19.

Listening to word of God not enough. Anyone can do that. Even the none believer do. We are required, to be living word of God, and that is living according.

We let God, be our console. Especially, in time of need. If we walk, through the lights we will not trip. But, if we walked through the dark we will trip.

If we know, Jesus Christ he's the light Will lives, into our hearts, to lead us to the right path. Our Lord Jesus Christ wind up on the cross. He was able to do so, for the sake humanity. New testament.

Do you know, how to handle suffering?. Jesus do. We all know, we could not do it on our own. We will be wise, to ask Jesus Christ for help. Jesus know very well, how to take suffering. He will help us, to get up On the, cross with him.

If we take advice, of those, who are in the dark, as much as we are. It will be no way out of the dark. If two blinds, help each other walking. They will both trips and fall. Proverb 22:19

God will fully supply us, with what we needed. With according to his Glory, Rich's in Christ Jesus. Philippines 4:19.

When we humble ourselves. And asking for a little God will give much more, because with God, there's no limit, to how much. He loves to give.

There is no limit to his Glory.

The kingdom of heaven, is unclaimed fortune waiting,for us to claim Matthew 10:7.

By faith, devotion, and trust in God, we will get there.

We all face situation. It seem more like, no way out. But if we study, the situation to find. The safer, and easier, and peaceful way out of it.

Would you, rather,be stress, or happy? When you, have things wrong. You should fix, and get it over with without delay. If you postpone things for later Can you relax? Even for a moment, without no worries ? You are only. Hurting yourself. Also wasting that, time you could use, to think how to fix it.

Instead of worrying. When we, become frustrated, desperate, and alone. That's what pleases, the evil. Evil love trouble. God want us to feel, free all the time. Because, God is full of goodness, and happiness.

But you are a shield around me, Psalms 3:3.

God want us, to belong to him. Always, unconditionally along with all our obstacles hardships. We go through, in to our lifetime. Never give evil, the chance to come near us, Under, any circumstances.

God want to take control, over our life. So we can be safe. He want, to be our shield. Protector, against all the dangers. God promised, he will take care of his people. As long as, they obey him.

We worship, God in spirit, and in the truth Romans 12:1-3.

We pray to God so we can get a security. God grant us salvation. In the bible We were, given. The insurance, to guarantee us our salvation.

Mark, the blameless man, and be hold the upright for there is posterity for the man of peace. Observe the honest Psalms 37:37.

Those at, peace with God, have a future. Those who are, good, and honest. Wonderful they are Guarded, and guided by the holy spirit, of God always. They will never tumble The wicked will struggle, and terrible, miserable fearful, and stress full life

If we follow evil way all the time this a chance to suffer in next life. More likely there will be cut off, from kingdom of God. If we don't repent. We could critical. Some people think. This is, a living hell on earth. Maybe it is. So many, problems created for ourselves. Was not, necessary. Or something, doesn't make sense.

Many people don't know. God is, common sense, and common knowledge. He want to be inserted in every human being. We don't have, much of common sense anymore.

We often run to fix, the most simplest problems. But we don't do, anything about the issue of life. The most awful thing we do, is ignore the main things that is our families We can, remain free of any problems.

A mild answer, calms wrath but the. harsh word stir s up anger Ephesians 4:26-27.

If you speak, to people with anger. People retaliate back. But if you talk to them, with kindness, and gentleness. Will guarantee peace.

Whenever, we have dispute with someone. If we deal with anger, that anger should be, with mercy. In order for things to go smoother. To get it, fixed faster.

When, we are angry at someone. Would be wise, to fix the problem on the spot What makes,anyone think they are in, any that person concern. That person, could be happy celebrating, not even thinking, of us being stress, or angry at them. At the meantime, we will be hurting inside mentally. Could lead, to internal problems. This is. the main reason, to be wise enough, to clear disputes. No matter how big, or small. We get it, of our heart, and mind. To remain, at peace. We should never let, the devil put us on hold.

Usually, if I have issue with, any one. I take care of it on the spot. I may scream, yell, with mercy. I don't rest until, I fix it. Once I have a dispute with someone I don't rest until everything, is fixed. Of course some people, they could be persistent not to give in. We pray for them.

Good persons, when they make mistake. They make up, and fix their mistake. Once you're done makeup, and fix things. If other site remain disappointed, or upset with you That is, their business. They lose.

Also what make, us think ? If we are disappointed or mad, at someone. We are, at any of their concern. They could be enjoying their life, vacationing, celebrating something While you, are hurting. The best thing you can do, is to join them. Once upon a time, I was disappointed at relatives. He did not even know. At the meantime, he was celebrating, and having good time with his friends, and family. Anyway, I said to myself look, at him having fun. All I, was doing is hurting myself. Being mad at him.

As oft answer turn away wrath,but a harsh word stir up anger Proverbs 15:1.

When we, speak gentle words. We could bring Almost anyone, to reasoning. Because every, human being is born with mercy of God, in their heart. Begging brings compassion in others hearts. There is compassion, and every one heart. Sometime, people don't know how compassioned, they are. Until someone go, under their mercy.

This is why, God depends on us, to bring his mercy, and compassion. Pleading, and begging for anything, and being a persistent. We end up, bringing compassion,and mercy out of someone's heart. Especially, when asking. For forgiveness, from someone.

We can easily teach, people how to become kind. Because, kindness is, in their in heart already. They just don't know it. Just by reaching people. Showing them we are there for them, to help them finding themselves. People, go through, so much throughout life. So many, their hearts harden. When they, do not get an answer, for their problem. They feel locked, don't know how to get out. They get relieved, once they find someone to lean, and depend on.

We need, to be in constant communication, with people around us, to be open forward, honesty, pure at heart. Will lead us, to successful life. I often say to a good person, with faith. If you are good persons? You deserves, to be happy always. Don't let anything ruin your happiness?

People who, play mantel games. Always lie. They are, deceived. They are, in the dark, they are, only fooling. Themselves. They live, having false dreams. Whom, never come true.

Our prayer, go like incense before God, he listen to every breath,we take, and every word we say. Psalms 141:1-2.

If we ever need of anything, or have any difficulties in life. We take, all our problems, and complaints to God. We plead, with God, for his mercy to pour on us. We should always pray, before making, any decision. For God to help us, decide what to do.

God give teaching. To believe, in him mainly. Also how, to deal with each other How to love, and respect, the people around us. God teach us in the bible, to team up together. Because God know, we are not able to do it alone, all the time. Bible also teach us how much,we are connected to each other.

One good thing someone do, it could benefit so many. One bad thing someone do could hurt so many. That's how Life is. Sometime we do things, without knowing how much ? We are hurting ourselves.

If you have, a personal gain, is only yours, and not no one else. And if you lose. It is not no one's lost, but yours. This is why your life. Should not become, any one concern or business first, but yours. The only thing people, out to do for you is, if they love you. They should be proud, and happy, for you, for your gain. The same people who love you. They should be, standing next, to you to comfort you. In times of hardships.

If any of you lacks wisdom, let him ask God,who gives to all men, generously, and without reproaching. It will be give him. James 1:5, God become, our guidance from A to Z. God will show us what to do, and how, to go, about our life. From the time of birth until our death.

Unfortunately so many, are afraid of, even reading the bible. They think God punish us. But God he is, perfectly good, he does not punish anyone. His wishes are, to gain every single person living on the face of the earth. It is not God's fault when we, fall into temptation.

When we sin we suffer. That is, asking for evil rewards. When we do good, it is asking for God rewards. Of course, they will be good rewards. Because, when we ask for Gods rewards, happiness follows.

Every time someone sins, is giving the evil, the chance to escape from hell, and go around the earth,to find more victims.

By practicing our faith, that is. When we discover the insurance. God give. That's salvation. You need, to be comforted. If you have a depression, need to learn how to handle emotion. Feeling guilty, or embarrass need encouragement. Need to have a grace hope, peace.

About jealousy, integrity, about the assault, kindness. Responsibilities. Problems of all kinds, laziness, leadership, pride, purity, about trials, and stress, criticism, emotion. We have answers in the Bible. If you're worried, about your employment you have an answer About gossiping. About pride, and envy. How to be patient. All that is, in the bible and teaching us how to fix. Everything.

Courage, and caring, how to be honest. Humble down to earth person. It is all in the holy scripture (the bible) Try to read it. If you just do that ? You will be able to control every issue. Fully, safe from evil.

Someday, we can be with God in heaven. God is not selfish. He want us, to share his glory forever, and ever. With him.

God wants us to be strong, no matter. What we, go through. Our lifetime. Always try to overcome temptation. Evil put us through. To concord evil with good. Whenever, we do any good, entire heaven rejoice. When we, continuously do good. We disappoint, the devil, and put him to shame. Knowing, we love God.

Evil hate God. This is, why evil. Use us to disappointed God. Evil able to do so. Because of our, free will. Was given to us from God.

When, anyone uses. God's name in vain. There's rejoice in celebration in hell. Evil hate God. Evil is, jealous of humanity. Because we are, granted the chance of salvation. I am not sure the evil have chance. If evil has chance of salvation ? He would, not be going around the earth. Causing all these catastrophes, he's the tempter.

We are human being victims, deceived, very weak. When it comes to Sin. Because of our free will. We face, our own consequences. They, could be very terrible.

We have no more common sense. God is, wisdom of common sense. No one was ever born with knowledge. We learn, as we go. We suppose, to learn on our own.

Sometime we do make bad decisions. We have the step back. What we, need to do is move forward, never stop. If we don't know much about certain thing. Never, become persistent Immediately seek, advice of someone, who is knowledgeable. Myself If, I am not sure what to do. I usually, seek few advices, not only one advice. So I can have many ideas. I study it, to figure out. Which one, sound good. I can go with it. Take five people advise, and will compare At least two, or three matches, the same idea, or similar. Our choice, to be patient. In order,to get things done, the right way.

I would more likely go with that. Three out of five agree. Hoping to be, what is best for me It is good, to take advice of a wise person. Someone with a lot of experience. In the field you are looking into.

Our Anger could lead to murder, and gives evil power, to put us. Through more temptations Showing anger, is foolish. Only make things worse, and spread quick. We must treat anger with mercy, compassion peace. Anger with mercy, in our hearts.

If you are mad, or disappointed at anybody, and if you don't fix. All you do is hurting yourself. Because other individual. May not care, about your feelings, or concerns: Some people cares only about themselves. Especially, the ones with no moral.

Therefore, will always, be best to make up, for our own health. When, we meet someone half the way, to make peace. More likely, put them to shame. Knowing they were, not able to do that, them self's.

Throwing a fit, and having temper is very critical. Anger can, lead to catastrophe. Sometime murderer. Anger, brings, and spread

Evil. Being gentle, loving, peaceful, and merciful. That is what faith, in God is about.

When Cain, murdered his brother Abel, he did that out of anger, jealousy, and hate. Genesis 4:8.

Why get jealous?. When at, the meantime, could be into our best interest to join. Who have more. There a chance, we can get their help. I we ever, we need them.

Be angry but not sin ; do not, loses sight sun set down on your anger. Ephesians 4:27.

Whenever we, get angry. Should, be with mercy. Especially, when, we to seek justice for someone. for less fortunate.

After a day, hard working. We need, a break time to relax, clear our heart and mind. So we can have, full peaceful night, hopefully. We have sweet dreams. God want you to be happy.

When it comes to love, be honest, and sincere. The love, we have for each other. Will reunite us with God.

Who have heard, it was said to your ancestors, you shall not kill, and whoever kill, will be liable to judgment. Matthew 5:21-22.

Jesus said, who is angry with his brother, will be liable to judgment. When it comes to a brother, he is part of you. Therefore, if you hate your brother. You are hating, yourself. We are, all made image of God. This is why, murdering anyone is blossoming. Abortion, as well.

When we have, boldness of speech confidence, of excess through faith in him (God) Psalms 138:8. Ephesians 3:1.

When it comes to faith in God, we should be persists: Take strong pride in God. Never lose his side. If we trust in God. We never have, any fear. Trusting God will guarantee, our salvation The lord is with us, to the end of time. God never abandon his people.

I will make with them, an everlasting covenant that. I will not turn away from doing good to them. Jeremiah 32:40.

Fear of God is loving father, and doing his will. God will continue, to do good for us unconditionally, for the rest of our life. Into our hearts, God will. Always put desires to worship him, and love him. God chooses, not to lose not even, one of us. God walks next to us even. When we are in state, and stage of Sin. God waiting, and willing to forgive us. Once we repent. God forgive every time. He knows we are only human. We are weak, when it comes to sin. He does not give himself, any other choice.

Because he want, us all for himself. Jesus Christ, said A men, a men, I say to you will ever hear my word, and believe, in the one, who's send me has eternal life, and will not come to condemnation. John 5:24.

Jesus said, all that the father gave me, will come to me, and I will not reject, anyone who comes to me. John 6:37.

Jesus Christ, our lord he is face, and heart of God. Jesus call us, to believe in him, and have like his heart, we'll see, God someday. Because, Jesus is the way. If we go to Jesus he will show us, the way to God.

What will separate us, from love of Jesus Christ ? Romans 8: 35.

When our, lord Jesus was carrying the cross. Was thinking of us. He's telling his father

I love them, I want to die for them.

Can any of us, go up on the cross alone. Like our lord Jesus. He was able to. For our sake He did it, for all humanity to open the door of heaven, for all of us. For anyone who chooses, to go on the cross. Ask Jesus. He knows the way. Because, he knew suffering. He is, willing to take all our suffering. If we can only count on him ?. He will not, send us empty handed.

Paul letter said, for which. I was appointed preacher apostle, and teacher. On this account I am suffering, for I am not ashamed Timothy 1:11-12.

Paul preaching from jail. He did not care about suffering. He was, focusing on Jesus. His main concern, was doing well of God. Knowing he had, a mission to accomplish, and for fulfill He also knew, there's nothing in the world. Can come, before God. He trusted in God.

Whenever, we know God, nothing matter anymore. Whenever, we are depressed. We go to God.

When the just cried out. lord hear, and rescue them from all of distress. Psalms34:18-19.

God never depart from, the ones, who are, depressed lonely, hurting, and broken heart. Lord saves those, whose spirit is crushed.

When we, turn to God, he comes to us for rescue before it's too late. He is, our spiritual inspirit.

Abraham believed. he, became the father of many nations. Genesis 4:18-22.

Abraham's faith in God was, very strong. He know that God is all powerful beyond anything That existed here on earth.

Abraham, never wavered in believing. God's promised. Abrahams, his faith grow stronger. By faith, he brought Glory to God.

At the final judgment, God will wipe, every tear from our eyes, and there shall be no more deaths, or morning, whaling or pain. Revelation 4:18-22.

God will remove all sorrows, and or crying, of good ones.

Evil will be gone forever. I believe, at the final judgment. All the people. we done good for, will be present, and all the people. We've done bad, or we put them down, persecuted there will be present. So we don't deny our wrong doing.

Those who Done, evil will vanish. They will, not have a chance to enjoy The kingdom of heaven with God. This is, why the faithful pray to God. Hell to be empty. For all humanity to be safe, at the end of time.

Have no anxiety, at all but in everything, by prayer, and petition with thank s giving make your request known to God. Philippians 4:6.

God telling us, not to worry. Always be, full of joy in him. Don't worry about anything instead pray about everything. Tell God what you needed, and thank him for, all he has done for you. If we only do this. We will experience, God's peace. Which is. far more wonderful. Than human mind, can understand. Because his peace, will guard our hearts and minds, to have heart, like Jesus Christ, heart. God want us, to live happy cheerful, and joy full life.

God did not give this life. So we can do nothing. But worry. Instead, he wants us to live this life to the fullest.

Therefore, next time if you are angry, with someone. Make sure, you make peace with them fast. You should do it on the spot. Anything can be solve. So you, can both be happy, and have peace of mind. Because, when you are disappointed or, more upset at someone. Always seek, a solution, and immediately. Think of, ways to correct the problem If we cannot face, the other individual. Do it in writing, that might be easier, to get it, off your heart. Hopefully, to replace it with, love, and peace. Be persistent, when making peace with anybody.

It is joy full. It is good when you are, begging for good things. Everyone, in the world was born with mercy of, God in their heart. Even if they don't know God, or believe in God Still have his mercy. Many of people, don't know. They are, compassioned.

We need to assure others. Help on the way. We also need to teach others how to be good.

Be assured, an evil man will not, go unpunished. But those, who are righteous will be delivered. Proverbs 11:21.

We can let them know that. Nothing will go unpunished. We also out, to know that even. When we make, an honest mistake. We still suffer, because of it.

Therefore, it is not worth it ? No way out, being disappointed, upset or unhappy keep working on everything at any given time 24.7.

Have concerns for your life. Waking up every morning. We should plan, to have another happy day. But not forget to whatever, obstacles comes ahead of us that day. We will fix it as they come,or at least try. It is very good to look ahead, in the future. Plan your future, set yourself goals. Be honest with yourself.

Be straight forward, don't be afraid. When, make bad decisions. People who, makes those mistakes, they worked on it to fix it. Once is fixed, they find it, very rewarding.

When you do right, most of the time.. You are, facing good consequences. When, you become a person, of integrity. You will be respected. Many will find you, trust worthy. People around you, will have confidence in you.

One thing we have in common. We Are born, one day. We all die. Therefore, we have the beginning, and the end on this earth.

Our life, is so similar. When it, comes to suffering, and struggling. We all cry. morn worry. We all have, responsibilities. We all have ups, and downs in life.

We don't, know common sense, any more. There isn't, hardly resting moment, in life There's, always something.

Once upon a time, my job was driving. Dropping off customer, and pick up. That's how I made living. One day, I was taking customer home. The lady looked, so depressed. At the meantime I was thinking of ways to comfort her. While riding together. I said, to her I see myself in every human being eyes. First, she was in shock thinking, and wondering. What, I was trying to say. Surprised, she was thinking. I was trying to make passes, at her. Actually, she had no idea. What I meant, to tell her. I immediately, answered telling her. That all human being have similar life. We go through good, and bad times. Our life so much alike. I explained to her. Life is, battle for everyone. This is, why I feel compassioned. For every, single human being. I have unconditionally mercy. She began, to have lots of tears in her eyes. I handed her paper towel, to wipe her eyes. Life itself. It is not fair.

Because, of the temptation. Which evil, put us through. Of mistakes, we make. We continue to do bad, toward each other. We just don't know. How much, we are connected to the other. If one person, one good thing. Could benefit, a lot of people. If one person do one bad thing, can hurt lot of people. Before you begin your day. Whatever you are going through, you need to remember. There are, millions, and billions of people like you. Having same issues. Like yours. May be you will run, into some of these people. With same issues May be you can find, a solution together.

If you feel, terrifying, stressed, troubled, and lonely. Don't be alarmed, or afraid. You are not alone. If anyone, tell you. They don't worry. They are, exaggerating. In fact we worry the 24.7. That is, part of daily thing. There will be, more coming ahead. Therefore, if you don't fix, the ones you have, now. Immediately, will double the amount of the things. You will have to fix. Will be no way out. You'll drive, yourself crazy.

Lost a loved one, by death. I have news, for you. We are, all orphans, in this world. We all lost, someone. May be parents, grandparents or anyone of our relative. In fact when, attended funeral. I love to comfort people. I often say that dead, are gone. There's, nothing, we can do for them. or either. They can, do for all of us. I continue by saying. Us the living, we need to take good care of each other. Our loved ones, are part of us. In the spirit. We are all made in the image of God.

Even when, our loved ones depart from us. They still live through us, in the spirit. We accomplish, what they did not have, a chance to finish. When, they were alive. Faith is being positive, decisive.

Now faith, is the assurance of things hoped for, the conviction of things not seen. Hebrews 11: 1.

We should be, confident when it comes to faith. If we have the faith, we should have confident in our self. Therefore, nothing work without faith. The world fell, without faith conquer evil with good.

Family, and relatives are part of each other. God forbid if I hate, any of them. Then I am hating myself. If I love them, I am loving myself.

In life the only way, you are able to make something, of yourself. If you trust, yourself things work out always.

If you have, self a steam. Just the way, you hope for things, to work out for yourself There are, so many like you. Should find, some of these people, so you can work, with them hopefully together. You will be able, to accomplish something. Always team-work.

Whenever you are stressed, take deep breath, then think of the things you can, be thankful for. Think of something, it has to be something out there, you are pleased with. May be you should, think of people. Who have no one. There are, so many out there. Always there is someone, who's worse than you. If your job stress you, think of finding another job.

Usually people, who complain about, what they have. More likely they get worse You need to remember. Your job, is only to make a living. You don't, need to mix your emotion with it. In fact would be wiser. If you treat it like your own. Also will be wiser to let people tell you, what to do. The point is, when customer comes, they are, the ones who know, what they needed. You Should, be pleasing your customer. They, keep coming back. Customer come first.

When people, are humble, and grateful. They, often succeed. We set goals, and dreams for ourselves. Sometime, we may be able, to achieve. We have, so much in common.

People love to gossip, and spread rumor about others. For some time, people hear things about others, they believe on the spot. I don't like, to hear anyone else problems. All they do is, adding more to my responsibilities.

It is very bad, when others hear things about you. They believe on the spot. Is like assigning judgment on you. Especially, when they are not sure. Or some time just because they like the person they are hearing things from. Better, or more. They believe, on the spot. That's not fair. People always, assume things. They will, never change.

My responsibilities, are to have enough time. To take care of myself, and my family. If I had extra time. I will help others. I often do that very often.

A worthless man plots evil, and his speech is like scorching fire. A perverse, man spreads strife, and whisper separate close friends. Proverb 16:27-28,James 4:11.

Bible talk about gossips. When, you gossip about somebody. You are judging them There is, only one judge, that is God. It is wrong gossiping. Especially, spreading rumors about people falsely 'cause. Everyone, have the right to be there, to defend them self. If you speak behind any one back, it is taking their advantage. It is not fair for the ones. Who, you hear things about someone, who's not present. To instantly believe. What they're saying about someone. Who's absent. If any put someone down in front of us. Before passing, any judgment. We ask that person. So we, can hear the truth. Speaking behind someone's back it is taking their freedom.

You shall not repeat, of false report, do not join the wicked in putting your hand, as an unjust. Do not corporate, with evil people, will tell lies on the witness stand. Exodus 23:1

Some time, there are people. Who really, love you enough to trust you. To the point where, they are, able to tell you. What bothered them. Something, no one know except them and God. You should honor, their trust in you, and respect their privacy.

False witness, it is teaming with evil. You shall not curse the deaf, or put a stumbling block, in front of the blind. But you shall, fear your God. Leviticus 19:14-17

God said, I am the lord. You shall not act, dishonestly. In rendering judgment, you shall not go about spreading slander. Among your Kinsmen.

God said, we must be honest, and treat everyone equally. Whether, they are weak, or strong poor, or rich.

We must, treat everyone equally. Don't matter, if they are. rich, or poor. The only one who judge, is God alone.

We should only judge fairly, and justly. Because God is fair, good, and just. Slandering and putting out roomer against anyone is Evil. If we have, anything against anyone. We should confront that person. Will be only fair. Because, everyone deserves, to defend themselves Always, speak the truth. Speak your heart out. Makes, your heart pure, and crystal clear Evil love, to see us miserable, hurt suffering. He truly enjoyed that, very much.

I often say, whenever someone hurt my feeling. I told them off. Even, if I have to screamed out. So they can hear me. So they know, how I feel about whatever. I never walked away tell, I make sure everything is A, OK. I don't like, to be unhappy.

My father, and his brother, my uncle, always had business together. They were partners When the brothers, and sisters, and I. Our parents. My uncle his wife, and their kids. My Cousins. We all, lived together in one very large home. It was big enough, for all of us when we, were young. But when we grew up. We needed more room. Therefore, my father, and my uncle. Build another home, for my parents. Along with me, my brothers, and sisters. Anyway growing up, with our Cousins. Whenever, we had a dispute. People around us, use to think we're, becoming each other worse enemies. But we, prove them wrong. It was different than what they thought. It took only few minutes later. We were together happier, than ever Like nothing happened between us.

Power of love. Some time, we made people laugh, wondering if. We were out of our mind. Because, people they are, not used to this type of love.

People, often used, not to speak to each other for short, or long time. After disputes A wonderful woman once, told me her husband's. Hasn't, talked his brother for a long time. I told her, if I don't speak to my brother ?. I will be very angry, and hurt. I add may be will be wise. If your husband, call his brother, to hear what he is up to ? May be, they can do something together. Maybe they can help each other. Starting some kind, of business together.

A worth less man plots evil, and his speech like a scorching fire. Scandal hunt for scandal; their words, are destructive blaze. Proverbs 16:27-29

Trouble makers, they like to gossip. So they can separate friends, and relatives from each other. They are, the bad seeds among people.

Scandalous person, is wicked whom does evil work Scandal when you start fire among people, when allure of all people it is hate, and evil Romans 1:28-29.

When they refused, to acknowledge God. He abandoned them to their Evil minds, and let them do things that, should never be done.

In the event, when people take God, out of their life's. Their life becomes, full every kind of wickedness. Sin greed, hate envy, murder, fighting, deception, malicious behavior and the gossip. They become back stabbers, and haters of God. They abandon God. So they don't feel shameful, or guilty, or acknowledge, any wrong doing.

Without faith, will be abuse, bad behavior divorce struggling, suffering. Without mercy of God, will be catastrophe on earth.

And so they, incur condemnation, for breaking their first pledge Beside that, they learn to be idlers. Timothy 5:12-13.

There are so many, who spend, their time gossiping. About other people's business They have nothing else to do. But revealing, people's privacy's, and spreading evil without feeling guilty, or a shame. Also they are, deceived. Because, everyone have their own issues Talking about someone else issues. It doubles their issues. Because, they are carrying on theirs, and others.

The man who, deceives his neighbor, and says, I was only joking. That's evil lying, is deceiving. Proverbs 26:19-22.

Spreading, false rumors. It is evil. Some people, they only talk nice to you, just to act nice. They never practice, what they preach. People with hate, in their heart. They sound pleasant enough, around people. Eventually, we learn not to believe them. Therefore, we stay away from them. They act to be kind, their heart. But it is full of evil. We need, to pray for their conversion of heart.

The steps, of a man are from the LORD, and he establishes way he delighted of, even when we fail, God is with us. For the LORD is stay of his hand. Proverbs 20:24.

Those who trust in God. Their steps are. Even if they stumble. They will not full Therefore, the lord God holds them by the hand.

Sometime, when you think you fall down to the ground once. You begin to get up. That's when God is there helping you getting up. So you can start, all over again. While you are, in process of getting up. You needed, to help someone else getting up there with you. You will please God. If you are grateful to the people. Who help, and care about you. To be considerate toward others. They will, be the same way to you.

God loves, who is thoughtful of less fortunate. Because God think of us 24/7, throughout our life. He is always at work for us, to protect us to give us, what we need.

In the bible God, give us answer, to whatever comes ahead of us. During our life time.

We find, an answer in the bible. If you have, any problem at all. Any questions, about anything There's, an answer in the bible.

From the creation. From the birth, to death. There's, an answer, in the bible. We also get from Bible the wisdom. That is, the knowledge. Holy spirit give us. From the bible, we learn the common sense, Basically, in the holy book of the bible.

God is telling us. I created you, I stay with you. Along your side. From the time God give us life until, he take us back to him.

In the Bible, God is reaching to us. So we can learn forgiveness, peace, and mercy Unconditionally, compassioned. Whenever, we sin we separate, ourselves from God. Therefore evil takes over our life. Until we, return to God. When we repent. God gave us this life, and set a goal. For us is, to be happy.

God wants us, to celebrate whole, of our life. God want us, to live life, to the fullest There is, a lot more celebrations. Throughout, our life then sadness.

In the beginning our parents, celebrate our birth. As parents we enjoy every moment of our child life. Then kids grow up, all the challenges parents go through, somehow, they always find joy.

In the beginning. As new parents. There is, always many first times of course, all new things, about our children. Worth of celebrations, and is very common, only some of followings.

From the beginning. The joy of being parents for first time. When, the child crawl for the first time. Is a celebration for parents. When child begin, to eat for first time baby food, is a celebration for the parents. When the baby, makes first step, it is a celebration, for the parents. When the baby, begin to make sounds. Parents, begin to train the baby anxiously, to hear their baby, to say first word mom, or dad. When the baby, say the magic word. There will be huge celebration. Baby has first tooth, will be a celebration, and makes first to walk will be a celebration. First, birth day parents gather, all the children to come to share their joy, and happiness. The parents celebrate, when their children learn. A,B, C. Before, they know it. Child is ready, for preschool. That's another celebration. kinder-garden the first great. That is more joyful time, than anything else, in the world. Your child living your life, all over for you. You are watching, your image. That is, part of you growing. Before your eyes. How much happiness, out to be for you ? The love you have for your children, get you to work. knowing you need to support them. Any good, parents their children should become your stirrings To build their future. Your future, become your children life's. Try to raise your children. So you can be proud of them. You celebrate, when they make it, to the middle school. When they make it, to junior high school. Then high school, the final year. When, they graduate high school. You say to yourself job well done. Even if they don't graduate. But they grow up, to become good people. To be proud.

Hopefully, they will all graduate for you. Then Someday, they graduate from college.

Or should be the time, to team up with your kids. To start some kind of business. Or if you already have a business, made out. May to be wise, get them involve. So they can be strong back. What you own, It is, their inheritance anyway. Will be wise, if they earn. What they want to keep. Relative, who don't have children. Sometime, takes part of helping you raising you children, as well. Because, of the love they have for you. Raising children is huge challenge. The challenges, we face. Isn't everyone life ?. Therefore we take joy out of it.

If you think, you have it so bad. It is not God fault. It is not. Evil fault. If you have it very bad, it is not your fault. What you need to do, is get up, and keep going. God create us, and give us free will. We face, our own consequences.

God don't want, us to please Evil. That is, when we give up. Therefore, God want us to take to him all our goodness, mistakes, sine's, and challenges.

God because, of his unconditional love, for all humanity. He give us, the freedom to choose. The choice is ours. Which road to take, if we really want to Carry on.

The hurt, and stress it is our choice. If you want, to choose happiness. Look around you and enjoy what you see.

God give us, free will. Not without his will, for guidance along, with the promise, of salvation. Psalms 37:23-34.

Jesus said, so be perfect, just, as your heavenly father, is perfect. Matthew 5:48.

Jesus knew, all humanities Sin.

But almost anyone, can be a perfectly good person. Good person, is the one, who live life of virtue, grace, mercy, and peace. Good person is, humble and pure. Only speaks, the truth never lie to gain, or to deceive anyone. Never steal, or take advantage of anyone. Always, seeking justice for the ones. Who are, seeking justice. Never treat, any one different. Just because they are poor, or less fortunate. Always, feed the hungry. Never gossip, or spread rumors About anyone, or bear false witness against anyone. Never, judge anyone.

Good person usually, is the one. Who trust in God, and believe. He, or she do is being guided by the holy spirit of God, to do what's right. Good persons, also are the ones. Who always are, un conditionally forgiving. Loving everyone. No matter, who they are. Good person, is the one who treat everyone fairly, and equally. Never treat, anyone less. Just because, they are poor, or less fortunate. Good person is the one, who don't talk smoothly. Only to act nice. But good person, is who prove his, or her, what preaches.

Smooth talk from an Evil heart, is like glaze on Cracked pottery, your enemies shakes your hands, and greet you like an old friend, all the time while, conniving against you Proverbs. 26:23-26.

We need, to be careful. Who we are, dealing with all the time. Never to judge anyone But to work, with others, to make things better, and bring peace, mercy, and freedom around the world. To feed the hungry, take care of the poor. God is very, concerned about the poor and less fortunate.

By their, smooth talk, and flattering words, they deceive, the heart of, the naive people Romans 16:18.

Such people, are not serving, Jesus Christ, our lord. They are serving their, own personal interest. By their smooth talk, and glowing words. They deceive innocent people.

Everyone who lies, to his neighbor. Their flattering lips, and deceitful, full hearts, is evil. The ones who, speaks the truth. They are, children of God.

It is unfortunate thing. What truly ruining, the world, is the abortion. accusation, adultery and, premarital sex.

Anger that lead to murder, arguments, attitudes. So many people, stopped caring for each other. We are, losing our common sense.

People do whatever, they please. Not worrying about the consequences. Desires of material, becoming things of today. More than spiritual. So much of dishonesty, in the world today

Too much, evil in the world. Evil is, jealous of humanity, and don't like to see anyone to be happy, or have a good life.

Too many wars, and hate. So many who hate. For a very stupid reasons. Some who hate, and they don't know why.

Too much judging, in the world. So many, who are losing hope, and becoming too lazy to do anything. Hardships loneliness, lust, love of the money. Painful life, for so many. Too much murdering, pride, selfishness.

Abortion, killing unborn babies. Actually, murdering. What God created. From the conception. There was life every time,at the conception. God is at it again. I mean, at creation Evil stopping. What God giving. That is life.

God told, Jeremiah. God knew him before, he was born trying to encourage him To have trust in God. Jeremiah 1:1-5

Therefore, God told him before. I formed you, in the womb. I knew you, before you were born. I dictated you a prophet, to the nation, had appointed you.

Therefore, everyone, who was not born yet. Is known by God. Unborn, they are a spirit that's the image of God.

Abortion is refusing, the gift that God gives us. With respect prochoice, who want the woman, to be able to choose. That is fair, and just. But are they giving, the unborn, the right to choose. If they wants, to get murdered, or not. Or to choose. Whether they wanted to live or not. If the women have a choice. It would be, fair, and just to give the unborn the choice We need to be, the voice for the unborn, and to choose, for them. There are, so many, who desperately want a baby. They want to be a parent's.

Abortion is, blossoming against God.

Saint, and angels in heaven, they are praying. Asking God to put in our heart. So we stop murdering babies. To bring justice, to unborn. They have every right to. Because they once lived. Where God, only know. Before, he created them. Waiting to be born into this world. Just like everyone else. To have the chance, like all of us. Good mother, would say I would give my life for my baby.

Dream I had, So God help me. For I am telling the truth.

In the year 2010. Just before Christmas. I had a dream. In my dream. I was looking at the wall. I saw picture of Mary, mother of Jesus Christ, on the wall. I believe, being called, the sorrowful. Mary; for the pain. She went through. Watching her son, being tortured and put on the cross to die. Anyway, on the picture, in my dream. I saw her moving her mouth. I was not able to tell what, she was saying. Because, I don't know how read lips But there, were a bunch of people. She was preaching to them. In the picture, she had the baby, in her arm. When, I wake on the next morning. I knew what, my dream was about Because, of the baby she had in arm. Talking, to all these people. I knew, she was giving warning about abortion. Especially, she had baby, in her arm. More likely the scene was by the abortion clinic.

That morning, I stopped by my sister, to visit her. Because, she is on my way to work To have a cup of coffee with her. As I sat, on the couch. I looked on the wall. I saw identical picture of Mary. I see, in my dream. I asked my sister, when did you get the picture ? Because I didn't even knew she had it. She replied, someone give it to her, as a gift a day before That was a hint, and based prove, my dream, was accurate.

One more time, on August 15th of year 2011.

I often attend, and hear mass in Saint Thomas, Chaldean, catholic church On maple road West Bloomfield, Michigan. By the right side of the Altar, in the church. There is, a door, on each side. One to the left. One to, the right. The priest, and the deacons, celebrate the mass. The above date, it was on Sunday, attending mass. As I was standing looking at the door to the left. I was able to see image, of Mother Mary. The same picture, I seen the year before. Only this time look like real life, as image, from the top, head to the feet Mother Mary She have the baby, in her arm. Real life. Every Sunday, I go to church. I see the, same image I wish more people can see her. I wish I can speak sign language so. I can tell what she's trying to tell me. Or If someone else, can see her. So they can understand what she is trying to say. I know, it is very important. It is for our sake, and for the sake of the babies.

Just to let people know. Mother Mary, her spirits play big role in our life. When we pray for her. We humble ourselves. We say to God, we are not worthy praying directly to you Because, we are sinners. We ask mother of Jesus. Mary. Along with all the angels, and saints in heaven, to be our mediator. Between us, and God.

Mother Mary, and all, the saints in heaven. Takes, our prayers to Jesus. He takes it to the father, our God. So they can be answered.

Like if you, need someone to do something for you. If refuses to do it. You go to his mother, or his father. To ask, on your behalf. Hopefully. He will lessen. Because, that is his mother, or father.

Also in the year 2008. In the same church. I see another image, on the right door. This images. I call it image of mercy, compassion, peace, and love. The reason, I call it this name Because the image look like, an old man. Who looks very sick, but look humble. Suffering, but he is pure. The image, look like a person. If anyone was look, at him immediately. Will have mercy on him. Just the way, that image look like.

When people worry. God love, to carry them. The image is telling me. I give you mercy You give me, mercy. The image, also have his two hands, on the two doors. Which are, in the Image, on the door. He is pushing the, two doors within the door to open, the two doors They are, on the same door. He is telling me he's. The door, and the way. To life. Every time I go to church. I see the Image.

Now supposed people, are fighting in process, they may not hurt a pregnant woman her child will born prematurely. Exodus 21:22-25.

If any harm done, the person responsible. Must pay for the damage. Any harm results Then the offender, must be punished, according, to the injury. It's the result in death, the offender execute.

Give justice to the weak, and the fatherless, maintain the right of the afflicted, and the destitute. Psalms 82:3-4.

God give fair judgment, to the poor, orphans uphold the right of oppressed, and the destitute, rescue the poor, and helpless, deliver them from the grasp of evil people. Psalms 127:3.

We should defended, the unborn. Because, they are, all alone. We should help, many who are troubled. The unborn need to have, the chance to be born. Like everybody else. So we can, have better world. Children, are gift from the lord. The fruit of the womb. Children are truly from God.

Adultery one of, the main reasons the couple, end up in divorce. Adultery. Can be fixed it happen once, and promised to stop. But if commit adultery, your spouse is committing adultery with you. Because, you are one. The person, who's involved with you, he, or she is stealing you From, your spouse.

To take advantage of, the young woman, knew that he must marry her, and One was as a wife to a man. Exodus 22:15.

God is protecting, the dignity of, the woman. Premarital sex, is forbid by God. Any man who fool a virgin, and have a sexual relationship, with her. That man is, obligated to take her as a wife, and keep her. So she don't be put, to shame by others.

It is crying shame, even religious, and faithful with kids. They don't train, or talk to their kids, about consequences. Of sexual relationship before marriage. Even, if they don't listen. We did our duty toward God.

Not too many, people explain, to the young. What is the meaning, of relationship. So many young people. First thing they have on their mind. For sex relationship. Younger people don't understand. They don't, have common sense. We need to, teach them from, early age. Their agenda goal, is to find someone. Who can be potential partner for life.

Dating, and finding someone, to love, to grow up with. It is the most profound thing anyone can go through. Building a memory, to last forever. Sometime, when one individual lay down his,or her eyes, on someone called love at first sight. They think this is it.

We need, to teach the young ones. God created us with pride, and dignity. Pride into ourselves.

Some people, are not a shame. Going around, expos their body. Going from, one person to another. My father often told me, save yourself, for your future spouse. I did, and I am on 34th. Years with my spouse. He meant purity.

People, who date many, only for sexual pleasure. They are, taking a chance of having terrible future. I mean sexual relationship, with different people, at same time. That's lust and evil. These, type of relationships creates, hate jealousy, and separations.

Too many broken hearts People. They still don't understand. How much,they are, suffering They are, blinded by the pressure, they think. They are, getting. People who date many, at same time. Would be hard for them, to find a decent relationship. Because a lot, of them live in the past. It is hard for them to let go. Or chances are, ending up with abusive relationship Mentally, or physically. Or both. Pride leads to disgrace. But with humility, comes wisdom.

People are guided, by their honesty. treacherous people are destroyed by their dishonesty Proverbs 11:12.

God hates cheating. But he is pleased, and delight with honesty. The Godly are showered with blessing.

The earnings, of Godly enhance their lives. But, evil people squander their money on Sin Proverbs 10:6,13,16.

Wealth from get - rich - quick schemes, quickly disappears. Wealth from hard work grows. Proverbs 13:11.

If you work and deal, with others with honesty, honor, and loyalty with everyone. God will bless you, in very special ways. Also in many different ways. God multiply for you, and fortune you. With many, great things.

People who gather, their money, and treasurer. By not working very hard, at dishonest and croaked ways. They might have, a lot of money. They struggle more, they have more terrible things, goes in their life. Not too many blessings. It is unfortunate thing, to these people. Because, love of the money, and greed makes them blind. To see how much, they are going through. They need to change, their ways. Maybe, God will come, into their life more often. So he can, give them more blessing. Is better to be poor, and honest. Then, to be a fool and dishonest.

People who steal, and take advantage of others. They are, deceiving themselves. Because nothing goes unpunished.

Even when, we make an honest mistake, or decision. We still suffer because of it. If you set, a trap for others. You will get caught in it yourself. If you roll a boulder down on others. It will roll back, and crush you. What goes around, comes around, and twice more for anything you do. If you throw rumor, against anyone, will back fire. If you hurt anyone They will come back to hurt you. If you curse, anyone will curse you back. If you hate anyone will hate you too.

If you get all the help you need, from people. Who are very considerate, and thoughtful If you don't show consideration they will eventually, stop helping. There are, so many people if you help them, all the time. They love you. But if you don't help them, one time. They hate you. They don't like you anymore. Those are, very ungrateful selfish.

Myself If I, get so much help. Whenever I needed. Some- time people tell me no. I respect that Because, we don't know everyone's situation, all the time, and just can't expect it to get help every time. Besides, there's always next time. If you expect, to get help from people You need to be loyal. Always truthful. Always trust worthy.

If you think, you are head of your household, and you want to be in control. All leaders they serve. Before, they get served. Leaders usually, are people of wisdom, and knowledge Leaders job, is to make sure. Everyone, is protected, having a peaceful life. and freedom.

Merciful, loving. Prospecting, and community to grow together with happiness.

Often in the marriage, were the man wants to be in control. In the wrong ways. Which is selfish ways, with no consideration, for greed.

Marriage - to last life time. should be, hundred percent. Marriage is built, on Mutual Trust and respect e very - things couple owned. Is hundred percent. Not 50,50.

Talking about woman right ? How about, asking your mother, If she would give you, right to be born, or not. How would you feel.

It doesn't matter, who work, or don't, or who makes more, or less. Everything, goes on in their life. It is one 100%, as one 100%.

Talking about woman right ?. None us wouldn't, being born. If it was not, for a woman. Who need, to ask for their rights ? man, or woman. people who debate, whether to give woman, right or not, is a joke. They are, out of their mind. What about. If all woman refuse to get pregnant and to have a baby. Are you going to exists ?

In marriage, should be, the final step to paradise with God. Nothing is perfect. people always have ups, and down in life, good time, and bad times.

Naturally something, that happen. To most of people. There will always, be disputes arguments, small, and large problems, illness financial problems, hard time raising children, and much more, and hard ship. So many people go through, naturally.

Good, marriage is the one. Who's never deceived. Who also know, life is full of challenges To make great marriage. For the couple, to have a wisdom, and the knowledge. They receive from holy spirit of God. Their love, will be ready to challenge, any problems, or obstacles. Might come their way. Parents are very, very important to God. Because that's, where the life began.

Are you having, any problems ? Are you worrying, about some things bothering you, every day. Are you counting, how many days, hours, and months. During that time. Your blood pressure may be going up. Or you beginning to get sick. At the meantime, all you are doing wasting your time. What you can do instead. Is work on, the problem to fix it. Instead of wasting all the precious time.

There is, a solution for every problem. The ones, who don't bather fixing their problems They are, being lazy or they don't care about them self, and they don't want to be happy.

Everything is possible. It is not the end. There's a way, to fix everything. One thing, out of time. I say as long, as you are alive. There is hope.

The only hard thing. We have, is death. We cannot solve. That's, naturally. Everyone has to take this road. We all die one day. When I go, to a funeral, relatives, or friends I usually have something, to say. Which is, the dead are gone. The living need, to take care of each other.

So many, they leave behind. Young children. Spouses of the dead, become widows Therefore, God is very concerned, about orphans. God knows, everyone must die. On their own time. God want us, to take care of the orphan. To make sure. They are, doing OK.

God bring justice. For the orphan. Your loved ones, are not really gone. Because children's are, the image of their parents. Myself every time, I see my nieces, and my nephew's, just like I see my own brothers, and sisters. Whether we're alive, or not.

We should also pray, for the orphan for God, to bring them the help. They need. We also pray for, the poor, the less fortunate, and people. Who do have no one.

The great God, mighty, and awesome, who has no favorites, excepts no bribes; will executes justice for the orphan, and the widow. Proverb 26:27.

God defends, the fatherless, and widows. God demand that. We care of the widow Who lost their spouse, and children. Who lost their parent, or parents. Especially, at younger age, for us to look out for them. Because, they are not forgotten by God. If we cheated an orphan or to take advantage of one. We don't go unpunished. If we take care of one. Will be blessing, If we care for fatherless orphans. Should be under God's law, and not to forget that.

Worried ? Rather worried sick to make extra buck. Then take care of your own health. How about, our own health, and family. It seemed like, times going by, so quick. We are, forgetting about our loved ones.

We don't care about facing, our own consequences. Our mind. Gone astray. We are lost. We need to find, our way back. To the, old tradition. We need, to have that sense of humor people used to have more often. Ask the Companions, for guidance. That's God.

Forgiveness requires, to be spiritual, sharing each other, emotion. Is spiritual. Stress, and loneliness. Can cause health problems. Anger, and hate can cause, health problems. We are so persistent. We rather be sad, and miserable Always worrying, about something.

I say if you, truly love a person, and they have the habit, and ways you don't like. You don't have, to do their ways. But because, you love them. You need to get, used to their way. As long, as they are, not hurting them self and others. You have no choice. Because, if you love that person. You could not stay away from, or live without. The one you love. What other choice, you have. Or else you choose to stay away from the one you love. Just because they act. You will become sick, and miserable without, the one you love.

It is all about unconditional love, is about loving someone as they are. Guilt, and fear can get you, in big hole. Will be tough, to claim out.

Focus on forgiveness accept. The fact is. We are all human being. We all make mistakes Do not be afraid, to let others share your feelings. Because, a lot of people, feels the same way, you're feeling. Sharing with others, your feelings. It is the first step, toward healing.

When you face conflict. If you run from it. You are in self-denial. All you are doing is hurting yourself, weakening yourself. Hurting yourself mentally. If you think you are, the only one who have problems ? You are not alone. We are, all children of Adam, and eve.

Money, and richness, have nothing, to do with our struggling. Humanity have identical struggling life.

God want us to, be brave, and cheerful. To accept all the problems, and turn it into happiness. It is healthier, physically, and mentally. To accept, all the responsibility. Commending our self, to the truth to be positive. Recognize, what was wrong. If you are harming yourself and the ones around you. Especially, your loved ones.

We are, God's inheritance. We are valuable, and precious to God. Solving problems, helps us grow, mentally, emotionally, and spiritually. It help us to go deeper, of understanding ourselves.

What is it, the meaning of believe in God ? Do you have an answer to that ? Majority of people claim have faith. They think faith is only, to believe in God. I say, there's a lot more They need to know. For instant. First of all believe in God means. We trust in God, for all he give us. We can use it, to conquer the evil, with good. To wipe, evil of face of the earth I know it's not easy. But we try over, and over again.

Faith in God, is not 1,2,3. It is lots of work. From the moment, we are old enough to understand.

We were born, until the day we die. continue to trust in God. Deuteronomy 10:17.

So God created man, in his own image, he created him in the image of God. He created us. Genesis 1:27.

Gods heart was, revealed through, the old testament, and it was established. By our Lord Jesus Christ. He did not only explain to us, also told us. What God's heart really want of us, to do for each other. That what, will please him. God created, every human being Like his own image, and likeness. God also give us, the gift of free will.

We face, our own consequences. I also know God, is the only creator. Who created what was seeing, and not was seen. Out of, the love he made us, so we can be, on guard Against evil, here on earth. To defend God, in every way, and field.

Religion is rules, and regulation. We put, over ourselves. So we don't skip out, on ourselves to control the way we behave. We get it, from the bible. We can judge ourselves knowing how good, or bad. We are doing, for ourselves, and the people around us.

Going to church, is the most profound thing, anyone can do. When you go, to church. We feel holy, humble, spiritual. Instantly you'll, know God's is there. He is in church, for sure the way you are feeling. You will, know automatically.

Through old testament, heart of God which, revealed spiritually, and prepared, for his coming. In the new testament heart of God, was revealed. Through, our lord, and savior Jesus Christ. Real life heart, flesh, and blood.

Jesus explained to us, meaning of faith. Love everyone around us. It is faith. Generosity it is faith. Being considerate, it is faith. Seeking justice, for others who don't have. It is faith Being fair is faith. Being hundred percent good person it is faith. Have a holy marriage, it is faith. Taking care, of less fortunate, it is part of faith. See Jesus, in new testament. It is faith. Taking care of sick, needy, and special needs, is part of faith. Give hope to the ones who are seeking, it Is part of faith. Serving others, it is part of faith. Being patient is part of faith. Kindness is part of faith. Tight relationship with your family. It faith.

When you Protect, your dignity, and dignity of others that is part of faith. Being peace maker is part of faith. Serving others, in line of duty, it is part of faith. Seeking freedom for others, it is part of faith. Having mercy on others, is part of faith. Feeding the hungry, is a faith Because, everyone deserves to eat. Finding job for someone that, is part of faith. Being humble generous, pure peacemaker, it's part of faith, Being thoughtful, considered, it is part of faith Speaking, the truth always, is the key to win. Serve others, is part of faith.

Comforting, and bringing joy, and happiness into someone's heart, is the most profound faith. Giving, true **hope to anyone, is part of faith. Being fair, and treating everyone equally, is part of faith. See Jesus, in New testament.**

Faith is not, to worry about anything. But focus always on God. You will have the answer Because when we, worry about anything. We lose, our freedom. God give us. When things are

bothering us. We feel locked up, and it feels like no way out. It is better to be, Concerned about things. Concerning about things, is to find, a way to fix it. without worrying.

Throw out our life. We need to focus, on doing good. Because of goodness. Evil will shrink, in our life. We need to keep, working on making, evil disappear. With the guidance Of the holy spirit of God. Makes it possible.

Gossiping about anyone is evil. It is taking advantage. Everyone has the right, to be there to defend themselves. You are taking, their freedom of defending themselves. It is not fair to, put out rumor, against anyone.

You need, to go, to people's face, to clear things. God gives right. Especially, if you have problem, with anyone. Every time, that we sin against anyone. Somehow, we pay Sometime, in big way, or small ways. There's, no way out. No one, can get away, with anything.

If we always try to, do good, good come. It works right. Goodness is the key to, the success, and happiness. For what - ever we go. Through life. Being bad, does not work. If we ask for God's rewards, we get good things. Doing good, it is asking for Gods rewards When we sin,we are asking for evils rewards. Will be terrible, and critical rewards.

Doing good is knowing, we have father. Who is in heaven waiting for us, for our return In our society everywhere people, blaming each other. So many who, blame God for all their problems. God give us, the resources, and knowledge. How to control our behaviors, and how to be good.

First began, with abortion, our God did not ask the world, to kill millions of unborn In fact God cares, for the unborn. He want us to protect, not only the unborn. Also the less fortunate. God is at the creation. The moment of conception. God takes spirits of, our parents, and give them us. and we are all made of God's image. God, knew us before we were born. Every child is born, into this world. Has calling, and reason why. God put him, or her. On this earth. Every child supposed, to have a future. God protect, who are abused, in any way. Or persecuted.

God protect those, who are helpless. No one, should ever get abused. God rewards, for us, according to, how much good we do.

No one ever force us to do,anything wrong. All our doing, is our choice. Which road We want to take. There is more, than one road. We need to check, and see. Which one, is the right path. So we don't make mistakes. Life is too short,to worry, about anything. How far we carry, the heavy load. When you have people, around you. Who are always considered helpful, and thoughtful. Never use you, in any wrong ways. You should do the same thing for them, or

else. You'll lose,a lot of friends. If you are thoughtful, considerate, helpful.

If they don't do the same for you. Instead of judging them. Especially, if you love them You need to teach them, to be like you. Not to be judgmental. But explain to them and tell them. Would make you happier, if they were just like you.

Sometime people, don't know how to be, thoughtful considerate. It is always good, to teach them how. There are, so many things. We can do, to make our life, easier to live.

Sometimes. We take our life, for granted. We don't appreciate it. The help we receive from others. We need to be the person's, of our words. To keep, our promises. Not to pick, on each other, or take advantage, of each other. We only lose.

So many cries to me, how terribly. Financially, they are doing,and they have good jobs. But unfortunately, not making enough money. They do, borrow money from friends and relatives sometime. Never pay back. Eventually, they lose the help, they are getting Because, no one trusts them anymore. I often tell these people, don't borrow money, from anyone. Unless you are, able to pay back. You can always find someone. If is friend, or relative If they are able, to lend you some money. Out of your, weekly check pay them, partial payment. Until, you pay them off. Make sure, you

show appreciation. If you continue, to do so They will always trust you, and help you. Also if you are not able, to make a payment, to them once a while. Be honest give them, good explanation. They will, understand.

Adultery lead to divorce, not only children, become victims. But also the people, who love you get hurt too.

Being controlled, by alcohol is foolish. doesn't make sense. Many say they drink. So they forget, about their problems. Not thinking that, the problems, will be there. Being drunk Does not solve anything.

Having bad attitudes, can hurt your relationship. Not only, with God. But also with everyone, around you.

Anger, and bad attitudes. Will leads, to a poor decisions. Always trust in God for, any decision. Being positive, is very rewarding.

If we only believe in God. He will make it, right for us. Believing in God, will make everything right, for us Keeping, word of God, is very important. For our, salvation.

God will stand right, next to us, through bad times and good times. God gave us, his word. Through old, and new testament, to keep.

God blesses those, who obey him. God blesses, the faithful, and the Godly people. God will bless, who fear him. Fearing him is loving him. God want us to bring all our complain to him.

God he is problem solver. He makes, our problems disappear. He comfort us when, we are suffering. We get comfort. When we, are hurting. Our duty toward, God it is giving our self's, courage. To help those. Who feels crushed.

Are you mad, or disappointed, at any one ? All You are doing, wasting your time, and more likely suffering, and hurting insight. Therefore, your heart is troubled.

But what makes you think that individual, you are mad, and disappointed at. Have any consideration for you. More likely, he, or she going on with their life. They may be, on vacation, or having good time. Not even wondering, or even thinking about you. He or she could care less.

A lot of people. They are, like that. They just don't care. Or maybe if they are, your loved ones. What If, they move away ? Or

God forbid. If they die. More likely, you will have something, to feel guilty about. The rest, of your life. Therefore, it would be wiser. If you make peace. What ever happen between you, and others. Would be wiser healthier, to make up, on the spot.

If you live always with peace, in your heart?. You'll have more friends. Than you can ever dream of. Or more than you, can ever imagine.

If we are mostly, concerned about, our rights. The door can easily be open. Through negotiation. If you give yourself, and others the chance.

Resentment, anger, hatred, fearing, guilt. Those are, self - destructive Instead. We should focus on forgiveness. Acceptance of others, apology. We must first forgive ourselves, than for the others. We should accept, the fact. We all make mistakes.

Once the people, around you. know how, you feel. They will exactly, share the same feelings. You have for them. That's, the first step, toward healing. Whenever, we face conflict. We should, never ignore. Because, it is first sign of weakening. If we don't face and solve, our problems. We can easily get, our self in deep hole. More likely. If you are positive. You can always, win over your emotion, and always working. Toward changes in your life. Often begins,

when you're willing, to accept and recognize. You are not, being harming yourself. But also, the people around you.

Rejoice you are, precious. Isaiah 43:4

We are, valuable to God, and he love us. Our God, made us not to be lonely, not to get hurt, not to worry, not to be alone To be loved, and enjoy this life. God is good,and will never let us down.

Married couple deserve, to have the freedom to solve any issues, or problems. On their own. If you let people know your private business. There so many, who are trouble makers Some who like, to side with one of you. Some who have, failing relationship like to see you fallen. There's some, who are jealous of you. Because, of the love you have, for each other you will be able to overcome everything. That comes ahead of you. You fix things at once It is good to take advise, of someone. Who's wise enough, and You love, and trust. Whenever you have, anything wrong. You close your, doors be private. The reason is, that people like to be nosy. When people, don't know. None of these people are with you 24/7 Like you are and your spouse together. Therefore, you only know about. Each other fully

In life if you lose ? It is you're a lost. The only thing people. Who love you, can do for you, is to comfort you. Also to see, if they can be, any help to you. The second thing they can do for you, is to bring you hope. If you gain, anything. People, who love you. They should be proud, and happy for you, and not jealous. If you gain people, who love you They need to celebrate with you.

Stress, and worries will never get you anywhere. Instead, you should be concerned, about things. That matter, and the ones. Who means, something to you.

In life we need, to be awake focus, on our surrounding. We run into. So many ungrateful inconsiderate people around us. They might be friend, or relatives alike.

Rejoice in the lord. Philippians 3:1.

There's so many, who are like, Pilate don't care, what will happen to other, as long, as they gain Matthew 27:19,24.

He had the power to release Jesus. Instead he sent him, to be crucified. He was able to protect Jesus. If he wanted to. He knew he was innocent. He did not care. he was afraid of people. He was afraid of people. He was afraid may be they were able to make him powerless.

Just then, as Pilate was sitting, on judgment seat. His wife send him this message; to leave the innocent man alone. Because, I had a terrible nightmare. About him last night.

Pilate saw that he, wasn't getting anywhere. He was not succeeding, at all. Riot was breaking out. Instead he took water, and washed his hand. In the sight of the crowd Saying I am innocent of this man's blood. Look to it, your selves. Then, he had Jesus scourged and hand him, to be crucified.

Well Jesus, he was meant to die. For the sake of humanity For us to, be saved from Sin.

Unfortunately now these days, there are so many, are like Pilate, and the governor during Jesus time.

The governor was guilty, as charge. He was easily able to arrest, and convict all the people. Who wanted, to hurt Jesus. He thought by, only washing his hands. He declared himself, innocent. But what he did, was for his own gain. He bribe himself, and he was afraid of the people. Uprising against him.

There are, so many. Who accept bribe. From the guilty, and hurt the innocent, and those were seeking justice. It is a shame. The ones whom, give bribes to the ones, who are like that governor.

So many, because of greed. It became a habit. Taking bribes. They are hurting many They could be hurting, one of their friends, or relatives. As well. There are, so many who are innocent. They become victims, on the hand, of people like Pilate.

He thought, by only washing, his hand. He was innocent. In fact he was more guilty than, any of these people. Who crucified Jesus.

We need to find. Those people, taking bribes to hurt the less fortunate. The morals and the faithful need to team together. To protect to honor, and respect. The human dignity.

About the Pilate, that was 2000 years ago. What happened to Jesus. It was meant to happen. But still the point is. He give an innocent man, in the hand of criminals, to be mocked to restrict, then crucify.

It is a shame, there so many. Will accept bribes, to let others get away with murder The innocent become, the victim. For many, who judge for themselves thinking, what they are doing, is right. Even, when they are wrong. There are, so many who do not care. What will happen. To the less fortunate. They justify, what they're doing, is. A, OK and right thing. When they are, hundred percent wrong.

There are so many, who laid off workers. So the company, can save. Without, worrying, or have, any consideration. They can care less, how these workers will live without job. There are some, who reduce workers- pay for their own gain. Without having, any conscience.

May God, save Pilate soul. Because he was, born for that reason. But those ones, Who except bribe. They were not born, to hurt anyone.

Throughout history, many were killed, murdered. Because, of their beliefs, hate, greed and money. Typical, and civil human being. Supposed, to kill only to eat, or to protect (Self-defense), her or himself. In comparison between people and animals. It is that animals only kills. To eat, or to protect them self's only. Therefore, animal are more civil. Then many, who hurt other, people for, any type of gain.

People who, hurt others. It is in their own choice, to do or not. But what reason have, the ones. Who abuse, use neglect, and persecute. The innocent. Nothing go unpunished. If we sin against anyone.

It is unfortunate. So many people, they only help you. When you are, doing some work for them, Or only when they need you desperately. They act like, and makes you feel they would do anything for you. But when, you need their help, some other times. They would not help.

There is, so many who really want to help. making things right for the people, all the people Unfortunately, always trying to stop them.

Finally God, is very concerned, about the poor. They are mentioned, in the bible many times. Feeding, helping clothing, doing charities for the poor, and the less fortunate. It is our key, to paradise. kingdom of God. God favor the ones whom are motivate, and never give up always trying. Because, when we give up. All we are doing, is pleasing evil.

If always do good. Good will come to you. If anyone try to do act of Evil against you,will never succeed.

Chapter 11

We Pray To Have Like Jesus Heart

Having like Jesus heart. That's, how we know God. We feel, and touch God.

So many people in the world. Who know Jesus. But they don't have, heart like Jesus heart So many people in the world. Who don't know Jesus. But they have heart, like his heart.

Christian around, the world are shaking. By their faith, and belief. Many, who are ashamed, and embarrassed, to know Jesus anymore. Evil himself, don' t know the truth.

The media, trying to make Jesus a joke, nothing less.

They forgot, that. Because of Jesus, we have the civilized world. First all the goodness in the world.

The world, it was reformed, and shaped to what it is today. The poor, and the less fortunate, they get the help, they need. The hungry are being fed, the sick are being taking care of.

Because of Jesus, all the hospitals, of the world. Were build. Charities foundations, of the world, started.

Justice was brought, to the ones who were seeking it. The peacemakers, became The braves, laid down themselves. For a friend.

We become sons, and daughters of God.

We will be with God someday. The great, Samaritans became. We received mercy of God We know what God's is thinking. We know, what God's heart wants us, to do for each other Mercy of God was, revealed to us. Doors of heaven, were open for us.

We learned how, to be in contact with God. We learned, how to pray to God. We learned how to love, and forgive.

We have performed miracles. Because of Jesus. We received, the holy spirit of God We acknowledge God is spirit. We learn, what's wrong, and was right, and the truth. We have the shelter, for the homeless. We have the Food Banks, to feed the hungry. Because, of Jesus all the good came out of our world, and the people on it.

We have the gospel, of Jesus Christ, the new testament. We have, the good news. Which is, that Jesus intention, and mission is, to unfold. The evil off face of the earth, and replace it with goodness. Every dot, every word in, the old and New testament, is to concord Evil with good. Jesus also shown us how, to cast. Evil, out of our life. Through, love mercy, compassion hope, grace, and kindness. How become our brother's keeper.

Living life of virtue. Not to judge anyone regardless of who they are, or where they come from, or what they look like, or what they believe in.

Through Jesus, God gives the freedom, to the poor, and the less fortunate. To the ones were taken, as a slave to be free, to be able, to liv e like everyone else. He's assured, us and taught us how, to be free. Explaining to us, we were all created by God, to be free not to be controlled, by anyone.

Jesus also taught us, not to pass judgment, at anyone But first to judge, ourselves. knowing no one is perfect. We all sin.

No one ever, throughout entire history of humanity. Any put himself down for his friends Like Jesus did for us. He is willing, to do that over, and over again.

Every faith has some, form of prayer. When they are going through bad times seeking God's help. Christian we pray, to Jesus, for his spirit remain in us. Because he is the heart spirit, and divinity of one God.

He told us, he will take us to the father. Through our prayers we receive, the holy spirit of God. When we, pray for whatever. We are, wishing for God, to grant for us. Our duty should, be finding people. With same needs problems, and issues, to work together, to help each other to make things work. When God see that. He will intervene, and rescue us.

When we pray, we receive the knowledge, wisdom grace. God is very, well pleased. When we are, in continuous communication with him. We need, to practice. What we preach. When we pray before. We wish, God to do for us. We ask God. What he wish us to do for him.

God wish, and hope is to do, his will 24/7, and teach it. God would like us, to bring, his mercy, love, peace, grace and hope to all people.

Through Jesus. God was revealed to us.

Millions of people, around the world are praying daily. To get answer, for their problems, and issues. God he is spirit, he do his work. Through the faithful, and the ones who know him. We don't only pray, to save our soul. We also pray to save, souls of others. Gods wishes are to, remain in our hearts, minds, and soul. Through, our Lord Jesus.

Jesus said but, seek first the kingdom of God, and his justice, all these things. Shall be given, to you beside. Matthew 6:33

Jesus remind us, to pray for God, to bring justice to the poor. The less fortunate, and sufferer. All of the suffering, in our world today. When we pray. We Humble our self. God already know, what we need. Before, we ask. God know, what is best for us. Jesus explained to us. What heaven is about, and what it takes to get to heaven. It is by feeding the hungry. Taking care of, the sick, and needy. Comforting the lonely. Give drink, to the thirsty Take care of everyone. Even if they, were strangers to you. Comfort the ones, who lost their freedom, and hope. Over the mistakes, people do. I mean the once, who are in prison. Hoping God, would convert their hearts, to show them. God still love them, and want them back.

Clothes the naked, also help people. Who do not have nothing, and the homeless. Heaven is, showing unconditional mercy. Compassion. Forgiveness.

Sometime we are too, persistent. We have, no choice but to do what's right. God will be pleased with us.

At the last judgment. Matthew 25:31-46.

We will be reminded, we will also be, face, to face with people. We done good, or bad for them. God will be very specific. About everything. We did, through our life here on earth. God will focus on, our goodness. At the last judgment.

The king will answer, to the righteous. Truly, I say to you, as you did it, to one of the least of these my brethren, you did it to me. Matthew 25:40.

I believe God, don't want to lose anyone. He want, to gain every single person living on face of earth. Therefore, the faithful must work. With those whom are, sinful, wicked Selfish, not very, considerate, abusers, and greedy. Not to judge them. But to help them come to the light.

So many good, and faithful people. Often asking them self this question. Why, do we suffer, when we, always do, good ? My answer to them is. The better person you are, the more you are liable, for evil temptation. Evil always trying to test us. Hoping, we fall. Because evil hates good.

Jesus said we will be blessed. If we carry, all the burdens, of this world. Matthew 5 :1-12 Jesus speaking pointing, to all the ones. Who were always on, Gods side no matter. How much they suffer in this life. Still kept their faith. When they mourned. Or if they were persecuted. Hardly, any justice, was done for them. People always spoke falsely, about them Jesus spoke of, the faith, and said. If you have enough faith to move the mountains ?. It is not enough faith, without charity.

Jesus promised his apostles, he will send holy spirit to sanctify, and guide, his church Acts 1:1.

Spirit of Jesus, stay with church forever. He is heart of God. Until the day on which, he was taken up, to heaven. Jesus give his commandments. By the holy spirit, of God. To the apostles. Whom he had, chosen. To be the witness, for the word of God.

Jesus told the apostles. They will receive, the holy spirit. Will come upon them. When they were, all together continually praying, along with, Mary mother of Jesus, several women, and his brothers.

Jesus did not, have any brothers. During time of Jesus, did not have title : cousin Therefore, their uncles, or aunts, children, they were called brothers. During Jesus time, and before that. People did not, use the word cousin, very often.

When Jesus saw his mother, and the disciple whom he loved standing near, he said to his mother," Woman, "Behold your son. Then he said to the disciple," Behold, your Mother And from that hour. The disciple took her to his own home. John 19: 26,27.

Besides, when Jesus was on the cross Saw, his mother standing there beside, the disciple he loved. He said to her Woman he is your Son. And he said to his disciple. She is our Mother too. From then on the disciple took her into his house. She is, our heavenly Mother, as well. Therefore, if Jesus had, any brothers. He would told his mother. You have, the rest of your kids, to take care of you. Go to them. He didn't not say that. Another meaning. Jesus give his mother. To be mother, for the entire humanity. Because, he died for every single person Lived, and will live on, the face on the earth.

For our salvation, and the holy spirit was descent from heaven, as a sound of violent wind blowing, and filled whole house, where they were sitting, and they were, all filled, with holy spirit. Acts 1:2,8,14.

Therefore, they had the power to speak, and preach. They received a gift, of the holy spirit Not to keep, for themselves. But to share it. With entire world.

When or, if we pray. We should, ask the holy spirit, to make our will. To be his missionaries, and disciples. Also our will to be. For the holy spirit, to give us instruction to bring God into people's hearts and minds, and to bring. What, lost back. Holy spirit calls to find. The less fortunate, neglected, and abused. To bring, God's mercy, peace, and freedom to the entire humanity.

God told Jeremiah. I knew you before you were born, there for if God knew Jeremiah before he was born. Jeremiah 1:1.

God know, every single person. Before they, were born. Everyone was born, has a reason. Why God, give life on earth. God wants us to be. His agents here on earth In particular, to protect the unborn. God knew us, before we were born. Abortion is refusing God gift.

Paul explains, and make it clear. That's how in prayer to the holy spirit, will play big role in our life. God has promised he is able to perform; We most fully, and gratefully pray appropriate precious promise to God. Romans 8:26.

We pray for forgiveness,and strength.

Jesus taught us how to pray. Matthew 6:8-15.

Jesus said do not be like them. Your father knows. What you need before you ask him. This is how you pray; Jesus, said. Our father who in heaven Hallowed be your name. Your kingdom come. Your will be done. On earth as in heaven. Give today our daily bread. and forgive us our debts. As we forgive our debtors, and do not subject us to the final test. But deliver us from the Evil one.

We say our God, the father, you are holy, forever, your kingdom to, come here on earth to put justice, peace, and mercy.

Therefore, we will not do evil no more. We humble our self. We promise not to be materialistic. Even if we live, on bread alone. Will be, grateful to you lord, help us live our life to the fullest, and to overcome sin.

Put in our hearts, to forgive others. Because, we forgive them through you. Please God save us, from evil temptation. Don't let Evil put us through, any test. Please God help us, put full trust in you.

Lord prayer is, promising God to be good. Pleasing him, in every way. If we do otherwise. We are deceiving, and lying to God. Every time, we say this prayer.

How can we, say to God. We already forgive someone. If we didn't yet. Heart of God wishes us to forgive unconditionally. If we do, were evil will fit. Jesus, is heart of God.

Jesus he is, the word of God, who was always one with God. John 1:1,14.

In the old testament, God prepared his coming, to save entire human being. In the New testament. God became, the son, and lived among us. Through his son, he revealed his glory.

Jesus Christ, he is full of grace, and truth. God become flesh. So we can feel, and touch our hearts, so we believe in him.

Through Jesus. He became, our salvation. He called sinners, to repent. So they can belong to him.

Because of Jesus. We all became children, of God. The father. The father loves, the son and has given all things into his hand. He who believes in the Son, has eternal life. John 34-36.

Everything under heaven, was given to Jesus. Jesus said for the one. Whom God sent Speaks the word of God Jesus Christ, gave us. The gift of the holy spirit. Jesus is power of God.

Jesus said, to Samaritan woman. I am he the one who is speaking with you. Jesus said I am the one God of Israel. Who had promised salvation. John 4: 26. New testament

Jesus said, whoever belongs, to hears words of God is, the good shepherd. Who gather His sheep's together. John 10 :1-6.

If he loses one, he do not rest. Until he find, the one which was lost. God does not want to lose, not even one sinner.

The washing, of the disciples feet. Jesus washes his disciples feet. John 13:1-17

Showing God wants, to serve us. So we can, serve each other. Jesus said love your enemies. Love your neighbor. Matthew 5:43-48

God want us, to work. Work, and work. Toward, good always.

The good, Samaritan. Luke 10:30-35.

God want us, to take care, and help anyone, even if they were strangers.

Jesus perform miracles, heal the sick, fed the hungry. He showed us. God is love. God wished to die for us. Jesus said, for just, as the father raises the dead, and give life. So also does the son, give life to whomever he wishes. John 5:21

God wished to, become man to suffer, and die. For us on the cross. So we, can be saved John 19 : 1-20 New testament.

God want us, to put our hope, and trust in him always. Therefore, he said the salvation, of the just, is from, the lord. He is there, in the time of trouble.

God will rescue, the just from the wicked. Because, they have hope in him. But for the un just. Shall, be destroyed, and shall perish. Psalms 25:31-44. Psalms 36:38.

Because, all statements Jesus Christ, made. People throughout, history were inspired, by the statements. Therefore, people put everything into prospect.

Once they, learned. What truly, God want us to do. In order to please him. Jesus Christ he is the wonderful wisdom, and mighty, power of God.

Which we truly, and fully learned. What will please God. Especially, the statements Jesus Christ made, in New testament.

In the Sermon on the Mont. Matthew 5 : 1 - 12.

Also in the story of good Samaritan. Luke 10 : 1-12.

And the final judgment. Matthew 25; 31- 44 Corinthians 1: 24.

Chapter 12

Inspiration, Miracles, And Dreams

Priest once upon a time said, it is difficult for anyone, to believe in miracles Unless that person gets a miracle, or be witness to one.

People had visions, sights, and countless blessings. Many around the world for centuries, experienced many miracles. Being proved, and recorded. Myself being blessed I had some of these experience.

Hopefully, it is about the next life. I am expressing, some of my blessing. So you my believe. A friend once told me. She did not believe in miracles. I answered miracles are being positive, decisive, and emphatic. Whether I am good, or bad. Sin or not I continuously. Pray every day, for short, or long time.

I always feel. I need to pray. I believe, purity, and charity. Will increase, and deepen our faith. I always felt that. I had no choice but to forgive unconditionally.

I always learn, if I know mercy, of God, I should never be afraid, of anything I always pray, pleading with God, to give me a string. And will power to continue loving him.

God hear, and listen, to our voice. Miracle is, Once a while, when we become critical in danger thinking something bad, about to happened but is not meant to be Evil make it feel this way, so we lose our hope. Therefore, at last minute, God intervene and save us. That Is the miracle. This is, the way God showing people wasn't meant to happen. Also improve our faith in God.

Most of the dreams. I have they become, true and evidence are, in place for it Before, and after. I see the images real live miracles. All these experience I believe. Because I get prove for it.

Being inspired by It give me hope, and increases my faith. I am writing, some of them. l like to share it with, who ever want to read it. at the meantime. We know we are made of image of God in spirit. Genesis.

I believe God takes, part of our parents spirit, and give them us. Prove of that parents, and children resemble each other. They are part of one, and another.

I also believe, when one of our relative past away. Their spirit, never depart from us. Because we have same identical spirit.

When, we dream, of our deceased loved ones. We see their spirit, and what they look like. When they are alive. Because their spirit, is part of our spirits, we know what they're thinking.

Our physical body full, to sleep, but our spirit never sleep. When we see someone who's dead. Face to face. We are, in contact with their spirits. Also the way we remember them. I also believe that, the dead don't even know, they are dead. Their spirit, live on like if they are alive.

I am fortunate enough. God reveal to me more than others. When we dream of people, who are alive. We see them, as they are. But we are truly, in content, with their spirit. One of the best thing happened me. The image, of sacred heart of Jesus appear to me, on the door, in one of the homes, I lived. Another image appeared, in front of me. On the door at back of the church. Next to the altar. In the church, I attend (saint Thomas. Chaldean catholic church) I called image of mercy.

I pray for saints. In heaven to pray for me. Everyone, in the world, can pray directly to God. It is very good. Many people, in the world pray asking, the saints, who are in heaven, to pray for them. They humble themselves. This is, the reason why they go to saints to pray them. Because they are closer to God. They speak to God. Myself first before I began to pray. I say please God, I am sinner. I am not worthy of speaking to you directly, please hear your saint, on my behalf. Whom went to heaven before me To pray for me. And all world.

Most of my life, until this day. I pray the rosary call on Mother Mary. Mother, of our lord, and savior Jesus Christ. To pray for me, along with all the saints with her. Mainly angels. Because, they are powered, by the holy spirit of God.

I believe. Mary, spirit is next to her son, Jesus spirit. Because, not any son, would want his spirit to depart, from his mother. I Pray for Jesus to help me. If he doesn't answer quick. I go to his mother. He will listen to her. Because she is his mother.

Once upon a time, I told one of my friends. I often happen, to have dreams of mother Mary. She comes, when I need help. He answered, I believe, her son Jesus send her, to help you.

One of the main experience, with God. He answers to everything. I asked him Ever since. I can remember the more. I struggle the more I prayed.

It said knock, and the door. Will be open. Matthew 7:7.

I continued to knock, and many doors. Have being opened. Every time, one door closed. Another, one open.

God send me, many wonderful. People along the way to help me. Almost in every way. Because, I've been inspired, by the gift God had given. I like to share, with everyone.

No exaggeration. I have proven, or base according, to every experience. In the most profound way.

1- My wife, and I were visiting friends, on one summer day in mid 1980s. We're playing, on front lawn. I was, running. I tripped,and failed, and strained my ankle. At first I thought it was broken. I did not have insurance. So I can go to the hospital Therefore, my wife took me home maybe. We can do something, to ease the pain. At home. I had hard, time climbing the stairs. Before I went to sleep. I prayed, asking Mother Mary, to help me. I could not, afford to miss work. The following day. In that same night in my sleep. She came to me, and said. Don't worry, you are healed. When I woke up in the morning. Without thinking, of the pain, or my dream. Slowly I put my foot on the floor. At the same time Began to think, of my dream, and remembering the pain. My foot was. It was a little sore. I was able to manage, going downstairs. It was much easier than a night before. I was able to get ready,and go to work. By noon, form that morning I felt, no pain. I thank God, he send me. Mother Mary.

2 - Another time. Mother Mary, came to me. I my dream. When. I was, desperate for money. I applied, for a loan. Was taking, a long time, for the paper work to go into effect. I was praying every day. Hoping to get the loan. Until one night. I had a dream standing in the

middle of crowd, of people. I looked, at one direction. I suddenly saw a lady pushing her way through. I recognized her. When she finally came. Close enough to me. Noticing she had, her hand folded closed. Once she, was by me. She opened her hand, and hand me the paper. She was holding. When I woke up next morning. I did not have to wonder, about my dream. Because, I knew, my prayers were answered once again. I called my loan officer. She said, to me my loan. It was approved. Once again I was truly, grateful to mother Mary. I believe, she is continually. Praying along, with all the saints in heaven for all of us.

3 - Early to mid1990. My wife, and I were visiting some relatives. On the way back trying, to get home. It was getting late. Through, the night while I was driving. My wife notice it. I was, getting tired. She asked me to pull off, the road. So she can drive By then, I was falling asleep. Therefore, instead of shifting the, car to park. I shift it to the drive. While, the car was still moving. I opened the door, to get off the car, for my wife switch to driver seat. My wife notices it something is wrong. She act very quick, to hold the steering wheel. Pushing the break to stop. By that time. She saw me under the car. The tire, rolled over me. At Last, she saw me. Behind the car, on the ground. My wife, was in shock. After the car, was stopped. she came running to me screaming. Thinking, I was may be dead, or badly hurt. I was fully awake. She saw the car rolled over my body. Thinking, I was dead. I did not feel, any pain, and I was ok The only thing, she did help me off, the ground. We were on, our way home My wife can never, forget that day. I believe, it was a miracle. Was not, my time yet. 4- One day, I was on my way, to work. l always pray, for protection, not only for me. But for all the drivers. Anyway, that same morning. I stopped for gas. Another person next to me. I recognize was doing the same thing. I tried to start my car,

after I got some gas. Unfortunately, my car did not start. The person I knew he, was just about to drive off. I immediately blow my horn, to get his attention. He stopped asking me. If I was OK. Explaining, my car would not start. Asking him, If he can give me right to work, and I will call someone help me fix my car. Anyway he helped me pushing the car to the side. Out of the way. Driving me, to work. He told me, he never came that way to work. Something made him, do that. I told him, I just finished praying before. I stopped, at the gas station.

5 - Mid 1990s. My wife, and I want to rent home. Because of, our bad credit. We had hard time renting one. We did not, give up we were critical. While I was working my wife. Was gone, trying to find us place to live. I was praying. One day, before we found home to live. Same night. I had a dream, in that. I've seen myself, walking to this one home. As I approached the front. Door open automatically for me. There was, a lady sitting in front, in site, with the smile, on her face sitting on the couch. I woke up the next morning, to go to work. My wife, once again went out Hoping, to find home. We can rent It was around noontime. My wife called me telling me. She found the house she liked, and the owner agreed, to rent it to us anyway. I was very excited, and relieve at the same time. Asked my wife. If the owner can showed me the house, the next day ? When I went to see it. I was surprised Because, it was the home. I dream of the nights before. The owner showing me the house. At last, took me to the garage. There was statue, of blessed mother Mary. He told me. I can keep the statue. If I want ? because, he wasn't catholic anymore Because, of the statue I knew that, was truly her, who came in my dream. That statue was prove to my dream. Once again, and I was, very grateful to her. God change hearts

6 - Living, in same home, we had one year lease. The owner remind us.

He is not willing to extend the lease. Therefore, will have to move once again. We become critical. Because our credit there was no way, we could get another home. But with help of one of our relatives. We were, able to try to buy a home. But without, any guarantees One day we did find, home to buy. I thought, we were only fooling ourselves Especially, having very little chance. Anyway we, apply for a mortgage, one of my relatives supposed to cosign for me, and my wife. He still had hard time getting. The mortgage was taken a long time. I was very critical, and when I am in any situations. My answer continuously praying. After a while before having, any luck. One night, I had a dream lady walking through hallway, in the house. I was trying to buy. I walked to her my dream. When I approached her, she handed me. The keys, for the home. That same morning, when I woke up, immediately. Called mortgage company, they give me the good news. We were approved for the loan. I was grateful to her.

7- In the year 1997. My brother, father in law passed away. Two months after He was dead, he came in my dream. Walking in, my house hall-way looking sharp dressed very nice. In my dream, I knew he was dead. Therefore, I asked him. What are, you doing here ? I thought you are dead ? He immediately, said to me, I am alive. Stretching his, hand toward me saying here. You want to feel my hand ?. I was very scared. It became like a nightmare. I immediately woke from my dream. Later, I remember, when he was alive. He promised, my five years old son. He was going, to bring him bunny rabbit. He had, unfinished business.

8 - In early year 1993. My son, was only six weeks old. One night in my dream sitting in my living room. I heard, someone knocking, on

the side door. When, I went to open the door. Was my deceased brother in law. He shook, my hand congratulate me, for having my son. After word, in my dream. I gave him, a tour through the town I lived, at last I took him, to see his sons, new business. After that I woke up. Few days after that. I happen to stop, at my nephews business, his son. While visiting with him, he mention. How disappointed, he was. Because, his father did not get a chance, to see his business, to be proud. With a smile, on my face. I told him how I brought, his father in my dream. To see his new business. I don't think he believed But I knew, he felt better.

9- I lost another, brother in law. On April 28th 1995 his favor daily lottery, he played for long time was (428). And, he happen to die on 4/28. Any way he did not get lay out in funeral home, until Saturday. I want to, see him very bad. But I, was hurt I decided to go the following day, Sunday. Saturday night. Before, I went to bed. I prayed, asking Jesus to show me. Where my brother in law go. That same night I had a dream Seeing my brother in law. Walking from, funeral home In motion. Outside was expensive car, with two body- guards waiting for him. One of them opened the door for him. The other one, he was the driver. I was able to see. My brother in law getting in the car, and they took off. The next day, on Sunday I went to the Funeral home, to see him for last time. I was surprised. They had him, wearing the same suit That I saw him, in my dream. He was very generous. Loving person. The suit was prove to my dream. He left this world first class.

10- It was, in the middle of the winter. One morning. I was driving to work, in very bad road condition. I suddenly, had flat tire. I immediately pulled on the site (shoulder) Opened the trunk, got my s pare tire out. Trying to change, the tire. It was a lot of snow, on the ground. Temperature, felt like below zero. I had no hat, or gloves on. I struggled setting up the jack. Because, of the snow. I finally managed to get jack up the car. Car pulled, behind mine. Man came, out of the car. Offering, his help. I told him, I was almost done. Thanking, him anyway. He said good luck, and took off. Just before, I was done, the jack begin slip. The ground, was not even Because of the snow. I stopped for, a minute trying, to take a break. Another, person stop offering, his help. I said, yes please. I did not want, to take any more chances Finally finished, because of his help. I wanted, to thank him, looked for him. He was gone, he was very quick. I did not realize, who was that person. Until, I remember his face. He looked like, my deceased uncle. From 40 years prior to that. I believed I had angel, to help me. He took on, form of my uncle. Because, I was his favor nephew

11- May of year 1998. I was working, in office building. I was new there. I did not, have too much experience. Therefore, I always went to someone, for any question. Or advise. One morning, I went to one of my friends office. As I walked in, after asking for excuse. When, I was talking to her. Suddenly, image appeared on the wall. Behind her with open arms. Giving her, sign her of protection. I informed her immediately about the image. So she believe me. I asked her for pen, and paper. I was able, to drew picture, of the image. After I did, that I show it, to her. She was amazed. She immediately, put her hand in purse, and took out medallion. It looked, exactly identical like the image, and the picture I drew. Then she, told me. Showing me, the medallion Her son was ruined over, by the car at age of 5. When, she got to him. She found that medallion, next to him. Her son was ok. She was being carrying it, in her purse ever since.

12 - I was saved, by the spirit. In the year 2003. One of the night while asleep I had dream. In it I was laying, on my back looking up. I was able, to see dark spirit coming toward me, trying to get me it was very fast. Just before, it got to me. I saw light spirit coming behind it, very fast. Then the light spirit got the, dark spirit. When, I woke up. I realized was not my time yet.

13- It was year 2002. Doing, real estate trying to sale homes. One of the time I was at home on lake. After I was done that day. In night time, when I was a sleep. I dreamed of an old woman, standing on the balcony overlooking, the lake at, the home. I showed to my customer a day before. In my dream, she was standing in the middle between, my wife, and I. I was only able to see her back. All night long, she was bragging, about the home convincing me to buy it. When, I awoke the next day. Immediately called the listing agent, telling her about, my dream. Prescribing the old woman. She told me that was her father's mom. Trying to help, her father. Selling, his house. Because, she knew he was desperate. It was message, from beyond the grave.

14- On August 25th Year 2003 About 7:00 AM I woke up. First thing, I want to do, is to use the bathroom, as I approach the door an image begin, to appear in front me on the door. First, I thought, I was imagining. Continued looking over, and over again to make sure what I saw. When, I was sure it was the image, of sacred heart of Jesus Christ I immediately woke up my wife. I showed her, the image. She saw, and believed. I try to tell the priest, he did not pay attention to it. A couple of days later. I found small picture, at my home look like the image.

Since then, I moved from that home I moved that door were ever. I moved to with me.

15 - Blessing. One day, I had to pick a friends from the Airport. I stopped at fast Food Restaurant to get something to eat. I ordered my food. Almost 100% of the time for drink I order coffee, but that day. I order soft drink. Also the cashier said. I will bring, the order to you. When she finally, brought it to me,as she was trying to put, the tray, on the table. She spilled, the drink, on me, it by accident. She apologized. I told her. You know, I am lucky. I did not order coffee. I could, got burned. It was a blessing. Something, told me not to get coffee. So I, don't get burn.

16 - My younger brother died. On February 22nd year 2001. We were, very close to each other. From the first day, he was dead. I felt his present around me Whenever, I run into, anything. He was associate with him. My hair on, the left side stand up. Like he is trying to say something to me. It is happening again. While I was writing this. We were, the most closest brothers ever. First dream, had of him. It was June 26th Year 2001. He came in my dream, he was sitting in the car. Front parking lot sitting behind, the wheel I went to the car, and looked at Back seat. One of my nephews, was also in the car. My deceased brother drove off. While driving. I knew he was dead. I begin ask him question. How our deceased, father doing ? He answered, he is doing fine. Then I also ask about my deceased mom. He said find but, she seems very upset, and sad all the time. I believe she felt that way, because he died at such a young age. Left very young kids behind. Anyway, my deceased brother drove me, to a location showed, me a person I also knew. I

believe he was, trying to tell me. That person owed him. Some money. My brother, was very generous, he helped whenever. He was able too. The next day I was thinking, about my dream knowing. I could not, do anything because. No one, will believe or either, that person would admit. When I saw, his face in my dream. I knew who that person is. May be someday, his conscience will bother him and pay back. The money to my deceased brothers children.

17- One of the Christmas season. I drop off my wife, at the department store. To do. Christmas shopping, and also told, her to. Make sure to, buy my deceased brothers young children. Some gifts I left for about one hour. So I could go, and do some work On the way back. I begin to have, those feelings. My brother trying to tell me something My hair on my left side, felt like a wave. I begin to pray if that, was the message, from my deceased brother. Give me clue, or hint. Anyway, I parked the car in the parking lot. Going In the store. My wife, was approaching the cashier to pay. My wife, seeing me she said. You are, just in time. While standing, quietly in line. Suddenly, my wife said to me, look, to your right. There was necklace. Carved on it, my deceased brother's wife name. Just the way, her name spelled. My wife asked, if she can buy it. For my brother's wife. Because, she did not, get her anything. After word I told my wife. She believed that. Was a, message from, my deceased brother, thanking me. I also believe because my spirit, is part of his. This is, why we could never depart.

18- Once again, when my brother, passed away. He left for his wife. One single investment property he owned. I always, helped her managing it. One year rental permit. It was due, for renewal. Usually the city inspect, the property prior, to renewal At the inspection city give us, some repairs. My sister in law hired people to fix whatever, was needed. At last. She called, city inspector. Hopefully, to prove the property Any way a day, before my sister in law, called asking me, If I could meet the inspector at the property for final inspection. Of course I said Ok. Night before that day, had a dream. I saw my brother wife, and his older son, at the rental house. Hanging new blind (curtains) on window. In my dream, my deceased, brother turn his face looking My way he began, to walk toward me. When he, got very close to me almost, his face touching mine. He opened his mouth trying, to say something to me. I became very frightened, and scared. Because. In my dream I knew he is dead. I woke up. With one thing, on my mind, is go to the home. To meet the inspector. I made it there, before the inspector, the house was fixed nice, he OK it, and approve it. Leaving the house I thought, of my dream, in it I seen blind identical, like the ones, I saw in my dream, a night before. While driving, I called my sister in law, telling her, about my dream night before. She was too surprise. She told me. Your brother was trying to thank you.

19- I usually go to, Saint Thomas Chaldean catholic church. On June of the year 2008. On one Sunday, morning. I was looking, at the door to the right. Where, the priest say the mass, by the alter. Image, appear on the door. And it is still there. The image. I always see when I go to the same church. I called, image of mercy Because looks like, a person. When you, see him you will have mercy, and compassion for him. The message I get from the image. He is telling me. You received mercy from me. You give me a mercy. Also the message I get from the image he's telling me. I am the way the truth, and the life. On the door. I am able to see the image, with each of, his hand, on one side of the door. Pushing it open. He's shown me. He is a door to the true eternal life. The two doors are. With then. the door.

20- It was year 1995. Managing, convenient store. One afternoon telephone. Begin to ring. I picked up, the telephone, answering was my friend. He was calling me, to be friendly. While speaking with him, he asked if I was ok ? I answered, don't worry about me, as long, as God, is with me. I am not, afraid of anything. As long, as God is with me. At that exact second. I felt energy, behind me, it was like if someone was very close, Like, common saying stop breathing over my shoulder. That's how it felt. Then I felt, hand taping on my shoulder, comfort me, gives me, the Goose bumps. Whenever I talk about it. Right away while this, was happening. I was trying, to tell. My friend, what was happening. He could, not believe it. I believe was, my guardian angel. With the power of holy spirit.

21- I lost my fourth brother, passed away year 2005. At his funeral. I was sitting myself, on the sofa, by myself being sad, and hurt. For my brother Of course praying, as usually. Suddenly, I was able to see light dust long with, white light look like crystals. I was able hear voice, whispering in my ears. Saying I am. OK. My brother he was kind, merciful, generous giving always want it to feed, the hungry. Very pure at heart. I got off, the coach. Went to, my niece his daughter, and told her, about my experience. She said he always sat, on that sofa.

22- My third brother, also passed away year 2005. His daughter, he came in her dream, telling her mentioning, my name something.

About change bag. My brother, he is about, 23 years. Older than me in comparison, he was older man. I have, often took good care of him. I drove him everywhere, and he used to save change. Whenever he took it to the bank, to cash it, into dollars. As a respect. I always carry, the bag of change. Into the bank. The dream meant. That my, brother thanking, and appreciate me.

23 - It was middle, of winter year 1982. My wife, and I were visiting friend up north, Michigan on the way back. We were having, car problem. We immediately knew will not make it. I was praying while struggling, on the Highway, looking for exit, so I could get off, for safety finely next sign I seen, it was another 30 miles To exit did not, know what to do. Suddenly. It is, so hard to explain. The process took, only a few seconds felt like, the car was spinning off. The Highway, next my wife and I, were off the highway. I looked down the street, I was able to see and get the help. We need, it was small town, people they treat us like a family. When we were strangers to them.

24- In the bible, it said to pray, for the dead. Therefore, I usually pray, for all my loved ones, and all the dead, who passed before us. Especially, when I drive by cemetery. I pray for, the departed souls One night, I had a dream passing, by certain cemetery. There was, big bus parked, and big number of people lined up trying to get go, into the bus. When, I wake up. I learn my prayers, were answered for some of the dead.

25- My father, and my other brother, were dead for a long time. One day, in my dream. I saw m y deceased younger brother. In my dream, looking critical sitting, on the couch. I went to him holding his arm. I helped him walk out to, the patio back of his home, where my, deceased father, and other brother, were sitting. I believe, my prayers, were answered, for my younger brother. Because of my prayer. I was able to take him to next level.

26- I used, to have same dream, at least once a year. That's my hands holding on the edge of shaking building before falling down. I wake up, from my dream Last time, I had the same dream except this time I looked down below on the ground I was able to see So many people trying to catch me If I was to full. It was last time I had that dream. That dream Increased my faith Knowing that I will always, have someone, to back me up, and I will never be alone.

27 - One day I had a dream, I believe was not my time, to die. Because, I dreamed I was standing In the, long line of people waiting. For their turn When my turn came A person, sitting on the chair Behind the desk. He told me, is not your turn yet And I woke up

28- Always being my goal, to preach, and teach wisdom I always,practice, what I preach. I even preach about, the mistakes I make. For people, not to make them but to learn from it. One day I dreamed, of a man sitting on high chair with two guards One on, each side Leaning, on my knee. One guard to his right, begin to ask him, on my behalf telling him. I was being good. If he would, allow me to preach.

29 - I moved from the home, we lived for a long time, the next day. My wife and I went back to clean, she was clean downstairs. I was up, in the attic cleaning While, doing that, I heard, rumbling noise, and looked where the noise was. I saw baby crawling, very fast, only took few seconds, he vanished he had, and blue short pans When I told, my wife, of experience. What, I saw. She said. I saw same child roaming around, our bed. She did not, want to scare me.

30-One of the year's, my wife was complaining from having allot, of pain. She is, very persistent, and refuse to see a Doctor. The only thing, I am able to do is praying for her. One night, had a dream Mother Mary, came to me, and said, my wife name telling me. To tell my wife, to take medication, and she will be ok. Soon after that my wife was fine I thank Mother Mary. I know Jesus, always send her to help.

31-When my father. Passed, away on June 6th Year in 1989. He died, at the age of 89. He had a strong faith in God. Everything, he did, was according to the bible. The day he died, my mother she was also deceased. My sister she was, to do, funeral arrangements. I remembered, my father's wishes was always, to be next my mother When he died Immediately. I called my sister, and told her. She said will call, the care giver. Few minutes later, she called me, and said, at first they told her that wasn't any next to my mother's grave. Then after they checked next to my mother's grave one more time. But when they checked. They said, to my sister. They just moved someone. Who was next, to my mom grave To plot his family purchased. it was a miracle. God grand, my father's wishes. On earth,also in heaven.

32 - A lady friend, had Cancer, she was not able, to work. I helped her paying rent. I asked her can I give you picture. Of the image, of sacred heart of Jesus that appeared, on my door. I explained. If She had faith, and accepted. She was also desperate to heal. I was sure I told her pray to Jesus, in heaven, and keep This picture, for blessing. Myself, I prayed to Jesus, to heal her. And she did.

33 - Relative, she was in the hospital, very critical. When I was there. Doctors said, there wasn't Too much hope. I was, by her bed standing. My heart was full of sorrow. She was not, moving at all Holding her hand. I asked Jesus to heal her, and give me. One more miracle. She began, to squeeze my hand. I told everyone in the room. We, immediately called her doctor, on the spot. She was moved, to care for recovery. She was better every day. God can extend life.

34-On Thursday July 7th. Year 2005. I dreamed of my deceased father. I see him going up stairs, and my deceased uncle was downstairs, dead lie in the coffin. Next morning, I woke not thinking, of my dream. On Saturday July 9th. Year 2005. My oldest brother past way. On July 11th Year 2005. My younger brother passed away, only two a part days. After the funeral. Finally remembered my dream. My father represented in my dream, my older brother, he was going upstairs meant, he went to heaven first When at meantime, his younger brother was not gone yet but to go next. After my older brother died first. Then my younger brother. Died second, that is when I understood, the dream. I thought of this dream about week after. My two brother were gone. The dream it was about them.

35- My son, at the age of four. He woke up one day. He came to me, and told me, he had dream of my. Deceased, brother in law visiting my son, in dream he said, my name is Sam, shown my son the scar, he had it always on thumb. He passed away when my son, was young. He loved children, he did not get a chance,to watch my son grow up.

36 - My father, and his friend Priest, both deceased. In my dream I saw them sitting talking. On sofa. The next day my wife, and I were cleaning the garage. I found picture, of my father, and his friend the priest. With another priest, in the picture. With them. I believe, the only reason. I did not see that priest in my dream. Because, he's still alive today I made copy, and gave it to the living priest. I also made another copy and gave it. To the deceased priests, nephews. He was very happy.

37- Mother Mary, image appeared, on the door to the left of the alter at Saint Thomas Chaldean catholic, church August of the year 2011. I can see her standing, some time with baby in her arm. Sometime without, any baby. She is very concerned. About millions of babies being murdered. Through abortion.

38 - My wife, and I, had couple, friends Husband, and wife with children. They were, very poor. Days before, Christmas. They were, visiting us along with their children Kids were, very excited. To see, our Christmas tree. With gifts under it. As they were staring, at the tree saying. They wished, they can have. Christmas tree, with gifts. I felt very bad the next day. I went to pick. With their, father while they were in school I get them Christmas tree and, I also put some gifts under it. I give them great Christmas. Anyway the following. Year on Dec 23rd Year 1992. Two days before Christmas Baby boy was born. God loves us, and blessed us with child. Gods rewards, are unlimited. When we do good.

39 – I have picture of Angel. Every home I lived in. My wife hung it on the wall next to the front door. Anyway in this home we live for the longest time. My wife and I we loved this home very much. Our hope was we live there the rest of our life Unfortunately, certain circumstance made us move out of the home, with no hope of return. About a year and half later I had a dream. The Angel from same the picture of the Angel picture we owned. He was sitting on driver seat driving me somewhere, I was not sure. I completely forgot about my dream. Few months later. By miracle we end up moving to the same home we love. After we settled. My wife she made sure she hung the Angel picture on the same wall, at the front door. When I saw the picture That is when I remembered my dream. I told my wife, in my dream the Angel brought us back to the house we love.

(Repeat)One of the best miracle, that was granted for my dad to happen. As following my father passed away, on June 6th 1989 My sister was, in contact with caretaker, to prepare. To berry, my father, and his funeral. At the meantime I remember, my father always wished, to be next to deceased, mom. I immediately called my sister told her about what my father, always wished, she told me. She will call the caretaker, to ask if there's spot. Next to my mother. My sister called me About 2 hours later, and told me the good news. She said, to me. When she called, the caretaker asking him At first said, he didn't think so. But he told my sister. Wait a minute let me check again. Luckily he, said to my sister. Someone. Who was buried, next to my mom His, family bought. A family plot. Therefore, they moved him. Therefore, that gave My father, a spot next to my mom.

I believe that was, a miracle. Because, my dad always he was, great man faithful kind, and generous, always practice. What he, preached. Because in, my family. Seven brothers, and four sisters. Eleven sibling. I want it this book to be. Eleven chapters. When I finish my book. I remember, I had written another chapter. I had to, find it In the computer. When I did so. I was very disappointed. Because I want to, have eleven chapters. When, I located my missing chapter. I was wondering, what to do. Then again remember that my mother, first born she said that to me, were twin boys. Unfortunately they died at birth. She was pregnant, for nearly five month. I believe God is, telling me My two brothers Whom did not had, a chance to born, and come alive. Into our world they are, alive with him. Therefore I was happy, I made my book. Thirteen chapters Because. We are thirteen sibling. That what God told me to do.

I have, many other dreams, miracles, and blessings. God reward me, throughout my life. I only mentioned few so. I proved, there is meaning to everything. That happen, in our life. Nothing can be done without God. I have many, more dream. That is all for now. All my dreams, and miracles. Proves to me there is life after death.

Chapter 13

Avoiding, And Defeating Evil

Temptation of Jesus. Luke 4:1-13. Evil is in the dark. The truth is taken away from him He was not sure. That was our savior. Evil didn't even know he was testing God. But, Jesus put evil to shame. Jesus said, to evil in reply. It is also says, you shall not put the lord, your God to the test. When, the devil had finished. Every temptation, he departed.

Jesus taught us, how to conquer evil, with good. Evil loves, to gain whole world. We should be awake, on guard. For the sake, of our spirit. We find our refuge in God.

We let God control our lives. When we, put all our goodness in his hands. We will definitely belong to God. And we put all of our sins under God mercy. Evil will, not be able see us. Ever. To Evil. We will, become invisible to Evil. Because, of the goodness we do.

Evil always want, to steal the joy, we have. In the salvation, It was given to us. From the, beginning of time. It was through, our savior. Jesus Christ, Our lord. God loved us so much He became, God the son, in flesh.

Now we know that, those who love God, above all things. Work together, unto good for those who, according to his purpose, are saints through his call. Romans 8:28.

Saints are people, just like you, and I. The only different is between us, and them. They did exactly 100%. What pleases God. They became saints. When they went to heaven.

Some people give up hope in God. Especially, the ones who are always spiritually. They feel very weak.

My friends was talking, to me about the good things. We can, do to please God. But he said, we all sin. I agreed with him. I added it by saying to him. How do, you think saints did it. They are, human being just like you, and I. I added no one was born as saint. We are, all being called by God, to become saints. When we get to heaven.

Saints are, the ones who loved God, and did everything. According to, his wishes all the time 24/7. They trust it. In Jesus Christ. They knew, God revealed himself to us through Jesus Christ, and he is. God the son, which he took flesh. Became a divine human, to suffer and die. For all of us. So we, can be saved from sin.

Those ones they only become saints, when they get to heaven.

God took form of man, so we can see him. Jesus Christ, himself said he is here to bring us to his father. John 14 :2-3 New testament.

Jesus said, in my father's house many rooms. He will come, and take us to himself. We will be. Where he is. John 14:2-3.

He died for all men kind, he gave us, the victory over Sin, and evil.2 Corinthians 5:19.

But if your enemy, is hungry, give him food, if he is thirsty, give him a drink for, by so doing that, you will have coals of fire, upon his head, be not overcome by evil, but overcome evil, with good. Romans 12:20-21.

If someone hate us,and if we do good anyway, for that person, he, or she will be in shock, and speechless. Wouldn't know, what to say. If we treat, people with good. They would have no choice, but to do. The same to you, and me. Walking in light, that when we see, what is around. Romans 13:12-13.

The truth is to do, what is right. That is how, we can get trusted, by everyone. We should always, be true in everything we do. Everyone, will approve of our behavior. If we walk in the dark, will trip, and stumble over things. If we walk in the light, will never trip, or stumble. God he is the light shines forever if we let Jesus Christ, take control over our life's. Evil will never be able to come near us

Jesus Christ answered, one who's commit sin, become slave, to sin John 8:34.

Living in sin. We lose our freedom, and happiness. Beside the suffering we could endure

Jesus prayed, and he asked his disciple, pray to have power over temptations Luke 22: 45-46

We need, to stay awake. Evil Is real, ready, and full of temptation. Evil will always have power over, all of us.

If we don't continuously avoid sin. We are, really giving evil full power over us When we sin. When we sin. Spirit of God depart from us. Then. Evil will have 100% control over our life.

Be sober, be watchful. Evil is, everywhere. Your opponent the devil is prowling around like a roaring lion looking, for someone to devour. 1 Peter 5: 8.

We are, evil worst enemies. He is always, going around looking for victims. We're out to be careful. Watch out for his attacks, and that's is temptation.

We need. to be firm, and stand, against evil. That is, when we have strong faith, and When we seek God through, our savior Jesus Christ.

We should, have no fear. That is, when can be surely confident.

The lord will rescue me, from every evil,and save me for his heavenly kingdom. Glory forever, and ever Amen 2 Timothy 4:18.

God will deliver us, from every work of evil. God chooses the righteous. For his heavenly kingdom. If we have like heart of Jesus Christ. His spirit, will be in us. If we take the right path 100%. Guidance of, the holy spirit. We will belong to God.

God guidance for the simple, and the just. He will bring them from death, to life, and deliver them from death, and they will prospect. The wicked, will lose. Proverb 11:15.

The good, always win. Because the, truth always reveal, and prevail. True faith, with action. Perfect faith, is to follow. All God commandments, and laws. He has given to us.

To have perfect faith, is to believe in Jesus Christ, and to be just like him.

The different, between good, and evil. Goodness, makes everything feel great, happy, and gives peace of mind. Always peaceful, surrounding.

Doing Evil Sin, is living in misery. Sin it is not playing a poker game. Either lose, or win

Sin it is like, if you have a pot of fresh food. If you only drop a spit, of spoil food into that pot. Will ruin, all that food. Will become spoil 100%. If anyone eat from it,more likely will get sick. Therefore, you have to start all over. Making, new pot of fresh food starting all over. Same thing with us once. We repent of all our sins. We cannot say to our self we did 99% goodness. Then we make it OK to sin only, one time. That does not work. Because one wrong thing we do, will lead to another one. So on, and on.

When we give evil an inch, he takes us for mile. When we sin. It is giving an opportunity to evil, to tempt us more, and to turn. Our life's upside down. If we sin one time. We repent and start over again.

So submit, your selves to God. resist the devil, and will flee from you. Draw near to God, and he will draw near to you. James 4:7-8,11.

Continually doing good, we will automatically belong to God. evil will never be able to come near us. In fact we will be invisible to evil. And visible to God.

Every time we sin. We take It, to our Lord Jesus Christ. Because, he know how it is to suffer, for our sins. He did that, on the cross.

When they were testing him, about the image on the coin was Caesar. They want, to know who belong to. Jesus replied, what belong to Caesar, it is Caesars. Matthew 22:18-22 What belong, to God it is God's. Just if we continue to do good. We will certainly, belong to God.

If we do evil we could be belonging to evil.

There's no such thing following, and going by 99% Of the commandments, and break one, or do, away with it.

If any of us break one, of the commandments, we broke them all. Believe me we all sin Jesus know it is not hard at all to sin. Every single, human being living, on face of the earth sin. This why Jesus, always ready to forgive.

It is a lot easier to obey, all the commandments. We ask God to make our will, to do what he command us.

Do not be, overcome by evil, but overcome evil, with good. Do not be conquered by evil but conquer evil with good. Romans 22: 18-21.

If we continue, to do good. We are, Summiting our self to God fully. Therefore, when evil. See mercy of God. He flee, from all of our hearts, and minds. We resist evil with good

Should sinners notice you, and say, come along with us getting away from evil. Is walking through the light. Proverbs 1:10.

Repenting it is, saying no to sin. At the meantime. We ask God, to give us strength and stand by our decision we make. Then the spirit, of God will remain In us.

Spirit of God goes through our blood stream. To live in, our hearts the rest of our life's Every time, we look up to heaven seeking God. He come down to rescue us always.

Not only being watched, as currying favor. But as slaves to Christ, it is doing the will of God. From the heart. Ephesians 6:6,10-11.

God have all the power, he will give us strengths. We'll finely get our strengths. From the lord, and from his mighty power. God will Put armor, we may be. Able to stand firm against, the tactic of the evil.

Evil is rulers, of darkness. God is master of the light. If we have, God on our side. No one, can ever hurt us. If we have like, Jesus Christ heart, and his spirit will remain in us.

We need, to examine our faith, in order for us to increase it. Then the peace of, God will quickly, crash evil under your feet.

The grace, of our Lord will be with you. Romans 16:20.

Peacemakers. They are, being called, children of God. He is love.

Good father, never leaves his children alone, or stray. God he is good. There is, no power above God. With our freewill, we can make our wishes, and will, for the spirit of God, to live among us. New testament.

Resist him, be firm. Be sober, and vigilant, your opponent the devil, is prowling around like a roaring lion looking, for someone to devour. resist, steadfast in faith. 1 Peter 5:8-9.

We out be a wake stay on guard. Continue praying. Because, the earth full of evil traps. Waiting to get us, into temptation. We need to be Strong In faith. Evil Looking for victims, and the ones. who are weak.

When it, comes to sin. Life is, like having pockets. From the time. When we, become mature enough. To understand, our faith. We begin, to focus, on our pockets. We fill it with goodness, holiness, charity. We live, life to the fullest. Just when, we think everything under control. Evil began to, pick pocket. Our faith, and it begin to slip off our feet

Evil is jealous, and he is always Looking for, the faithful, to put them through harsher Test.

Temptations are, not a joke. They are, like dropping, our self below ground. Hell people, lives through. It is lust, greed, hate, injustice, murder, adultery.

People who believe, and have faith in evil. Where, do they think evil live ? He live, in burning hell.

Evil loves, to torment human being. Because, we have the chance of salvation I don't know if evil have, any chance. For our life. God has given us. Many chances, and opportunities.

Jesus Christ said. Who does wicked things, hates the light, and does not come toward the light. John 3:20.

So many who, do wrong they don't want, to face it, or admitted, or even think about it. So they can continue, doing wrong, and not feel guilty. They also feels justified. They refuse to know the truth. They prefer, to stay in the dark. Many people, they justify what they, are doing is right. Even when they know, it is wrong, for their own gain. So they don't, feel guilty about anything. Those are people, who don't acknowledge sin. They are living in the dark.

God is spirit, and those. Who worship him they must in spirit, and truth. need to be cautious, and awake. So we can welcome, the holy spirit to dwell among us. John 4:23.

Power of the holy spirit, will crush evil, with our grace. We were all born, with grace of God. Lord Jesus Christ, his spirit, will reside into our hearts. He promised us. The power of God will be send to us. As holy spirit to be demonstrated in our life, and all the world.

Be subject. Therefore, to God. But resist the evil, and will flee from you. 1 James 4: 7.

We surrender, our life to God. Let him control it, and we will be, a winner. Always guarantee. God want us to be, pure at heart. Therefore, we become fully, and truly temple of God. Genesis.

When we commit the sin. We become, servant of sin. We get, hurt. With broken hearts Worries. Bad, and bitter memories.

Sin it is, production of the devil, and wage of death. For the wages, of sin is death But gift, of God it ever lasting. in Jesus Christ our lord. Romans 6:23.

When it comes to Christ Jesus. Evil is out of reach. Because, Christ put evil to shame Our life's in Christ he will save us from all the suffering, and he will lead to the true light.

Jesus said I am the way, the truth, and the life John 14:10.

Hate is, what evil, hold, to what is good. No one render, evil for evil. But provide good things, not only, in the sight of God. But also, in the sight, of all people Romans 6:23.

Good with goodness, go together. Bad, and good they don't. People who hate us We should, pray for God to put mercy in their hearts toward us, and not to take vengeance against us. We also pray to God, to transform their hearts.

Yet do so with gentleness, and fear, having a good consequence. So that, they reveal The good behavior, and Christ, and they might be, put to shame. For it is better to be, will of God, that you suffer. For doing good then doing evil. 1 Peter 3:16-17.

Because Jesus Christ, also died once, for our sins. For just, and for the unjust. So he can, bring us to God. Christ was put to death, indeed in the flesh. He was brought to life, in the spirit, flesh, and blood. Mutual love, comes from the heart.

Hate what comes from evil. True love built, on Mutual Trust, showing honor. Romans 12:9.

Love is, not only for spare moment. It is forever. Moreover love comes from our hearts, minds, and souls. Love is kind, mercy, peace, compassion, and is not jealous.

God made, covenant with us,and he said I shall take away, their sins. That was, his divine choice. Romans 11:27-28.

God at the end, will deliver us from evil. Jesus Christ died for us To please the father From falling of Adam, and eve. God promised us of savior. Genesis 3 : 15.

God wishes are, to share his. Divine kingdom with us forever.